These very stones cry out Luke 19:40

Stories on the history of the Diocese of Gaylord

Bishop of the Diocese of Gaylord
Most Reverend Patrick R. Cooney

Editor
Father Patrick T. Cawley

Editorial Advisory Committee
Mary Dickerson
Linda Floyd
Kay Hughes
Chris Jenkins
David L. Knight
Father Gerald F. Micketti
Father Raymond C. Mulka
Candace Neff

Harbor House Publishers, Inc., 221 Water Street, Boyne City, Michigan 49712 USA
Manufactured in the United States of America

ISBN 0-937360-47-3

THESE VERY STONES CRY OUT

Stories on the history of the Diocese of Gaylord

Cathedral of St. Mary – Our Lady of Mt. Carmel
Gaylord, Michigan

Introduction

This book is a collection of stories on the history of a diocese and the incredible people of faith and vision who have made the Diocese of Gaylord one of the great places to catch a glimpse of God and tell about it.

The title of this book, taken from Luke's gospel, are the words of Christ spoken to the crowd as He entered Jerusalem on Palm Sunday. The stories in the book speak of the incredible faith and courage of a people who walked the stones of this part of the northern lower peninsula, which is now the Diocese of Gaylord. These stones do cry out to us about a journey of faith over the years, and they will continue to cry out as this faith leads us to a new millennium.

This book captures this "telling" in an anthology of stories covering the long journey of this diocese dating back to when it was part of the first and only diocese in the United States, Baltimore.

This work is not a comprehensive history in the traditional sense but a "narrative history" made up of a collection of stories of people, places and events. Individually these stories are complete in themselves like a square patch in a quilt. When they are woven together, however, they make up a colorful quilt with a unique faith pattern that leaves one better for having been touched in some way by either a single patch or the entire quilt.

In order to bring this "telling" into the present form we solicited stories and information from throughout the diocese including parishes, offices and departments within the diocese. This process took over a year and the results were extensive and diverse. The authors include a Cardinal, bishops, priests, parishioners, and others who were able to tell of their special glimpse of God in such a manner to make us all proud to be a part of the Diocese of Gaylord.

The volume of "patches" received was more than we could manage so the history committee had to make choices. All parishes were invited to participate and many did. Editing and arranging were difficult but necessary and the committee did so with prayer and reflection. We are pleased with what you are looking at and know you will find this to be something to read with pride.

The book begins with a concise history of the Diocese of Gaylord titled: "From Baltimore to Gaylord" by Willard M. J. Baird, Ph.D. Following this are a variety of faith stories. You can read these in consecutive order or skip around covering those areas you are most familiar with and then go back to read the others. Any way you choose will give you a glimpse of God, a journey in faith and a good bit of pride in knowing you are a part of something very special.

A special word of gratitude to all who contributed to this history and to the members of the diocesan history committee whose insights and commitment were invaluable in bringing this work to completion.

We are most grateful for the support and encouragement of Bishop Cooney who initiated the idea of a diocesan history to commemorate the Twenty-Fifth Anniversary of the Diocese. He allowed us to develop this "narrative history" concept and we believe we have a history of which Bishop Cooney and all in the diocese can be proud.

The stories and histories submitted are accurate according to the authors who submitted them. The histories were collected during the year 1997 from a variety of sources, including the parishes. Some sources date back considerably and no specific author could be identified. More current histories are accurate according to the identified author. However, since they were collected throughout 1997 from the parishes and many other sources and since some of the histories were written prior to 1997, they will have varying periods of historical coverage.

Father Patrick Cawley

Table of Contents

Table of Contents

SECTION ONE

Roots of the Church in Northern Michigan

From Baltimore to Gaylord:
A genealogical history of the Diocese of Gaylord

By Willard M.J. Baird, Ph.D.

Twenty years after the signing of the Declaration of Independence, the Jay Treaty between the United States and Great Britain brought the territory of Michigan under American control. With that historic step in the nation's development in 1796, the single Catholic parish which then covered all of Michigan and most of Wisconsin—Saint Anne in Detroit—came under the ecclesiastical jurisdiction of the first American bishop, the Right Reverend John Carroll of Baltimore.

Had there been any Catholics in northern Lower Michigan at the time, they would then have been under the spiritual care of Bishop Carroll, whose episcopal authority extended from Maine to Florida and westward from the Atlantic coast to the Mississippi River and the Louisiana Territory.

Earlier, of course, black-robed Jesuits from France who introduced the Christian faith among the Indian tribes of the upper Great Lakes region in the 17th century, had passed along the shoreline of northern and western Michigan, establishing several mission stations in the Upper Peninsula and at strategic points along the Straits of Mackinac.

Dependent as they were on waterborne transportation, however, their exploratory travels and accompanying efforts to spread the faith, guided by bishops of the colonial French Church in Canada, did not take them far into the interior wilderness of either Upper or Lower Michigan. A century and a half or more would elapse before Catholic priests might occasionally be seen in the settlements which suddenly began to appear in Missaukee, Wexford and other inland counties when northern Michigan entered its fabled lumbering era in the second half of the 1800s.

The earliest imprint of the Catholic Church in Michigan, therefore, is primarily associated with the voyages of the French missionaries and their explorer companions on Lake Superior, Lake Michigan and northern Lake Huron and their work among the Indians they encountered at Sault Sainte Marie, the Straits of Mackinac, the Keweenaw Bay area and elsewhere along the shores of the upper lakes. It would be many years later before another chapter in the early history of the church in Michigan would begin in the southern part of the Michigan territory. The locale for that chapter would be Detroit.

Saint Anne, serving a congregation of French-speaking parishioners, was dedicated in 1701 as the Chapel of Sainte Anne de Detroit by Recollect Fathers. The priests had accompanied the French colonial commandant, Antoine de la Mothe Cadillac, when he brought a number of French Canadian families to settle at Detroit.

Before the American takeover, Saint Anne Parish had served for nearly a century as a sturdy outpost in the far-flung ecclesiastical province of New France, administered by the Archbishop of Montreal. One writer has termed Saint Anne "the mother parish of the entire Northwest."

In tracing the lineage of church authority in Michigan, the Reverend John W. McGee, a Grand Rapids pastor with family ties to Missaukee County, concluded that Cardinal Richelieu of Paris was the first bishop of the territory which would one day become the Diocese of Grand Rapids. He could as easily have declared Cardinal Richelieu to be the first bishop of all of Michigan.

The jurisdictional status changed abruptly in 1796, when Michigan finally came under the flag of the United States and the Catholics of Michigan found that the Right Reverend John Carroll of Baltimore was now their bishop.

That very year, Bishop Carroll assigned the Reverend Michael Lecadoux, a Sulpician priest, to take charge of the vast Saint Anne parish. Two years later, the bishop sent a young assistant to the parish, the Reverend Gabriel Richard, who became pastor in 1801 and who later became one of the more notable figures in the early history of Detroit and Michigan.

In a few years, diocesan administration in Michigan was to change again. In 1807, Bishop Carroll recommended to Pope Pius VII that to serve a steadily growing number

of Catholics in the young nation it would be well to create four new dioceses. The Holy See agreed the following year. Baltimore then became the nation's first archdiocese, in 1808 — with Bishop Carroll, a native of Maryland and member of a prominent family in that state, as the first American archbishop. Meanwhile, new dioceses were established at Boston, New York and Philadelphia and, interestingly, at Bardstown, a remote settlement in the wilderness of north central Kentucky.

The new Bardstown Diocese embraced the states of Kentucky and Tennessee, but its bishop was also to be responsible for administration of the church throughout the Northwest Territory until the Holy See approved other arrangements. The Northwest Territory, created by the Continental Congress in the Northwest Ordinance of 1787, included Ohio, Michigan, Indiana, Illinois, Wisconsin and the portion of Minnesota east of the Mississippi River.

Saint Anne Church and neighborhood, Detroit, Michigan, c. 1850.

So, it happened that in 1810 Michigan passed from the direct jurisdiction of Bishop Carroll of Baltimore (by now an archbishop) to the diocesan control of the newly-consecrated Bishop Benedict Joseph Flaget, S.S., of Bardstown, Kentucky. Father Flaget, a Sulpician, recommended for the episcopacy in 1807 by Bishop Carroll, was appointed Bishop of Bardstown by the Holy See on April 8, 1808. A former seminary teacher in France and later a professor at Saint Mary Seminary in Baltimore, Father Flaget was, at first, extremely reluctant to accept the appointment but was finally directed by his Sulpician superior general in Paris to do so. He was consecrated November 4, 1810, by Archbishop Carroll and arrived in Bardstown on June 11, 1811, after a month-long, 700-mile journey over a circuitous travel route from Baltimore.

Bishop Flaget's report of April 10, 1815, to Pope Pius VII about conditions in the Bardstown Diocese provides interesting reading. Discussing the situation in Michigan, after having traveled extensively for six months in 1814 in other parts of his diocesan territory, he wrote:

"In the Territory of Michigan there is a parish called Saint Anne in a town known as Detroit. It is so large that it seems necessary to divide it into two parts. One contains 1,500 souls. The other is in a place called La Riviere aux Raisins, the name of which I do not know, which consists of about 500 souls. Each is in charge of a Sulpician. The parishioners pay their tithes to him.

"I could not visit these places on account of the war (the War of 1812) which was raging in these places at the time of my visitation. Besides these, on my journey, I heard of four French congregations settled in the midst of the Indians who belonged to my diocese, one on the upper part of the Mississippi, one in a place commonly called Chicago, another on the shore of Lake Michigan, a fourth at the head of the Illinois River. But neither time nor the war would permit me to visit them."

By 1820, Bishop Flaget was convinced a separate diocese should be established in Ohio, which had become a state in 1803, and submitted that recommendation to Rome. With the Archbishop of Baltimore in agreement, the Holy See authorized the erection of the Diocese of Cincinnati on June 18, 1821. A Dominican priest, Father Edward D. Fenwick, O.P., who had been stationed in Kentucky, was named the first bishop of the new diocese and apostolic administrator of Michigan, Wisconsin, and the remainder of the Northwest Territory.

Father Fenwick was consecrated a bishop on January 13, 1822, by Bishop Flaget in Saint Rose Church in Washington County, Kentucky. Most of the Catholics in Michigan who came under the jurisdiction of the new bishop of Cincinnati in 1822 resided in the southern part of the territory. Father Gabriel Richard at Detroit, reporting that year to his new diocesan superior, said there were 6,000 Catholics in his parish of Saint Anne, which embraced all of Michigan and most of Wisconsin, with only two priests—himself and an assistant.

In May of 1831, Bishop Fenwick escorted a newly arrived Slovenian missionary priest, Father Frederic Baraga, to his first American mission post at L'Arbre Croche, near the present Cross Village on the eastern shore of upper Lake Michigan, with a brief stopover at Mackinac Island.

Father Baraga remained at his L'Arbre Croche station, working among the Ottawa Indians of western and northern Michigan, for two years.

In the spring of 1833, Father Baraga journeyed south from L'Arbre Croche to the Rapids of the Grand River in Kent County, arriving June 15 and remaining about a week. There he offered Mass for the first time at the site of what is now the city of Grand Rapids.

In that same year of 1833, four years before Michigan became the 26th state in the American Union, the Holy See established the Diocese of Detroit, embracing the Territory of Michigan and what then remained of the old Northwest Territory.

The Reverend John Frederick Rese, born in Germany and a zealous missionary priest of the Cincinnati Diocese on February 25, 1833, was consecrated on October 6, 1833. His new diocese—all of Michigan, most of Wisconsin and the eastern part of Minnesota— had eight churches and three or four Indian missions. Saint Anne in Detroit became the cathedral for the diocese.

A year later, Bishop Rese could count 14 priests, besides himself, serving the 12 churches then in the diocese. Three years later, he had 18 priests and the following year three more.

On September 8, 1833, with the sanction of Bishop Rese, Father Baraga left L'Arbre Croche to establish a new mission near the Rapids of the Grand River, where he had visited for a week in June of that year. Traveling by canoe on Lake Michigan, the missionary reached the mouth of the Grand River on September 21, arriving upstream at the Rapids of the Grand on September 23. There, on the west side of the river, he established his "Mission of the Blessed Virgin," which he usually called Saint Mary's Mission. And there he remained until relieved in February of 1835 by the arrival of a replacement, Father Andreas Viszosky. Bishop Rese had another challenge in mind for Father Baraga, which impelled him to transfer Father Viszosky from a mission station on the Saint Claire River near the present Marine City to the settlement where Father Baraga had built the foundation for the Catholic church in western Michigan.

The task Bishop Rese put before Father Baraga was another missionary assignment, this time in the Lake Superior region of upper Michigan, Wisconsin and Minnesota. Father Baraga readily accepted, almost eager to be on his way to a new missionary adventure. His initial station was to be at LaPointe du Saint Esprit, on Madeline Island, an American Fur Company trading post in the Apostle Islands off the northern shore of Wisconsin. His assignment would carry him deep into the Indian territory surrounding Lake Superior, at times even into Ontario on the northern shore of the lake. Eight years later he would move to the Keweenaw Bay area of Michigan to establish a more centralized mission station for the Chippewa Indians at Assinins, near L'Anse, and in 1853 he would become vicar apostolic and the first bishop of Upper Michigan.

Bishop John Frederick Rese

Bishop Rese, meanwhile, suffered a serious illness in 1837 from which he never fully recovered. When the disability continued, he asked to be allowed to resign, but that request was not granted. Instead, the Holy See permitted him to retain his nominal status as bishop of Detroit while allowing him to return to his native Hanover in Germany, where he lived in retirement until his death in 1871.

In the meantime, an able replacement took charge of the young Detroit Diocese, the Right Reverend Peter Paul Lefevre, who in 1841 at the age of 37, was named coadjutor bishop and administrator. Bishop Lefevre served in that capacity until his death in 1869, while Bishop Rese remained inactive in Germany.

During Bishop Lefevre's tenure, the Wisconsin portion of the Detroit Diocese was detached and became the new Diocese of Milwaukee in 1844. The Reverend John M. Henni, a priest of the Cincinnati Diocese, consecrated by Archbishop Purcell in Cincinnati on March 19, 1844, became Milwaukee's first bishop. Thirty-one years later, Bishop Henni became Milwaukee's first archbishop when that see was made an archdiocese in 1875.

In 1853, also during Bishop Lefevre's tenure in Detroit, the Holy See created the apostolic vicariate of Sault Sainte Marie and Marquette, severing the Upper Peninsula of Michigan from the Detroit Diocese. Father Baraga, the kindly and patient missionary priest who had labored for 18 years among the Indians of the Lake Superior

country, often enduring almost unbelievable hardship, was named vicar apostolic and consecrated a bishop.

It was at Sault Sainte Marie that Jesuit missionary Fathers Isaac Jogues and Charles Raymbault had introduced the Catholic faith to native Indians in 1644. And it was at Sault Sainte Marie, in 1668, that Father Jacques Marquette had established a Jesuit mission station which became the first permanent settlement in Michigan. There, too, Bishop Baraga established his see in 1854.

In 1857, the Holy See created the Diocese of Sault Sainte Marie and Marquette, naming Bishop Baraga as the first bishop of the new diocese. Bishop Baraga moved his residence from Sault Sainte Marie to Marquette, a more central location, in 1866, and there he died on January 19, 1868.

In 1871, Bishop Casper H. Borgess, who was also born in Germany, succeeded Bishop Rese in the Detroit Diocese. He, in turn, was succeeded in 1888 by Bishop John S. Foley, who headed the diocese for the next 30 years.

As the years passed and the Michigan population grew during the second half of the 19th century, more Catholic churches began to appear throughout the western part of the state as well as elsewhere in the Lower Peninsula. Relating some of that development in his book on the history of the Grand Rapids Diocese, Father McGee mentions the cluster of churches and mission stations which flowered along the Grand River in Kent, Ionia and Ottawa counties and later in towns farther north, among them Newaygo, Big Rapids, Ludington, Manistee, Cadillac and Traverse City.

Father McGee notes that the Catholic Almanac in 1857 reported that priests from Grand Rapids occasionally visited and said Mass at Muskegon and Newaygo, which then had churches, and at Grand Haven, where a church was being built, as well as at Pere Marquette (later known as Ludington) and Manistee. Thus, as he observes,

Bishop Henry J. Richter

in 1857 Saint Andrew, the mother parish in Grand Rapids, extended from Ionia on the east to Muskegon on the west and from Yankee Springs, in Barry County on the south, to Ludington and Manistee on the north. That impressive growth within a time span of only 24 years could be traced to the original Saint Mary Mission which Father Baraga built at the Rapids of the Grand in 1833.

In 1878, the Reverend Andrew Herbstret, a Precious Blood Father and pastor of Saint Mary Parish in Big Rapids and its 15 surrounding missions, invited a small and struggling community of Sisters of Mercy at Grand Rapids to come to Big Rapids to open a hospital in his city. Mother Joseph Lynch, mother superior of the community which had run into financial difficulty while operating an academy in Grand Rapids, readily accepted the offer. The sisters moved to Big Rapids, began a school there and at the same time started planning for the hospital which Father Herbstret knew was so urgently needed to care for injured lumberjacks.

With the help of lumber camp operators and by means of $5 tickets sold to men in the lumber camps to insure their hospital treatment if injured, the sisters opened Mercy Hospital in Big Rapids in November 1879. That was the beginning of the hospital work of the Sisters of Mercy in the Grand Rapids Diocese.

Farther north, at Cadillac, construction of the first Catholic church to be erected in Wexford County began in 1880. Dedicated to Saint Ann, it was to become the mother church for a dozen missions in seven counties. Before Saint Ann was built, priests from Traverse City or Big Rapids occasionally visited Cadillac, offering Mass in the home of a Catholic family in a part of the community then known as Frenchtown.

When Saint Ann was built, Cadillac and Wexford County, and indeed the entire Lower Peninsula of Michigan, were still in the Detroit Diocese.

On May 19, 1882, the Holy See announced the establishment of the Diocese of Grand Rapids. Spread over nearly two-thirds of the land area of the Lower Peninsula, the new diocese covered 39 counties, reaching west from Grand Rapids to Lake Michigan, north to Beaver Island and the Straits of Mackinac and east to Saginaw Bay. The other 29 counties of the Lower Peninsula remained, of course, in the Detroit Diocese.

As structured in 1882, the Grand Rapids Diocese included all of the Lower Peninsula north of the southern line of Ottawa, Kent, Montcalm, Gratiot and Saginaw Counties and west of the eastern line of Saginaw and Bay Counties. That territory, embracing almost half of all

the counties in Michigan, included the cities of Saginaw, Bay City, Midland, Alpena and Cheboygan on the east, as well as Grand Rapids, Holland, Grand Haven, Muskegon, Ludington, Manistee, Cadillac, Traverse City and Petoskey on the west, and Alma, Mount Pleasant, Clare and Gaylord in the central part of the state.

Missaukee County, which had been organized in 1871, was among the 39 counties grouped in the new Grand Rapids Diocese.

After the announcement that the diocese was to be created, nearly nine months elapsed before Pope Leo XIII named the Reverend Henry Joseph Richter, D.D., pastor of Saint Lawrence Church in Cincinnati, to be its first bishop. Then 45 years old, the bishop-elect received the pontifical credentials for his consecration on March 4, 1883. Shortly thereafter he came to Grand Rapids to visit the priests of the city's four parishes—Saint Andrew, Saint Mary, Saint James and Saint Adalbert—and to choose the city's mother church, Saint Andrew, for his cathedral.

Bishop Joseph G. Pinten

Born in Germany, the new bishop had come to the United States when he was 16, living at first in Cincinnati. He studied for the priesthood in that city and later in Rome, where he was ordained in 1865. He was consecrated and installed as bishop of Grand Rapids on Sunday, April 22, 1883, by the Right Reverend William H. Elder, coadjutor to the aging Archbishop Purcell of Cincinnati. The co-consecrators were Bishop Casper H. Borgess of Detroit and Bishop William G. McCloskey of Louisville, then the bishop of the senior see in the Province of Cincinnati.

At the time of Bishop Richter's installation, Grand Rapids was a rapidly growing city. It had a population of 32,016 in the 1880 census, and 41,934 in 1884. Only 50 years earlier it had been a frontier trading post at which Father Frederic Baraga arrived from L'Arbre Croche on a missionary visit in 1833. On that occasion Father Baraga had offered the first Mass at the Rapids of the Grand River in the log cabin home of Louis Campau, the region's first white settler. Of that journey to the trading post on the Grand River, the missionary later wrote, "Never before had a Catholic priest penetrated this region."

In 1883, Bishop Richter's new diocese—then embracing most of the central and northern portions of the Lower Peninsula, presently divided among the Grand Rapids, Saginaw and Gaylord Dioceses—had 37 churches with resident pastors, 17 parochial schools with 2,867 students and an estimated Catholic population of 50,000.

Among the priests in the diocese at that time were Reverend Henry Grimme at Big Rapids, Reverend M. P. Willigan at Cadillac, Reverend L.P. Paquin at Ludington, Reverend D. Callairt at Manistee, Reverend George Ziegler

Bishop Edward D. Kelly

at Traverse City and Reverend Louis Baroux at Montague.

A few years later, while stationed at Reed City and Cadillac, Father Baroux was to be seen occasionally in Missaukee County, in the late 1880s and early 1890s, when he occasionally came to Lake City to offer Mass in the home of a Catholic family or in the courthouse or the Grand Central Hotel. He is probably the first priest to have celebrated Mass in Missaukee County, perhaps the first priest even to have traveled through the county. In any case, the zealous concern of Father Baroux, who had come to the United States as a missionary priest from France, made the Catholic Church a visible presence in Missaukee County.

With Bishop Richter's encouragement, Catholic churches were built in Lake City in 1896 and in Jennings in 1903, and in 1912, a small Christian Reformed Church

Bishop Michael J. Gallagher

was purchased in McBain to become a house of worship for the small Catholic congregation in that community.

At the silver jubilee observance of Bishop Richter's consecration on April 22, 1908, a purse of $28,000 was presented to him to establish a diocesan seminary. Bishop Richter said the project was suggested to him by Pope Leo XIII during his 1905 ad limina visit to Rome. The following year, Saint Joseph Seminary was established in temporary quarters in Grand Rapids. Shortly thereafter, a new seminary building was constructed, which Bishop Richter blessed on October 27, 1910.

In March of 1912, Bishop Richter appointed Father Michael J. Gallagher, who had been chancellor of the diocese since 1900, to be vicar general of the diocese. Three years later, in August, 1915, the Holy See announced Father Gallagher's appointment as coadjutor bishop of Grand Rapids, with the right of succession. He was consecrated a bishop on September 8, 1915.

When Bishop Richter died on December 26, 1916, at the age of 78 after an illness of only four days, Bishop Gallagher automatically succeeded him as bishop of Grand Rapids.

At Bishop Richter's death, after remarkable tenure of 33 years as the first bishop of the diocese, the Grand Rapids Herald noted that "during his entire administration, he kept his diocese entirely out of debt, and when he relinquished the reins, every church and institution erected in the diocese was paid for."

On July 18, 1918, the Holy See announced Bishop Gallagher was to be transferred to the vacant see at Detroit. Installed there in November of that year, he remained bishop of Michigan's oldest diocese until his death on January 20, 1937.

At Grand Rapids, Bishop Gallagher was replaced in 1919 by Bishop Edward Dionysis Kelly who, like Bishop Gallagher, was a Michigan native. During the tenure of Bishop Kelly, who came to Grand Rapids after 34 years as a priest in the Detroit Diocese, including eight years as auxiliary bishop of that diocese, new churches were built at Evart and Reed City in Osceola County, and a new rectory was built at Saint Ann in Cadillac. After his unexpected death on March 26, 1926, he was succeeded on October 26, 1926, by Bishop Joseph Gabriel Pinten. A native of the Upper Peninsula, Bishop Pinten was transferred to Grand Rapids from the Diocese of Superior, Wisconsin, where he had served as bishop for four years.

Bishop Pinten insisted at the outset of his administration of the diocese that after a period of rapid expansion and construction of churches, schools, convents and other facilities during the preceding decade, debts must now be paid and mortgages retired. It was well that he did so, for three years later the stock market crash of 1929 signaled the start of the nation's Great Depression.

Despite the unavoidable financial austerity imposed during the depression era of the 1930s, several projects were undertaken during Bishop Pinten's regime. Among them, in the upstate area, was the formation of a Houghton Lake mission parish and construction of a church at Prudenville in Roscommon County.

Bishop Pinten resigned on November 1, 1940, at age 73, after 14 years as head of the diocese and retired to his home in Marquette, where he died November 6, 1945. The Holy See named Bishop Joseph H. Albers of Lansing as apostolic administrator of the Grand Rapids

Bishop Joseph C. Plagens

Diocese until a new bishop could be installed.

To succeed Bishop Pinten, the Holy See announced on December 16, 1940, the transfer of Bishop Joseph Casimir Plagens of Marquette, who was installed as the fifth bishop of the Grand Rapids Diocese on February 18, 1941. Before he was named to the Upper Peninsula See at Marquette in 1935, Bishop Plagens was auxiliary bishop of Detroit under Bishop Gallagher.

When Bishop Plagens died March 31, 1943, the rector of Saint Joseph Seminary in Grand Rapids, Monsignor Thomas L. Noa, (later to become bishop of Sioux City, Iowa and Marquette, Michigan) served as diocesan administrator until the arrival of a successor.

On October 2, 1943, Pope Pius XII announced the appointment of Monsignor Francis Haas of Washington, D.C., Dean of the School of Social Science at the Catholic University of America, to be the next bishop of Grand Rapids. Monsignor Haas was consecrated and installed on November 18 of that year and served as bishop until his death on August 29, 1953.

It was Bishop Haas who authorized the establishment of Saint Stephen in Lake City as a separate parish on June 15, 1950 and who assigned the Reverend Edmund Farrell as its first resident pastor, effective July 3, 1950. Four years earlier, on June 21, 1946, Bishop Haas had approved separate parish status for Our Lady of the Lake Church at Prudenville which, like Saint Stephen, was previously a mission church.

During the tenure of Bishop Haas, new parishes — formerly missions — were also established at Roscommon and Irons; new missions were established at Kalkaska and on the north side of Houghton Lake; a new school and convent were built at Saint Philip in Reed City; and hospitals operated by the Sisters of Mercy in Cadillac and Manistee were enlarged.

He was succeeded in 1954 by Bishop Allen J. Babcock who was transferred from Detroit where he had served as auxiliary bishop since 1947. Bishop Babcock died June 27, 1969, and was succeeded by Bishop Joseph M. Breitenbeck who, like Bishop Babcock, was also transferred from Detroit where he had been appointed an auxiliary bishop in 1965. Bishop Breitenbeck was installed as the eighth bishop of Grand Rapids on December 2, 1969.

Bishop Francis J. Haas

Less than seven months after the death of Bishop Gallagher in 1937, Pope Pius XI raised the Diocese of Detroit to an archdiocese and, on August 3, 1937, transferred Archbishop Edward Mooney from the Diocese of Rochester, New York to become the first archbishop of Detroit. The Holy See's actions brought all of Michigan's Lower Peninsula dioceses, previously in the Province of Cincinnati, and the Upper Peninsula's single diocese of Marquette, which had been in the Archdiocese of Milwaukee, into one ecclesiastical province.

On May 26, 1937, shortly before raising Detroit to an archdiocese, the Holy See created the Diocese of Lansing, embracing 15 counties in central, southern and southwestern Michigan. The Most Reverend Joseph H. Albers, who had been auxiliary bishop of Cincinnati since 1929, was named the first bishop of the Lansing Diocese.

In February, 1946, Archbishop Mooney, metropolitan of the Province of Michigan, was elevated by Pope Pius XII to the dignity of a cardinal, one of only four American cardinals at that time. In 1949, Cardinal Mooney established Saint John Theological Seminary at Plymouth, a provincial seminary intended to serve all of the Catholic dioceses of Michigan.

Cardinal Mooney, who died in 1958 while in Rome for the funeral of Pope Pius XII, was succeeded by Bishop John Francis Dearden, who was transferred to Detroit from Pittsburgh. In 1969 he, too, was named a cardinal by Pope Paul VI while serving as the first president of the National Conference of Catholic Bishops. Cardinal Dearden resigned as archbishop of Detroit on July 15, 1980, at age 72 because of impaired health. He continued to serve as apostolic administrator of the archdiocese until his successor was selected.

The following year, on February 26, the Holy See announced creation of the Diocese of Saginaw, covering a large area in eastern Michigan and the Saginaw Bay and Thumb of Michigan region which had previously been in the Diocese of Grand Rapids and the Archdiocese of Detroit. Monsignor William F. Murphy of Detroit was appointed the first bishop of the Saginaw Diocese on March 17, 1938, and consecrated on May 17 of that year.

Again in 1971 diocesan boundaries throughout the

Bishop Allen J. Babcock

Lower Peninsula of Michigan were redrawn when the Holy See created the Diocese of Gaylord and the Diocese of Kalamazoo.

The Gaylord Diocese embraced the 21 northernmost counties of the Lower Peninsula, all of which were previously in the Dioceses of Grand Rapids and Saginaw. At its inception, the Gaylord Diocese had about 80,000 Catholics in an area with a total population of about 419,700.

The new Gaylord Diocese stretched across the upper part of the Lower Peninsula from Manistee County bordering Lake Michigan on the west to Iosco County bordering Lake Huron on the east, and northward from that line to the Straits of Mackinac.

In southwestern Michigan the new Kalamazoo Diocese embraced the nine counties of Allegan, Barry, Calhoun, Kalamazoo, Van Buren, Berrien, Cass, Saint Joseph and Branch. The greater part of this area was previously in the Lansing Diocese and the remainder was in the Grand Rapids Diocese.

At the same time the eastern boundary of the Lansing Diocese was realigned to include Lenawee and Washtenaw Counties, previously in the Detroit Archdiocese, while Clare and Isabella Counties in central Michigan were detached from the Grand Rapids Diocese and added to the Saginaw Diocese.

On June 5, 1971, Pope Paul VI announced the selection of the Reverend Edmund Casimir Szoka, chancellor of the Diocese of Marquette, to be the first bishop of Gaylord. At the same time he chose the Reverend Paul V. Donovan, a priest of the Lansing Diocese who had served for several years as secretary to Bishop Albers, to be the first bishop of Kalamazoo. Both were relatively young men; Bishop Szoka was then 43 while Bishop Donovan was 46.

Bishop Szoka was ordained a bishop by Cardinal Dearden and formally installed as the first bishop of Gaylord by Archbishop Luigi Raimondi, then the apostolic delegate to the United States, on Tuesday, July 20, 1971. The date marks the beginning of the Gaylord Diocese. The ordination and installation ceremony was conducted in the gymnasium of Saint Mary High School at Gaylord because Saint Mary, the city's only Catholic church, was too small to accommodate the turnout of friends and well-wishers.

The aging Saint Mary Church became Bishop Szoka's first cathedral. A larger cathedral church was to be built five years later.

Born September 14, 1927, in Grand Rapids, Bishop Szoka studied for the priesthood at Saint Joseph Seminary in that city, at Sacred Heart Seminary in Detroit, and at Saint John Provincial Seminary in Plymouth. He was ordained June 5, 1954, by Bishop Thomas L. Noa at Saint Peter Cathedral in Marquette. Three years after his ordination he went to Rome for two years to study canon law at the Pontifical Lateran University. After his return to Michigan, he served as pastor of Saint Pius X Church in Ishpeming and Saint Christopher Church in Marquette and as chancellor of the Marquette diocese before his installation as bishop of Gaylord.

Saint Mary Our Lady of Mount Carmel Cathedral, an impressive $1.7 million structure, was built under Bishop Szoka's direction and dedicated Sunday, July 25, 1976. Bishop Szoka was the principal concelebrant at the dedication Mass, following the blessing of the cathedral by Archbishop Jean Jadot, then the apostolic delegate to the United States.

The Gaylord cathedral is octagonal in shape, with

Bishop Joseph M. Breitenbeck

seating for more than 900. The adjoining Blessed Sacrament chapel provides seating for 96. Included in the design of the structure is a shrine area honoring Bishop Frederic Baraga. The 1975 date on the cathedral cornerstone marks the year construction began. The cathedral church and adjoining social hall and priests' residence were designed by Mayotte, Crouse and D'Haene Architects of Lansing.

In 1980 Bishop Szoka's appointment to the board of trustees of the Catholic University of America in Washington, D.C., was announced by Archbishop Philip Hannan of New Orleans.

With the creation of the Gaylord and Kalamazoo Dioceses, boundary realignment in Lower Michigan reduced the Grand Rapids Diocese to 11 counties in central western Michigan, the Saginaw Diocese to 11 counties in the Saginaw Bay and thumb of Michigan region, the Lansing Diocese to ten counties in south central Michigan and the Detroit Archdiocese to six counties in southeastern Michigan. The Diocese of Marquette, embracing the 15 counties in the Upper Peninsula, remained unchanged.

Bishop Edmund C. Szoka being ordained by Cardinal Dearden.

On Saturday afternoon and evening, March 28, 1981, the electrifying news spread through the Gaylord Diocese — and elsewhere in Michigan — that Pope John Paul II had chosen Bishop Szoka to be the new Archbishop of Detroit, succeeding Cardinal Dearden. Underscoring his personal interest in the assignment, His Holiness had called Bishop Szoka to Rome to inform him officially of the appointment at a private audience in the Pope's chambers earlier that day. (Bishop Szoka first learned of the appointment in a telephone call March 16 from Archbishop Pio Laghi, the papal representative in Washington.)

Bishop Szoka attended a farewell reception in his honor at Gaylord which drew hundreds of clergy, religious and laity from throughout the diocese, on Friday evening, May 8, after celebrating Mass in Saint Mary Cathedral. Proceeding to Detroit a few days later, he took possession of his provincial see and assumed his new office as head of the archdiocese at an early evening vesper service in Detroit's Blessed Sacrament Cathedral on May 14, 1981.

He was formally installed as the new archbishop of Detroit and metropolitan of the Province of Michigan on May 1 in an impressive two-hour ceremony in Detroit's riverfront Cobo Arena. Cardinal Dearden presided and the apostolic delegate to the United States, Archbishop Laghi, installed the new archbishop. "The Michigan Catholic", the weekly newspaper of the archdiocese, estimated that more than 11,000 people filled the arena for the installation ceremony and the Mass concelebrated by Archbishop Szoka and 11 other active and retired Michigan bishops. Cardinals from Chicago, Philadelphia and Baltimore, along with Cardinal Dearden, were among the 30 prelates attending.

Bishop Edmund C. Szoka at his ordination, accompanied by Msgr. Frank Kaminski, left.

In 1980, the 21-county Diocese of Gaylord had a Catholic population of 84,425 served by 55 diocesan priests and 21 religious order priests in 59 parishes and 25 mission churches.

After Archbishop Szoka's departure from Gaylord, the seven diocesan consultors, meeting May 15 at the cathedral in Gaylord, elected Father David W. Gemuend, vicar general and chancellor of the diocese and pastor of Saint Thomas Aquinas parish at Elmira, as administrator of the diocese. Father Gemuend served the diocese in that capacity for nearly six months.

To fill the vacant see in Gaylord, the Holy See selected a priest from the Grand Rapids Diocese, the Reverend Robert John Rose, pastor of Sacred Heart Church in Muskegon Heights and a former rector of Saint John Provincial Seminary in Plymouth.

Bishop Rose was born February 28, 1930, in Grand

Bishop Robert J. Rose to be ordained by Archbishop Szoka.

Rapids and was reared in that city. He began his preparation for the priesthood at Saint Joseph Seminary in Grand Rapids and later studied at Le Grand Seminaire in Montreal where he received a bachelor of arts degree and at the Pontifical Urban College in Rome. He was ordained December 21, 1955, in Rome and said his first Mass in that city. He later earned a master of arts degree in education at the University of Michigan.

When he was named Bishop of Gaylord, he had spent most of his priestly life in his home diocese of Grand Rapids where, for several years, he was on the faculty of Saint Joseph Seminary. Appointed rector of Saint John Provincial Seminary in 1971, he served six years in the position before his appointment as pastor of Sacred Heart in Muskegon Heights.

In the fall of 1981 he went to Rome for three months of study at the Institute for Continuing Theological Education at the North American College. He had been in Rome only two weeks, however, when he was informed on October 7 by the Vatican Congregation for Bishops of his selection to be the second bishop of Gaylord. The appointment was officially announced by John Paul II on October 13 and, after an audience with His Holiness a few days later, the bishop-designate returned to Muskegon Heights.

As he prepared to leave for his new post at Gaylord, some 120 priests of the Grand Rapids Diocese honored the bishop-designate at a farewell dinner at Saint Joseph Seminary in Grand Rapids. Members of his Muskegon Heights parish gave him an episcopal ring as a token of their esteem.

Sixteen bishops, including Cardinal Dearden of Detroit and Archbishop James A. Hickey of Washington, D.C., attended the ordination and installation of Bishop Rose on Sunday afternoon, December 6, 1981, in the new Saint Mary Cathedral in Gaylord. Archbishop Szoka of Detroit was the ordaining prelate, assisted by Bishop Joseph M. Breitenbeck of Grand Rapids and his auxiliary, Bishop Joseph C. McKinney.

The Gaylord Diocese remained under the guidance of Bishop Rose until August 30, 1989 when he was appointed as the ninth bishop of the Grand Rapids Diocese.

The Diocesan College of Consultors elected Reverend Isadore J. Mikulski, pastor of Sacred Heart Parish at Oscoda, to serve as the Apostolic Administrator after Bishop Rose left and while the See was vacant. He took office August 31, 1989, and served until the third Bishop of Gaylord was installed.

On November 21, 1989, the Gaylord Diocese learned of the appointment of its third bishop, Patrick R. Cooney, an auxiliary bishop in the Archdiocese of Detroit. Born in Detroit, the eldest son of Michael and Elizabeth Dowdall Cooney on March 10, 1934, Bishop Cooney attended Saint Edward Elementary and graduated from Sacred Heart Seminary High School in 1952. He entered Sacred Heart Seminary College and was awarded a Bachelor of Arts in 1956 with a major in philosophy. He next attended the Gregorian University in Rome and received a degree in sacred theology in 1958 and a licentiate in theology in 1960.

Bishop Cooney was ordained to the priesthood on December 20, 1959, by Bishop Martin J. O'Connor, rector of the North American College in Rome. Following completion of theological studies in Rome, Bishop Cooney returned to Detroit and was the Assistant Pastor at Saint Catherine Parish from 1960 to 1962 and Assistant Chancellor from 1962 to 1969. He was appointed Director of the Archdiocesan Department of Worship in 1969 and continued in this position until his ordination as a bishop. From 1977 to 1983 he was the Rector of the Cathedral of the Most Blessed Sacrament in Detroit.

In December, 1982, His Holiness Pope John Paul II named Father Cooney to the episcopacy and he was ordained titular Bishop of Hodelm and Auxiliary Bishop of Detroit on January 27, 1983, at Detroit's Cathedral of the Most Blessed Sacrament.

On the day of his installation as the Bishop of Gaylord, January 28, 1990, His Eminence Edmund Cardinal Szoka, the first bishop of Gaylord, presented Bishop

Bishop Patrick R. Cooney at his ordination mass.

Cooney to the Rector of Saint Mary Cathedral in Gaylord, Reverend James A. Suchocki, at the cathedral door. From there a procession of bishops, priests, deacons, church officials and lay persons moved into the cathedral proper. Archbishop Pio Laghi, apostolic pronuncio, read the official letter of appointment. Cardinal Szoka then led Bishop Cooney to the bishop's chair which serves as the symbol of his role as the shepherd of the diocese.

As a member of the National Conference of Catholic Bishops, Bishop Cooney has served on a number of committees: Bishops' Committee on Liturgy, Subcommittee of Bishops and Scholars, Subcommittee on Use of Exclusive Language in Liturgy, Subcommittee on Book of Blessings, Subcommittee on Cremation and Other Funeral Questions, Committee on Laity, and the National Advisory Council. He served on the Board of Directors of Notre Dame Liturgical Center, the Board of Governors of North American College and as a Board member for Sacred Heart Seminary, Detroit.

Since the time of the nation's first president, it can be said that northern lower Michigan has been successively in the Dioceses of Baltimore (1789), Bardstown, Kentucky (1810), Cincinnati (1821), Detroit (1833), Grand Rapids (1883) and Gaylord (1971). In terms of provincial jurisdiction, the Lower Peninsula passed from Baltimore (1808) to Cincinnati (1850) to Detroit (1937). ■

Note: This was excerpted from Willard M.J. Baird's book, "A Heritage of Faith," which traces the history of the Catholic Church in Missaukee County and northwestern Lower Michigan.

Reflections on the founding of a diocese

by its first spiritual leader

By Edmund Cardinal Szoka

On July 21, 1996 the Diocese of Gaylord celebrated its 25th anniversary with a special liturgy. Presiding were the present bishop, Bishop Patrick Cooney, and the two previous ones, Cardinal Edmund Szoka and Bishop Robert Rose. Cardinal Szoka delivered the homily at the Anniversary Mass and used the occasion to review the history of the diocese and offer some personal reflections of his years in Gaylord. Following are excerpts from this homily.

I was appointed by Pope Paul VI in June, 1971 to be the first bishop of the new Diocese of Gaylord. This new diocese was formed from parts of two other dioceses: Saginaw and Grand Rapids. It consisted of the 21 counties in the northern part of the Lower Peninsula of Michigan. Fourteen of the counties came from the Diocese of Grand Rapids, and seven from the Diocese of Saginaw.

In this new diocese there were about 70,000 Catholics with about 60 diocesan priests and about 15 religious priests. There were about 170 religious sisters and two brothers. There were five Catholic high schools and 22 grade schools. There were 58 parishes and 24 missions. There were also three Catholic hospitals.

The See City, the City of Gaylord, was and still is a very small town of only about 3,500 inhabitants. I believe it is still the smallest See City in the United States. It was chosen very wisely because of its location in the geographical center of the new diocese.

There was only one parish in Gaylord, a large parish with a very small church which would seat only about 400 people. Monsignor Francis Kaminski, of beloved memory, was the pastor. At the time he was about 70 years old and was without an associate pastor. He was assisted on weekends by a retired priest from the Saginaw Diocese, Father Dalbert Narloch, who was about 74 years old. Because the church was so small, there were ten Sunday Masses: three on Saturday evening and seven on Sunday morning. Monsignor Kaminski and Father Narloch celebrated these Masses themselves, with occasional help from a vacationing priest.

The parish had a large grade school and high school. The Mass of my episcopal ordination was held in the gymnasium of the high school on July 20, 1971. The consecrator was the late Cardinal John Deardon, then Archbishop of Detroit. The Apostolic Delegate, Archbishop Luigi Raimondi, was also present to canonically erect the new diocese at the beginning of the Mass of consecration.

It is a very unusual experience to be the first Bishop of a diocese. The practical realities immediately became apparent. I had no place to live, no office, no staff to assist me. In a word, I didn't even have a paper clip.

I continued as the Bishop of Gaylord for ten years. A unique relationship develops between the first bishop and his priests, a relationship so special that it can never be repeated. We all began the new diocese together without any particular traditions or procedures to maintain. We were not bound by past practices. The priests of the new diocese came from two separate dioceses and had to become acquainted with each other as well as with their new bishop. There was no past to haunt any of us. Each of us began with a clean slate. I assured the priests that I was not interested in their past record, only in the present and future.

Pope John Paul II and Cardinal Szoka who is today the President of the Pontifical Commission for the Vatican City State.

We developed a special fraternal, priestly bond which none of us will ever experience again. The same can be said about the relationship that grew between the bishop, the religious and the lay people. There was great excitement about the new diocese and there was remarkable coming together in the unity of faith. I think the outstanding characteristic of the diocese was that unity, a bonding in faith, which continues today in its full vigor.

The Diocese of Gaylord grew and developed, especially as a year-round vacationland tourist center because it is situated in the most beautiful, or at least one of the most beautiful areas of Michigan with lakes, forests, small mountains and valleys. My ten years here were among the happiest, most rewarding years of my life.

In March, 1981, our Holy Father Pope John Paul II, appointed me Archbishop of the Archdiocese of Detroit. The installation took place on May 17, 1981, just four days after our Holy Father was wounded by an assassin in Saint Peter's Square.

In the meantime, the Diocese of Gaylord was without a shepherd until October 13, when Father Robert Rose, a priest of the Diocese of Grand Rapids, was appointed the second Bishop of Gaylord. The consecration and installation took place on December 6, 1981.

Since I was then the Metropolitan Archbishop of the Ecclesiastical Province of Detroit, to which the Diocese of Gaylord belongs, I was invited to consecrate Bishop Rose and install him in this Cathedral Church of the Diocese.

Bishop Rose served the Diocese of Gaylord with great dedication and success. During his time as bishop, new diocesan departments were created to better serve the people of the diocese, and new diocesan office buildings were acquired. Above all, the bond and spirit of unity which had developed continued to grow and deepen under his leadership.

After eight years of service, Bishop Rose was transferred to the Diocese of Grand Rapids on July 11, 1989. Again, the Diocese of Gaylord was without a shepherd until November 21 of that same year when Bishop Patrick Cooney was appointed the third Bishop of Gaylord.

Bishop Cooney had been one of my Auxiliary Bishops in Detroit and I had consecrated him a bishop in Detroit on January 27, 1983. On January 28, 1990, I installed him as Bishop of Gaylord in this same Cathedral Church.

I have had the unusual privilege of consecrating and installing my two successors as Bishops of Gaylord.

I left for my present duties in Rome in June, 1990, so I have been away from the United States for most of the six years during which Bishop Cooney has served the diocese. However, everything I have heard about his ministry here as a bishop has been very positive and complimentary. I know he has given himself wholeheartedly to the service of the priests, religious and laity. He has not spared himself but has given totally and without hesitation of his time, his energy and his talents to his episcopal ministry.

My dear friends, I have said a great deal about the episcopal ministry and the bishops because the bishop is and must be the heart and center of the diocese. At the same time, however, it is obvious that a bishop must depend on his priests, who share in his priesthood, to serve more closely and on a daily basis the people of the diocese. I want to pay tribute to the priests of the Diocese of Gaylord who continue to serve so well and so faithfully, and who have developed a special, priestly fraternal bond of unity which in many respects is unique to the Diocese of Gaylord.

During my years as bishop, there were no Permanent Deacons. I note, however, that now there are about 12. I commend them and encourage them. I know from my experience in Detroit how valuable is their ministry.

I express as well my great respect, gratitude and admiration for the religious sisters who have shared in the life and ministry of the Diocese of Gaylord. Their commitment to the service of God's people is given with complete generosity in a way which is special and unique to the consecrated life of Religious.

Dioceses are established and bishops are appointed to serve God's people. Without people, however, there is no need for a diocese or a bishop. Without people there is no particular church, no diocese. From the very first days of the announcement of the new diocese, the lay people were most enthusiastic and pleased that they would have there own diocese and their own bishop.

During my ten years as bishop of Gaylord, I found the lay people of the diocese to be people of profound faith and love for the church. Their commitment and loyalty were evidenced in many varied and diverse ways, both on the level of the parish as well as on the level of the diocese. It did not take long, for example, to establish a diocesan Board of Education, a diocesan Finance Committee, a diocesan organization for the annual Catholic Services Appeal, the diocesan Council of Catholic Women, committees for the guidance of our work in the area of social services, and many others.

The people of the Diocese of Gaylord are a people of faith who truly love their church and participate in the life of the church, each in accord with his or her circumstances.

Today is a day of memories, recalling our beginnings and giving thanks to God who made it all possible. We thank the Lord for this wonderful, beautiful Diocese of Gaylord, this portion of God's people gathered together with their shepherd in these 21 counties of northern Michigan.

Today is also a day to look to the future. And we can certainly look to that future with confidence. The Diocese of Gaylord is going forward with great vigor and vitality. It is my hope and prayer that it will continue to do so in the years ahead. ■

Under Bishop Rose, the diocese grew in spirit and mission

By Father Patrick T. Cawley

Word came to Father Robert Rose while he was attending a three-month study program in Rome in the fall of 1981 that he was to be made a bishop and become the second Ordinary of the Diocese of Gaylord. This appointment was announced by John Paul II on October 13, 1981. Bishop Rose was ordained by Archbishop Edmund Szoka and installed at the Cathedral in Gaylord on December 6, 1981. Bishop Rose served the Diocese of Gaylord until 1989 when he was transferred to Grand Rapids.

Bishop Rose's vision and goal was to bring the people of the diocese together in order to develop a comprehensive plan for this young and growing church. He was very concerned about the unchurched in the diocese and for the isolation that several of the clergy faced.

The priests in the diocese comprised a mixture of backgrounds and formations. They included diocesan priests from both the Grand Rapids and Saginaw Dioceses, religious order priests such as the Franciscans, priests from other states, some displaced priests and some retired from other dioceses. The spiritual health and well being of his priests was a major commitment for Bishop Rose and this was much appreciated by the priests.

Another very important focus for Bishop Rose was to help the people understand and accept the concept that the diocese does not belong to the bishop, but to the bishop and the priests together. It is "our" diocese was a major point he stressed often.

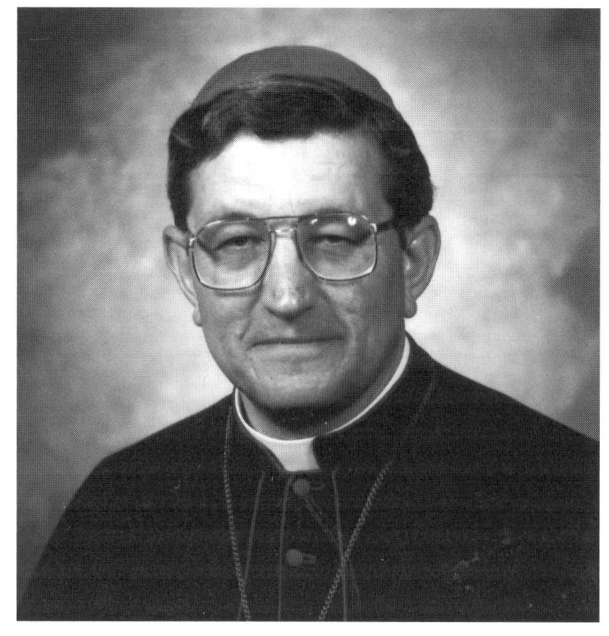

Bishop Robert Rose

He carefully and deliberately set up a process of consultation with clergy and people regarding goals and directions for the diocese. He developed diocesan assemblies with the assistance of Sister Virginia Phillips, O.P. These assemblies served to move ideas and thinking from the parishes to the diocese, and to develop implementation strategies.

Many ideas surfaced from this model, including the clustering of parishes and pastoral administrators. Bishop Rose also developed diocesan pastoral and finance councils as directed by the revised code of canon law.

Bishop Rose is quick to point out that he received assistance and guidance as he began his assignment in Gaylord from Archbishop Szoka and Msgr. David Gemuend who had served as administrator prior to Bishop Rose's appointment. Prayerful listening, consultation, honesty, involvement of all people and careful planning were necessary ingredients for Bishop Rose.

The process took a while but the results are fruitful and considerate of everyone.

Bishop Rose established an active priests' appointment committee, appointed Father Jim Suchocki as vocations director, introduced computers at diocesan offices and initiated the annual convocation of priests. He also introduced a parish deposit and loan program in Gaylord,

similar to one he helped establish in Grand Rapids.

Bishop Rose also obtained for the diocese the Augustine Center Retreat House in Conway, and made pastoral visits to all 82 parishes in the dioceses during his leadership.

Evangelization, liturgy and music were very important to Bishop Rose. He wanted to build on what was developed before him and very much wanted the people to feel that he was their bishop and that the priests and people could take ownership of their diocese.

During his leadership, the Diocese of Gaylord grew in many ways, not the least of which was making the Kingdom of God a reality for all members of the church. Cardinal Szoka was certainly the right person to establish the Diocese of Gaylord and Bishop Rose was the right choice to build on what he had initiated. Bishop Rose was the church's choice to take the new diocese to a direction and spirituality necessary to foster God's kingdom. Like Cardinal Szoka, Bishop Rose brought unique and spiritual gifts that were so significant in the development of the Diocese of Gaylord.

After eight years as Bishop of Gaylord, Bishop Rose was transferred to his home Diocese of Grand Rapids. He left in the summer of 1989 with some anticipation for his new See but he also left much love and great feelings of joy and peace for the Diocese of Gaylord he loved so very much. ■

Bishop Cooney carries on the diocesan 'continuum'

By David L. Knight

In November, 1991, having been installed as the third bishop of the Diocese of Gaylord eight months previous, Bishop Patrick R. Cooney issued his first pastoral letter to the laity, religious and clergy of the diocese. Entitled "An Agenda for the Church in Gaylord," the document provided revealing insight into Bishop Cooney's pastoral vision for the diocese, his spiritual emphasis and his managerial style.

"The Church of the Diocese of Gaylord is more than the Bishop and central staff," he wrote. "It is more than pastoral people and parishes. It is more than teachers and schools. It is more than monasteries and houses of prayer, more than Catholic social service agencies and Catholic hospitals, and more than Catholic organizations and movements of women and men.

"The Church in the Diocese of Gaylord is all of us and all of us together. Being one together is essential."

Thus the spirit of inclusiveness, which had been introduced by Bishop Edmond Szoka at the diocese's founding and which had been such a strong theme during the tenure of Bishop Robert Rose, was destined to continue and grow under Bishop Cooney. Indeed, Bishop Cooney characterized his first nine years in Gaylord as not a new era in diocese history, but just the next step forward in its ongoing evolution.

"What has taken place since the establishment of the Diocese of Gaylord is a developmental continuum carried out over the tenures of the three bishops," said Bishop Cooney. "The main accomplishment of Bishop Szoka, whom I consider the 'Father of the Diocese,' was the merging of two dioceses into one. That was no easy task.

"Bishop Rose continued the growth of the diocese with his development of greater roles for the laity and the Catholic faithful, which went hand in hand with clergy development.

"My part in the continuum has been to build an espirit de corps among the priests of the diocese, providing more meetings and opportunities for them to share ex-

periences. A second thrust for me has been continued development of the laity through such programs as adult education."

Obviously lay persons in the Diocese of Gaylord have come to bear many new responsibilities within their parishes as northern Michigan's Catholic population continues to grow while the number of available clergy and religious to serve it remains limited. Between 1971 and 1996, the number of Catholics in the diocese increased over 30 percent from 66,000 to 87,000, while the number of diocesan priests increased only seven percent from 70 to 75, and the number of religious sisters dropped by over half from 178 to 82.

Rather than look at the situation as a hardship, however, Bishop Cooney approached it as an opportunity.

"One of the great strengths of the diocese that I have observed is the increasingly strong relationship between the lay people and the clergy," he said. "Part of that is a result of a new attitude we, as the clergy, have taken toward the role of the laity. We now realize and accept that the lay people of our parishes want to make meaningful contributions. We understand now that our parishioners who wish to get involved in the work of the Church cannot be ignored or treated like children."

Through increased involvement in pastoral and finance councils, the liturgy, religious education, outreach ministries and other activities, the laity of the Diocese of Gaylord have acquitted themselves well as important partners in God's work, noted Bishop Cooney. And the Church, he added, is better for it.

"The days are gone when the pastor says, unilaterally, 'This is the way it is going to be done,'" he said.

The Catholic liturgy is another area in which Bishop Cooney has seen evidence of a diocesan "continuum."

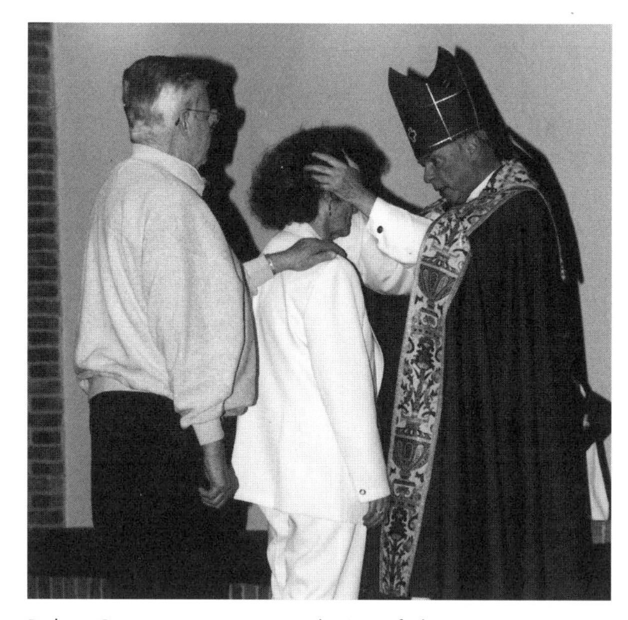

Bishop Cooney participates in the Rite of Election.

"The first 25 years of the Diocese of Gaylord's existence has been a very interesting time of liturgical development for the Church," he said. "In the immediate aftermath of Vatican II, people were very enthused about the new liturgy. We are just now, however, beginning to understand its real impact."

In his 1991 "Agenda for the Church," Bishop Cooney identified three primary goals:

- Worship the Almighty

"Much talent, time and financial resources will be needed for such an ongoing development of our liturgical celebration. Yet the very nature of liturgy calls for it."

- Cherish and Share His Word

"The ministry of cherishing and sharing the word will always be seeking a better understanding of the message, new horizons in which to share it and improved methods to communicate it,"

- Co-build His Kingdom

"Jesus modeled and taught what the kingdom is and what 'kingdom life' is like. We are challenged to make the effort to convert our world into that vision."

Another of Bishop Cooney's emphases has been to nurture personal and professional development among the priests of the diocese. He has stressed the importance of keeping alive such traditional responsibilities of the parish priest as visiting the sick and taking an active role in religious education. But he acknowledges that much more has come to be expected from the priests of the diocese, saying, "We demand more professionalism from our priests today. We are recognizing that the modern priesthood is a vocation that demands a high level of professionalism in all its different aspects."

So, how does a Catholic laity willing and able to assume more responsibility within the parish square with the priest's mandate to carry out his traditional roles?

"It is not a question of either a priest or lay people carrying out these responsibilities," Bishop Cooney said, "but the priest and the lay people."

Appropriately, his words in 1999 closely reflect those he first wrote in 1991, and which are worth restating: "The diocese is all of us and all of us together. Being one together is essential." ■

Section Two

People, places, institutions and stories

Father Baraga and L'Arbre Croche

Overcoming the hardships of early Northern Michigan

By Kay Hughes

On May 28, 1831, a Slovenian missionary priest, Father Frederic Baraga, arrived at L'Arbre Croche with Bishop Edward D. Fenwick, bishop of the newly formed Cincinnati Diocese, which at that time included Michigan.

L'Arbre Croche was an area between the present day Cross Village and Harbor Springs that the Ottawa Indians named Waw-gaw-naw-ke-see ("the crooked tree"). The name was derived from a large pine tree with a dramatic hook at its top which stood on a bluff and served as a navigational aid for all who traveled along the Lake Michigan coast. The French version of "the crooked tree," L'Arbre Croche, is still used today.

Father Baraga had spent the winter with Bishop Fenwick in Cincinnati and had learned the Ottawa language from William Maccatebinesse, son of an Ottawa chief who later went to Rome to study for the priesthood.

Baraga found life harsh in the north. As he recounted to his sister, Amalia, "Our church, schoolhouse and my house are of wood, roofed with tree bark. All of this the Indians have made alone; you can imagine how it may look. When it rains I must spread out my cloak over my table on which I have my books and papers, in order to protect them from an inundation. Over my bed I spread my umbrella, and I save myself, as well as I can, in a corner of my small room where it drips the least: nevertheless I am happier in my little room than all the European emperors and kings in their glittering gold palaces. Our church is rather roomy; it could accommodate 400 persons; but I hope that it will soon be too small for us.

"The Indians of this region have small and poor fields, they cultivate nothing else but Turkish corn and some legumes and potatoes, which thrive here very well. The principal product of the Indians is sugar which they produce from the large number of sugar trees existing here. At the beginning of this month of March begins the production, and it lasts till towards the end of April. Now, in this sugar time, there is no person at all in this village, with the exception of four individuals who live in the mission house. They are all in the forest, where, at various distances from here,(one, or at the most two hours), they have their sugar trees, then in receptacles of tree bark catch the sugar water which flows abundantly from them, boil this water into a syrup, which, then, after it settles and cools, makes excellent sugar, which in spring they sell very well to the merchants, or rather, exchange for clothing, provisions, utensils, and the like: since the Indians have no money, nor do they want to have any, their trade with the whites is only barter.

"As an interesting curiosity, I send you a little of the sugar of my Indians. Each of my Indians produces annually from eight to ten hundredweight's of this sugar.

"...I have already mentioned to you in my last letter how severe winter is in this desolate land, overgrown with immense forests. However, now I must give you some more noteworthy information about our winter. In my little room I have a rather large iron stove in which fire burns continually and intensely day and night, but there were many nights this winter when my drinking water froze which stood on a table only a step away from the stove. Yes, even the water in my washbasin, that I purposely placed under the stove, often froze for me during the night.

"Some days in January and February were so cold that I almost could not finish holy Mass that was begun. I brought the cruets, in which I have the wine and water for holy Mass, warm from the stove to the church, and before I came to the offertory everything was frozen so that I had to break up the ice in order to be able to pour the wine and the water into the chalice. Scarcely had I poured the wine in the chalice when it froze instantly, and when I came to the consecration I had to breathe into the chalice for a long time in order to melt the ice in it a little; even longer I breathed into the chalice before holy communion in order to be able to consume the sacred blood. The missioners of the northerly and wild countries, where winter rages terribly, are all in the unpleasant necessity of doing this."

The following spring Baraga baptized 251 Indians. He also brought the gospel to the Beaver Island Indians.

Another woman who helped bring the Gospel to the people was Marianne Fisher. She had been at L'Arbre Croche as a teacher when Father DeJean was there. She continued to work with Father Baraga and even later moved to Grand River with him. Father Patrick O'Kelly briefly mentioned her: "They say she is a very exemplary and virtuous woman, and well qualified to discharge the duties annexed to the female apartment of the Indian mission (at Arbre Croche)."

It was a general practice on missionary trips to take one or two missionary women along, particularly for the duties of helping the priest hear confessions. They also taught the women and children, while the priest and several men took care of the men.

In 1832, Baraga wrote: "As regards our school here, it is now in good condition. We have more than 60 pupils, boys and girls, the boys are instructed by Mr. L'Etourneau of Detroit in reading and writing, in arithmetic and in French languages. Arithmetic is imparted to them in the French language.

"Mrs. Fisher of Mackinac is conducting the girl's school. She instructs the girls in Indian and French reading, and after school, she shows them feminine handicrafts such as sewing, knitting, etc. For an hour every day all the boys and girls are assembled and instructed by me in religion."

Father Frederick Baraga

A Mr. L'Etourneau also instructed the Indians in carpentry, especially how to make sashes, doors and frames for their houses. Father Baraga wrote Indian prayer books, had them printed in Detroit, and brought them home to be bound by Redemptorist Father Aloysius. He also introduced the arts of blacksmithing and locksmithing.

Baraga left L'Arbre Croche in September, 1833, to establish a new mission at what is today Grand Rapids. He went on to travel and minister extensively in Michigan's Upper Peninsula and in 1854 was named bishop of a newly formed vicariate in Sault Ste. Marie. He moved his See in 1866 to Marquette.

Frederic Baraga, who is being considered for sainthood, founded churches and schools and lived in the harshest conditions. Adding to his ordeal was the fact that he suffered terribly from seasickness. This was unfortunate since the chief mode of travel from spring through fall was on the water by small canoe, large canoe, sail craft and steamboats. It has been said, however, that as soon as Baraga stepped onto firm ground he was just fine.

Winter was a different matter. He writes in February, 1860, that "the missioners said to me that I should come in winter in order to meet them. Therefore, in winter, in the first days of the month of February, 1860, I shall have to make a journey on foot, on snowshoes, to Mackinac and Saint Ignace. These winter journeys on foot are now difficult for me, first, because I am now already somewhat out of practice, and secondly, also because of my age, since next February, if I live, I will be in my sixty-third year. In these years, especially when one in past years has suffered hardships, one is already somewhat stiff and feels the cold.

"The marching throughout the day is still tolerable, but when it comes to the evening, to spend the night on the snow under the open sky in this northerly climate, that does not go well. By the tiresome walking on snowshoes, over hill and dale, one is in a sweat the entire day, despite the cold, so that all the underwear becomes wet; and in the evening, when one comes to a halt, he then soon feels extremely cold and begins to shiver as if he had a fever.

"If on these winter journeys I could come every evening to a house, then they would not be difficult for me. But in this desolate country one must often travel many days before he again comes to a house. Such is the lot of a missionary bishop, which however, I do not find hard, because I have been a missioner in this dreary country for so many years; only the years oppress me somewhat."

In the 1860s the Civil War encroached its ugly head on our fair country. One L'Arbre Croche schoolteacher's son was killed while burying his father before Petersburg. Lieut. G.A. Graveraet led nearly 100 men, almost entirely Indians, from the Little Tra-

verse Region. You can still see markers in local cemeteries of "Company K, First Michigan Sharpshooters."

In his letter to the Leopoldine Society dated August 30, 1862, Bishop Baraga expressed himself on the war then raging:

"This year untold misery and oppressive want as to the necessaries of life prevail on every account of the terrible civil war, which rages horribly in the interior of this once so happy and peaceable country. Thousands and hundreds of thousands of useful individuals, who were the support of their families, are torn away from their feeble parents, their helpless wives and children, and thousands of families are plunged into the most direful poverty, misery however must admit that there is less to be seen and heard of this misery in my out of-the-way diocese than in the southern part of this country, the actual theater of this most sad war."

In 1868, Bishop Baraga died at the age of 70. He is interred in a basement chapel of Saint Peter Cathedral in Marquette. ■

The intriguing tale of

Father Charlevoix, Secret Agent

By William H. Ohle

pparently no one knows who came up with the idea to name the northern Michigan community of Charlevoix after a Jesuit priest who explored the area in the 1720s.

The name was first given to the county when the state legislature in 1843 denoted it as Charlevoix County, as a replacement for the one originally assigned, Keshkanko County.

The change became official when enough settlers had congregated and the county was officially organized in 1869. The name Charlevoix wore so well that the village at the mouth of the Pine River also adopted it as a mellifluous replacement for its original Plain Jane title, Pine River. In 1926, the County Board of Commissioners, stimulated by an enthusiastic Grand Rapids tourism promoter, sought and secured state and congressional action to change the name of beautiful Pine Lake to Lake Charlevoix.

Pierre Francois Xavier de Charlevoix was an exceptionally bright French boy, born in 1682, who joined the Jesuit Order at age 16. While still in his 20s, he moved to Quebec in French Canada to teach grammar at a Jesuit college for four years.

Returning to France, he planned to settle down to a teaching and writing career. But by sheer accident Father Charlevoix became a key figure in international intrigue involving the famous Northwest Passage, which everyone believed existed and, when found, could provide an easy passage to the western ocean.

At the end of Queen Anne's war, France had lost the Maritime Provinces of Canada to Great Britain under the terms of the Treaty of Utrecht. To re-strengthen his hand in the New World, the King of France was easily persuaded that it was of paramount importance for France to discover the Northwest Passage.

Advisors came up with two proposals to accomplish the royal wish. One idea was to mount a deluxe expedition estimated to cost 50,000 francs, a large sum for that day. The other was the ingenious suggestion to dispatch a Jesuit priest as a secret agent. The ostensible purpose of the priest's trip was to inspect French missions throughout the Great Lakes and down the Mississippi River.

Arguments advanced in favor of the latter were that it would require minimal financial outlay and would not invite suspicion.

The priestly trip was quickly accepted as the most likely chance for success and Father Charlevoix, because of his recent Quebec service, was chosen to undertake the project.

So the Father returned to the New World, this time armed with orders to the French governor at Quebec to supply him with two canoes, eight companions and all the merchandise needed for the journey. He had become a foreign agent for the King of France.

Part of the plan was that he was to write a series of letters addressed to his "patroness," the Duchess de Lesdigueres, reporting details of what he saw and did. These were, in fact, a ruse to throw off suspicion as to the true purpose of his trip and actually were never delivered to the duchess.

They were published later in illustrated book form and translated into several languages in many editions. Fortunately for us, Charlevoix was a gifted observer and writer. He returned from his journey two years later with the disappointing news that no easy route had been discovered leading to the Western Sea.

He had toured the Great Lakes and made a leisurely voyage down the Mississippi River, visiting mission stations as planned, and had seen wonderful things. He reached New Orleans in 1722 and returned to France in 1723 after a harrowing shipwreck experience in the Gulf of Mexico.

Father Charlevoix

Father Charlevoix spent the rest of his life teaching, editing a Jesuit journal and writing his experiences. As a teacher he had the reputation among his pupils of being full of words. (Incidentally, one of his students was the famous author Voltaire.)

But, as the author of his *History and Description of New France*, which was the first general narrative history of French Canada based on both personal experience and existing source material, Charlevoix made his mark on history. It, too, was translated into several languages and has been through numerous editions and remains today as one of the most important bits of source material pertaining to France in the New World, giving a clear picture of the flora, fauna and manners and customs of native Americans.

A copy was one of the items in George Washington's private library and copies of both the three- and six-volume editions are to be found in the Charlevoix and Petoskey public libraries.

From time to time there has been speculation concerning Father Charlevoix's direct connection with this area. This should be laid to rest in a quotation from one of his letters to the Duchess dated July 31, 1721:

"Madam,

"I set out (from Mackinaw) five leagues westward in order to make Lake Michigan; afterwards I turned south...advanced three leagues farther, and a strong wind obliged us to stop at this island...

"On the first day of August, after having crossed under sail a bay which is 30 leagues in depth (Grand Traverse Bay), I left on my right 'Les isles de Castor' (the Beaver Islands) which seem very well wooded. Some leagues further on the left I perceived a sandy eminence, which when you are abreast of it, has the figure of an animal lying down: the French call this the Sleeping Bear."

So we know for sure that Father Charlevoix was an early explorer of Michigan's northern Lower Peninsula and that he spent at least one night in Charlevoix County, on what is now known as Fisherman's Island.

William H. Ohle, who died in 1997, was a writer and historian who lived in Horton Bay. This account first appeared in 1983 in Petoskey's summer newspaper, "The Graphic". ■

The Church in Northeastern Michigan

Memories of the Alpena Deanery

By Kenneth J. Povish, Retired Bishop of Lansing

A hundred years ago, all of the present-day Diocese of Gaylord was in the Diocese of Grand Rapids. Before that, all of Lower Michigan belonged to the Diocese of Detroit. Before that, both Michigan peninsulas were part of the Diocese of Cincinnati, from 1821 to 1833. Before that, Michigan was the northern most portion of the Diocese of Bardstown (Kentucky) from 1808 to 1833. Before that, Michigan was part of the original United States Diocese, Baltimore, established in 1789. Before that, from the days of the French missionaries and explorers, Michigan was part of the Diocese of Quebec, established in 1674.

All this history was beautifully pictured for years in the soaring Gothic arch above the sanctuary of Saint Mary Cathedral in Saginaw. Painted on the archway were, in historical order, the coats of arms of all of Saginaw's predecessor dioceses: Quebec, Baltimore, Bardstown, Cincinnati, Detroit and Grand Rapids.

In 1938, a new diocese was established for northeastern Michigan, with its bishop in Saginaw. After 56 years as part of the Church of Grand Rapids, 13 eastern counties of that diocese were transferred to the new Diocese of Saginaw; among them were Alcona, Alpena, Iosco, Montmorency, Oscoda and Presque Isle. When the first Bishop of Saginaw, William F. Murphy, set out to organize this diocese in 1939, he divided the territory into four subdivisions called "deaneries." The six counties enumerated above were called "the Alpena Deanery." All six of them were, in turn, transferred to the new Diocese of Gaylord in 1971, when, after 30 years of growth in northern lower Michigan, the Churches of Grand Rapids and Saginaw were further divided to provide 21 counties for the new See in Gaylord.

I was born and raised in the old Alpena Deanery. After my ordination to the priesthood of Saginaw in 1950, I was assigned to that deanery for two years. For 18 years thereafter I visited family, friends and priest classmates in the old Alpena Deanery almost every month. This essay is a record of my recollections of Catholic life in the easternmost counties of the present-day Diocese of Gaylord between my First Communion in 1932 and my ordination as bishop in 1970.

The First Centuries

French missionaries, most well-educated, zealous Jesuits, explored the upper Great Lakes and were probably the first Catholics to touch the shores of northeastern Michigan. They were at the Straits of Mackinac, where they founded the mission of Saint Ignace in 1671. In May of 1675 the famous Pere Marquette died near Ludington in northwestern Michigan. In December of that same year, Father Henri Nouvel offered the first Mass in what is now Saginaw. In 1679, the explorer LaSalle sailed his ship, the *Griffin*, from Lake Erie to Mackinac and encountered a severe storm in northern Lake Huron. From the description in the ship's log, many believe that Thunder Bay, on the 45th parallel, is the bay in which LaSalle took refuge.

With all this traffic around the Straits and in upper Lake Huron, it is hard to believe that French Catholics did not camp, pray, and perhaps offer Mass in the counties of the former Alpena Deanery. But if they did, there is no record of it or any identifiable site. The church at Michilimackinac was moved early on to Mackinac Island, and the settlement and evangelization of northern lower Michigan was left to French Canadians from Quebec and to European immigrants a hundred years later.

Later Missionaries

Father Frederic Baraga, native of Slovenia, missionary to the Chippewas, first Bishop of Marquette, candidate for sainthood, began his apostolic labors at L'Arbre Croche in 1831, in the Upper Peninsula in 1835. It was as bishop of the Upper Peninsula that he volunteered to look after the faithful at and around the Straits, so far and so difficult for the Bishop of Detroit to pastor. It was in that capacity that Bishop Baraga organized the first parishes in Alpena and Alcona counties.

Father Henry J.H. Schutjes, a Belgian, was a pioneer missionary in outstate Michigan. Schutjes spoke several languages; his name was pronounced "Shoo-zhay" by the French and Walloons, "Skoo-chess" by the German and Flemish. It was the influence of pioneers like Father Schutjes that brought more than a dozen Belgian priests to serve in the parishes north of Saginaw Bay. Names like VanGennip, DeKiere, Van der Bom, Schaeken, Kindekins and Takken appear often in the oldest parish records of northeastern Michigan.

The third missionary of these eastern counties was Father Francis Xavier Szulak (pronounced "Shoe-lock"). This Jesuit missionary worked among Polish immigrants for 50 years. Wherever he went, mission parishes were organized and churches were built. This was the origin of the parishes at Posen, Rogers City and Alpena Saint Mary's. From Michigan, Szulak followed the immigrants to Wisconsin, Iowa and Nebraska. He died doing the same kind of work among Polish exiles in Argentina in 1920.

Immigrant Communities

The development of northeastern Michigan came fast after the Civil War. The Homestead Act of 1862 gave great impetus to this development. It granted a farm of 160 acres, free of charge, to any citizen over 21 years of age who would settle upon it and cultivate it for five years. Aliens who had declared their intention of becoming citizens were also eligible. Imagine how land-hungry immigrants of Europe viewed this opportunity! Thousands of hardworking young Catholic families from Ireland, Germany, Poland and Quebec, anxious to own land of their own, flocked to Michigan via New York, the Erie Canal, and steamers on the Great Lakes. One of my great-grandfathers homesteaded 160 acres in Maple Ridge Township, Alpena County.

Two railroads crossed the eastern counties. The Boyne City, Gaylord and Alpena line (BCG&A) went east-west. It folded by the 1920s when the lumber was gone, but, when I was a boy, the roadbed was still clearly visible in many places bordering on M-32. The other system was the Detroit and Mackinac line (D&M) going north-south along U.S. 23. The name was a misnomer because the terminals were Bay City on the south and Cheboygan on the north. However, the D&M flourished for generations and still carries freight profitably along the Lake Huron shore. Irish Catholic immigrants were prominent in the building and operation of these railroads. My paternal grandfather was a cook and parlor-car cleaner on the D&M for 49 years before his retirement in 1939.

A First Communion card.

White pine forests covered the eastern counties and lumbering, sawmills and shipping were the chief industries from the 1870s until the forests gave out 50 years later. French Catholics from Canada were attracted to these jobs and to commercial fishing in Lake Huron. It is no accident that there was a "French church" in every town along the lake shore from Cheboygan to Saginaw. That's where the saw mills were located and where fresh fish could be sold. The parish at AuSable (now Oscoda Sacred Heart) numbered 900 families in 1900 and was then the largest parish in the Diocese of Grand Rapids.

When the land was stripped of trees, rich deposits of shale, limestone and gypsum began to be quarried in Alpena, Presque Isle and Iosco counties. These operations also drew immigrant labor in large numbers, and many of these workers were Catholics. My maternal grandfather worked in the quarry of the Michigan Alkali Company all his adult life, and five uncles of the next generation were employed there or in the adjacent Huron Portland Cement Company plant, a principal user of limestone and shale. As well as Poles and Germans, the Michigan Limestone & Chemical Company quarry at Rogers City attracted a significant number of Italian Catholic families who enriched the life of the parish there.

With all the scrap from the saw mills, the sawdust and the stumps, forest fires in dry weather were always a

danger. The eastern counties suffered two major fires with a loss of life and property. Metz Township, Presque Isle County, was ravished by flames the afternoon of October 15, 1908. Eighteen persons perished when the train sent to rescue them was derailed with fire all around it. On July 11, 1911, sparks from a locomotive ignited a fire in the woods near AuSable. A wind-driven fire destroyed the town, including all the property and the records of Sacred Heart Church. Saw mills and homes were destroyed, and many people moved away for good. There were few deaths, however, because Lake Huron provided a safe retreat from the flames.

Monsignor T. D. Flannery

The Immigrant Parish

When I was growing up in the late 1920s and the early 30s, the immigrant parish was already beginning to change but was still well represented in Alpena, the largest town in the eastern counties of the present-day Diocese of Gaylord. The different national groups tended to flock together, the elders of each convinced that the old language and culture were necessary to preserve the faith.

So Alpena had the "Irish church" on West Chisholm Street, the original parish founded by Baraga in 1866, where English was spoken and to which the German and Italian Catholic families also belonged. Saint Bernard parish had strong pastors over the years; the legendary Monsignor T. D. Flannery led the parish from 1883 to 1921.

The "French church," Saint Anne on South Ninth Avenue, served the large number of French-Canadian families concentrated in Alpena's West End. By the 1930s, French was heard publicly only in the lovely carols at Midnight Mass of Christmas and when the periodic preaching mission featured a Jesuit from Quebec. However, one could overhear the older parishioners murmuring their private prayers in French and conversing with one another on the church porch in that language.

As a young priest in the 1950s, I heard confessions occasionally at Saint Anne; and my high school French was adequate to understand and give a penance to the many faithful who confessed in that language. A German-American penitent at Saint Bernard in those same years prefaced his confession this way: "I say the sins in English, Vater; aber the prayer goes in German." I am sure many confessors heard explanations like that in those days from the different nationalities.

The pastor who stands out in Saint Anne history is Father Louis T. Bouchard, who was pastor from 1919 to 1944.

Alpena's "Polish church" was Saint Mary on Second Avenue, north of Thunder Bay River. Most Poles lived on the North Side, with a considerable overflow in the West End, where both my paternal and maternal grandparents lived. They were only three blocks each from Saint Anne, but in those days it was unthinkable that they and their children would not walk the mile and a half to the "Polish church" and school. In the 1930s, three of the four Sunday sermons and all public devotions in Lent, in May, and in October were in Polish.

Msgr. John E. Gatzke, a native of Cedar, in Leelanau County, is the pastor most associated with the history of Alpena Saint Mary. When he retired in 1963, he was only a few months short of finishing his 50th year there. When the deaneries of the new Diocese of Saginaw were organized in 1939, Bishop Murphy named Monsignor Gatzke as the first Alpena dean. For the rest of his active ministry he was the bishop's special representative in northeastern Michigan, calling the clergy together periodically each year for deanery conferences and visiting each residential parish annually to inspect the parish records. This quiet, soft-spoken priest was held in honor by virtually all Alpenites; I hold him in honor for having baptized me on April 27, 1924.

The immigrant parish was an interesting sociological unit. It was the center of much of the social life of its membership, united as they were by the common language of the elders. The constant money-raising projects usually involved dinners, card parties and dances in the parish hall. Parochial schools to this day are a unifying factor in parish life; in the decades of the Immigrant Church that was all the more true, since the members saw the school as a way of maintaining the ethnic values and traditions.

A multitude of parish societies existed in every ethnic parish, each usually having its own badge and banner to be worn or carried in processions or at funerals. Often these local societies were affiliated with national fraternal and insurance societies. As the oldest grandchild on my mother's side, I was entrusted at one time with making the payments for my grandmother. I would go by bicycle across town to the home of the treasurer with the monthly premium (ten cents) and Grandma's passbook. The treasurer would put her initials after the name of the month. When members got sick, the benefit paid was $2 per week to help with expenses. When Grandma died in 1943, the death benefit was $25 for burial expenses. In earlier years, that was about all the immigrants could afford to pay in premiums, and in uninflated dollars the benefit was much bigger than it would be today.

For 15 years or so in the twenties and thirties, Saint Mary's YMC (Young Men's Club) had a baseball team that competed against the town teams all over northern Michigan. Home-and-away games were played on Sunday afternoons with amateur teams sponsored by the merchants of Cheboygan, Gaylord, Harrisville, Millersburg, Onaway, Oscoda, Rogers City and the Tawases. The YMC played the other Alpena city team (the Eagles from F.O.E. Aerie 1242) on Memorial Day, the 4th of July and Labor Day. In addition, at the end of September, these two teams played a two-out-of-three series for the city championship. These games were hotly contested, with neutral umpires imported from out of town and 900 or so partisan fans on hand.

For us youngsters, to follow the YMC's baseball fortunes was practically a religious act, akin to today's Notre Dame loyalties. This was true even though the Eagles had enough Catholic McDonalds and Kellers on their team to field a team of nine by themselves. The YMC nine won the city championship about half the time.

In the Immigrant Church, people did not move from parish to parish very much. It was very rare in those days for a person to attend Mass in a church where he was not an enrolled member simply because it was closer to his home or because the Mass schedule was more convenient. In fact, when a young lady from the "French church" married a young man from the "Polish church," it was half-jokingly referred to as a "mixed marriage." I say half-jokingly because young people were under intense pressure from the older generation "to marry their own kind." And by older generation I mean not only parents and grandparents but also pastors.

Yet by necessity there were some activities in which the parishes cooperated. There were Catholic hospitals in the larger towns, a Catholic orphanage in every diocese and Catholic cemeteries in every community. The Immigrant Church avoided public agencies, services and institutions as much as possible because these were all dominated by Protestantism and seen as dangerous. This was especially true of the public schools.

When I was growing up 60 years ago, six parochial grade schools and three parochial high schools served the Catholics of the old Alpena Deanery. The elementary schools were: Saint Ignatius in Rogers City and Saint Casimir in Posen; Saint Anne, Saint Bernard and Saint Mary in Alpena; and Saint Joseph in East Tawas. Three others had closed earlier; Sacred Heart in AuSable way back in 1893 when some lumber mills closed and the population sagged; Saint Dominic in Metz in 1920, when the mission at Rogers City began to grow and its new school began to require all the resources; and Saint Paul in Onaway in 1927, after the rim factory burned and the company moved to Alma.

Saint Anne and Saint Bernard in Alpena both had a parochial high school as well in those years, as did Saint Joseph of East Tawas for a period of years before 1940. Saint Anne and Saint Bernard high schools closed in June 1950 to make way for the new Alpena Catholic Central. That school had a brief but glorious life before it closed, beset by the budget problems that afflicted the Catholic school system in the United States in the late sixties. Nothing welded the Catholic community of Alpena together into one as much as the academic and athletic pride generated by the young Thunderbolts of Catholic Central.

For sheer excitement and fun, however, the rivalry between the Saint Anne and Saint Bernard basketball teams in the 1930s and 1940s will never be beat. They played each other on New Year's night every year; and Alpena's Memorial Hall was packed for THE social event of the holidays, THE athletic event of the basketball season, and THE Catholic event of the year. The Saint Anne Big Reds won the State Class D Championship in 1927, a feat not matched, as far as I know, in any class in any sport by an Alpena team ever.

The immigrant generation made great sacrifices to erect brick school buildings for their children and grandchildren and to furnish them as far as possible as well as any tax-supported school was furnished. On the wall below the clock in my grandmother's living room was a postcard-size, tintype photograph of the parish school. One spring when I was helping her clean the wallpaper with that absorbent pink stuff, I asked her whether I should throw away the tintype; it was so dark that it was difficult to make out the picture. "No," she said, "we'll keep it there. We had to pay $50 for it." That was the amount asked from each family to build the school in 1905. Fifty dollars in 1905 from a quarry worker with a growing family was a big sacrifice.

Catholic Leaders

Among the Catholic leaders who left their imprint on the communities along the Lake Huron shore, John Emmett Richards, the longtime editor and publisher of the *Alpena News*, certainly stands out. Under its name on the front page was the slogan, "Northeastern Michigan's Newspaper"; and its eight pages, six days a week covered the happenings of Alpena, Alcona, Montmorency and Presque Isle counties. Richards was a proud member of Saint Bernard parish and sent his sons to the University of Notre Dame.

J.L. Bertrand's deep bass voice, whether in the adult choir or leading the Holy Name Society in "Holy God, We Praise Thy Name," made him "Mr. Saint Anne's." He ran a successful insurance and real estate business and was active in the Union Francaise.

While Saint Mary was very much a parish of working people, it had many businessmen, both in the Polish neighborhoods and among the downtown merchants. One such entrepreneur was West End grocer James S. Szczukowski (pronounced "Shoe-cuff-ski"), known for settling the dispute at the parish meeting called on a Sunday afternoon in 1911. The question was whether the catechism should be taught in English in the parish school. The debate went back and forth, pro and con, for almost two hours. Mr. Szczukowski finally secured a clear majority with this announcement of his view on the matter: "I think if Polish was good enough for Jesus, it's good enough for these kids."

Monsignor C.T. Skowronski's leadership in Rogers City was recognized by Catholics and non-Catholics alike when he left Saint Ignatius parish after a pastorate of 34 years. He organized the Presque Isle County Baseball League, the County Library with its bookmobile system, and the drive to fund and build the Rogers City Hospital. He attended the meeting in Cheboygan in 1923 that was the first to promote the idea of a bridge across the Straits of Mackinac, and 30 years later he took the credit for "Mighty Mac." He was a recognized expert and author on Michigan mushrooms.

Karl Vogelheim was one of Rogers City's business and cultural leaders. A Notre Dame graduate in the 1940s, he headed the Radio Apostolate of Northern Michigan during the following decade. Until television took away the audience, its popular "I Have a Question" radio program was regular fare for thousands in Michigan and Ontario on Sunday afternoons.

This essay has been dreadfully short on the Catholic people and history of the southern parishes of the old Alpena Deanery, those in Alcona and Iosco counties, also the parishes inland from Lake Huron—Mio, Lewiston, Hillman, Mikado and points in between.

The late James Mielock, representative for Iosco in the state House of Representatives for several terms, was a prominent lay leader at Saint James in Whittemore. Father Robert F. Neuman held the longest pastorate of East Tawas Saint Joseph and presided over its period of greatest growth between 1937 and 1959. In addition to his pastoral dedication, Father Neuman was an enthusiastic promoter of the German culture. Many a public gathering in the deanery was enlivened by his spirited direction of the fun song, "Schnitzelbank."

White Anglo-Saxon Protestants from the eastern seaboard and Ontario were the first people to settle in northeastern Michigan in sufficient numbers to organize congregations and build churches. But the mid-century immigration of Irish and French-Canadian Catholics, augmented toward the end of the 19th century by great numbers of Catholics from eastern Europe and the Mediterranean region, soon overtook the Yankee establishment.

In the old Alpena Deanery of the Diocese of Saginaw, Roman Catholics clearly constituted the largest denomination on the scene. Today, the 22 parishes in these six counties constitute the strong eastern flank of the growing Diocese of Gaylord. ■

The beginning of the Catholic missions
and fostering of the faith in northwestern Michigan

By Father Stanley Bur and Father Gerald F. Micketti

"Yesterday was an unprecedented one in the history of the Catholic society of this city. It was a gala day and all nature seemed to rejoice with the members of Saint Francis Church in the celebration of its silver jubilee. The flags which hung from pinnacle and the bunting which was draped in graceful festoons over the front of the church waved in harmony with the occasion to the wooing caresses of the breezes."

So reported the local Traverse City paper, *Traverse Bay Eagle*, October 11, 1897. Bishop Henry J. Richter of Grand Rapids came to Traverse City to confirm and anoint the bells of Saint Francis Church. The pastor at that time was Father Joseph Bauer; his assistant was Father H.P. Maus.

Earlier in 1897, an anonymous donor had offered to give $500 toward new chimes for the church, if the parish would raise an equal amount. It was decided to hold a spring festival for that purpose. The festival took place at the City Opera House for three days at the beginning of June. The additional $500 was raised and the bells were ordered. They arrived in September and were blessed October 10.

Three o'clock was the time appointed for the ceremony of the anointing of the bells. Two hours before this event people were gathering in the vicinity of the church in order to secure a good seat to view the ceremony. The streets were lined in all directions with people and carriages. Spectators were standing on tiptoe and fences to catch a glimpse of the dedication of the bells and hear the words spoken by Father Maus. At the close of the address, Bishop Richter blessed the water and the bells were washed in the holy water by Fathers Bauer and Maus. Then the bishop anointed the bells with Holy Ointment, marking the sign of the cross inside and out. Seven crosses were marked inside symbolizing the seven sacraments; four crosses were marked outside symbolizing the four gospels.

The total weight of the bells, including standards, is 7,860 pounds. The largest, weighing 2,501 pounds, is inscribed: "In remembrance of Reverend Joseph Bauer, pastor, and Reverend H.P. Maus, assistant, Saint Francis Church, Traverse City, Michigan, 1897." The second weighs 1,600 pounds and is inscribed: "In remembrance of the devoted members of Saint Francis Church." The third bell, weighing 1,351 pounds, is inscribed: "In remembrance of the humble donator of $500 towards the bells of Saint Francis." The fourth and smallest bell weighs 701 pounds and is inscribed: "In commemoration of the blessing of the bells by Right Reverend Henry J. Richter, Bishop of Grand Rapids." The four bells were placed in the tower and ready for use on October 14, 1897. They are now at the entrance of Saint Francis Church.

That was 25 years after the establishment of Saint Francis Parish in Traverse City. What led to the establishment of the parish? What followed?

He was ordained in Austria in 1837 and after he came to the United States eight years later, he offered his services to Bishop Lefevre of Detroit. He was Father Ignatius Mrak. Bishop Lefevre assigned him to L'Arbre Croche, succeeding Father Frederick Baraga who moved to L'Anse in the Upper Peninsula. The parishioners of L'Arbre Croche were Indians. L'Arbre Croche means "The Crooked Tree" and was located in Emmet County somewhere north of present-day Harbor Springs. Owing to the lack of priests in that part of Michigan, Father Mrak was obligated to minister to the spiritual needs of all the Catholics in the seven surrounding counties. Ten years after he began to minister to the Indians, some of them left L'Arbre Croche and moved to Peshawbestown - Eagle Town. Father Mrak went with them and made his home there, where he established a school for the Indians. From there he also attended to the needs of the Chippewa and Ottawa Indians at Manistee and traveled as far north as Petoskey. He traveled by Indian canoe, by Indian pony or snowshoes in the winter.

Father Frederick Baraga became the first bishop of the Diocese of Sault Sainte Marie and Marquette. When he died in 1868, Father Mrak was nominated for the office of bishop to succeed Bishop Baraga. He served as bishop for seven years. When

his health began to fail, he resigned as bishop. When he heard that the Indians whom he loved so dearly were without a priest, he returned to them living and laboring among them at Peshawbestown until failing health forced him to retire from all active work in 1891. He went to Saint Mary's Hospital in Marquette where he spent his last days in peace and rest.

When Father Mrak was appointed bishop, Father A. Herbstret was his successor. He, too, lived at Suttons Bay and visited Traverse City monthly as well as the other missions. When he visited Traverse City, he offered Mass in the homes of Martin Sheridan on Randolph Street, Dominic Dunn House on Union Street about where Arnold's Books was located, and Frank Phoral, location uncertain. Father Herbstret laid the foundation for the first Catholic Church in 1870. The church was a small frame structure, 24 x 30, located on Tenth Street between Union and Cass Streets. Father Herbstret did not finish the construction of the building because he was transferred to Big Rapids.

In the fall of 1870, Father Philip Zorn was appointed to Suttons Bay. He attended 21 different missions, though the Indians were nearest and dearest to his heart. He offered Mass in Traverse City once a month and he completed the church begun by Father Herbstret. Mass was offered in the new church for the first time in December 1870. At that time there were only about 20 Catholic families in Traverse City. Father Zorn was well traveled in his missionary work because he was serving the Catholic population in all seven surrounding counties, much like Father Mrak. He traveled by pony and many times the only canopy over his head was the stars. With all his travels and activity, his health began to fail and he was transferred to Harbor Springs, and from there to Hart in Oceana County. His health continued to fail and he retired to become the chaplain at Mercy Hospital in Big Rapids.

During the residence of Father Zorn at Suttons Bay, Traverse City was attended for about eight months by Father Schacken of Big Rapids. After him Father Zassa was given temporary assignment for three months. When Father Zassa was transferred, the needs of Traverse City area fell to Father Zorn. He served Traverse City until Father George Ziegler arrived in 1877.

Father Ziegler was the first resident pastor of Saint Francis Parish. During his eight years as pastor he organized the Catholic families into a parish. When he arrived, he found that the congregation had outgrown the little church. He started the construction of an addition, 40 feet long with two wings, 10-12 feet each. Father Ziegler established a Catholic school, founded a convent, and procured sisters from New York. He built a pastor's residence for himself at a cost of $1,200. He also, at the same time, cared for the smaller missions in the surrounding counties. A list of the places where Father Ziegler served includes the missions at Cadillac, Provemont, Leland, Frankfort, Suttons Bay, Northport, Maple City, Empire, Cleon, Hannah, Fife Lake, Barker Creek, Isadore, Arcadia and Mapleton. He built churches at Cadillac, Isadore, Barker Creek, Mapleton and Fife Lake, and the rectory at Provemont. After working faithfully for eight years, traveling day and night, exposed to all kinds of weather, his health was severely tested and failed him. He was obliged to retire. At this point in his life, he joined the Franciscan Order at Saint Louis, Missouri. As a member of the Franciscans he was sent to Ashland, Washburn and lastly to Cleveland, where he died at Saint Alexis Hospital at age 67.

Father Ziegler requested through Father Mendel in Saint Paul Parish, Greenville, New Jersey, that the Sisters of Saint Dominic of Second Street, New York City, come to Michigan to start a school. Five sisters accompanied by Mother Aquinata arrived in Traverse City, Thursday, October 23, 1877. The sisters were Mother Camilla Madden, Mother Angela Phelan, Sister Mary Martha Mueglich, Sister Mary Boniface Hartleb and Sister Mary Borromeo Ahlmeier. The superior was Mother Angela. After a short stay in Traverse City, Mother Aquinata returned to New York.

Their first residence was a house on Union Street purchased by Father Ziegler from his own private means at a cost of $1,000. The house was furnished by the congregation for church and school purposes as well as for a sisters' residence at a cost of $600. The ground floor contained two classrooms. In one of the classrooms Mass was offered on weekdays. The second floor, the sisters' dwelling proper, had a small chapel where the Blessed Sacrament was reserved, two bedrooms, a sitting room and a kitchen. The sisters lived in this house for nearly six years. On the Monday following their arrival, school was opened with six pupils. By the end of the school year the number increased to 50.

Perry Hannah donated six lots on Tenth Street to the sisters for the purpose of erecting a convent boarding school. In May 1883, construction began. The building was completed in the beginning of September of the same year. The total cost, including furniture and fences, was about $10,000. Of that figure, Bishop Mrak living in Peshawbestown, donated $2,400. The new Holy Angels Convent was dedicated by Bishop Henry J. Richter of Grand Rapids on the first Sunday of September. The next day school opened. Holy Angels convent was the first mother house of the province of Saint Joseph of the Sisters of Saint Dominic. In time the mother house was moved to Grand Rapids where it has remained at Marywood.

In the tradition of Second Order foundations, the convent was separated from the school area and a grille was installed to regulate visiting. On December 5, 1883,

the sisters completed the arrangements for the legal corporation of Holy Angels Academy. The Academy celebrated its first high school commencement in 1889 consisting of three young women: Anna Shane, Mary Donley, and Stacia Burden.

The convent-academy continued to benefit from civic improvements, such as the claying and graveling of Union Street in 1883, tree planting in 1886, and the installation of street lights in 1889. In 1891, Bishop Mrak purchased for the sisters ten lots adjoining the convent on the south side, at a cost of $1,200. A brick annex, begun in April of 1911, provided a new chapel, refectory and sleeping areas. This work was completed in May of 1913. The building continued to serve as a convent for the sisters who staffed Saint Francis Schools. In 1972, the original convent-academy was demolished. Modifications were also made to the 1913 addition to improve the living areas for the sisters serving at Saint Francis and later in the Grand Traverse Area Catholic Schools. That part of the building became known as the Saint Francis Convent. On Saturday, October 24, 1993, a prayer service and reception were held in the Saint Francis Convent. Shortly after the convent was demolished — the passing of an era for Saint Francis Parish and schools.

As Traverse City grew so did the need for a larger house of worship. Father George Ziegler was succeeded as pastor in 1885 by Father Theophile Nyssen, who served for three years. Father Nyssen urged the construction of a brick church, but lack of money was a problem. So a larger wood frame church was built. The cornerstone was laid May 15, 1887, and the foundation of the building, 48 x 100, was completed at a cost of $933. Father Nyssen, discouraged by the lack of financial support, did not continue building the church. When all efforts to raise the money failed, he resigned and left for Europe.

After spending three months in his native country of Germany, Father Nyssen changed his mind and returned to America. During these three months, Bishop Mrak of Peshawbestown offered Mass at Saint Francis Church every other Sunday. Saint Francis was still without a priest after Father Nyssen returned from Europe. He requested to return to Traverse City and complete the church building. On August 5, 1888, the work of constructing the new church commenced. One year later, August 18, 1889, Bishop Richter dedicated the new church.

Father Joseph Bauer came from Provemont to succeed Father Nyssen in 1889. Father Bauer was born in Alsace-Lorraine, Germany, in 1862. He was ordained by Bishop Richter in December of 1885. His first assignment was Provemont. He arrived in Provemont in January of 1886 and left three years later. When he arrived in Traverse City, the parish of Saint Francis was becoming the center from which all the Catholic mission churches of the surrounding counties were being attended. The missions under the care of the pastor of Saint Francis were Hannah, Mapleton, Barker Creek, Fife Lake and Kalkaska. Since the Traverse City parish was growing, Father Bauer asked Bishop Richter for an assistant to take care of the mission churches. The first assistant was Father Stephen Nowakowski who arrived in 1892. Father Nowakowski cared for the above-mentioned churches plus Isadore, Empire and Maple City. He remained in Traverse City until January of 1895 when he was transferred to Saint Joseph Church in Manistee. While at Saint Joseph Church, he still served the churches of Isadore, Empire and Maple City. The successor of Father Nowakowski was Father L.M. Prud'homme. He served for eight months, caring for the missions as well as Elk Rapids and Nessen City. He left for Saint Ann Church in Cadillac in August. Father H.P. Maus was sent to follow Father Prud'homme.

Father Bauer was the pastor when the new church building was dedicated in August after his arrival. The old church building now vacant was renovated to become an elementary school. In December of 1889, the children were moved from their temporary quarters on the east side of Union Street between Eighth and Ninth Streets, to the old church building on Tenth Street. Prior to the renovation of the old church, the children occupied the classrooms in the convent building until the completion of the new church. Father Bauer was the pastor of Saint Francis Church when the parish celebrated its silver jubilee described above.

Under Father Bauer the schools were expanded. Construction for a new parish school facing Cass Street began in June 1893, and was completed the following September. The school facing Cass Street had gray walls with chocolate trim and red shingles on the roof. There was a cupola on the roof for the bell. The building was 50 x 75, two stories with a basement and large attic. There were four classrooms on the main floor and two classrooms and a larger room on the second floor. The opening enrollment was 150 students. The total cost was $8,358.66. By 1898, the school enrollment was 20 pupils in the high school and 180 in the grade school. Father Bauer also saw to the construction of a gym in 1913.

Thirty-three years is a long time for a pastor to watch his parish grow. That is what Father Joseph Bauer did; he watched Traverse City grow too. Father Bauer served Saint Francis Parish for 33 years, the longest tenure of any pastor of the parish.

Father Bauer left Saint Francis in 1922 and was succeeded by Father Edward McDonald who served for two years. He was followed by two pastors who also served the parishioners of Saint Francis for over twenty years each. Father William J. Schueller came in 1924. He was the pastor during the tough years of the depression and World War II. Two years after his arrival the school was nearly destroyed by fire. Lillian Ludka records

that she and the other students went to school on Saturdays and late into June to complete the academic year. When he left Traverse City in November 1945, Father Schueller was succeeded by Father Joseph Kohler. Two years later, the parish was saddened when Father Kohler died March 14, 1968. He had served as pastor since his arrival in Traverse City in November 1945. He was born in Suttons Bay January 14, 1900. At one time he was a professor at Saint Joseph Seminary in Grand Rapids and served in the parishes of S.S. Peter and Paul in Saginaw, Saint Ann in Cadillac and Saint Patrick in Portland. The funeral Mass was at Saint Francis High School gymnasium.

In 1969, Bishop Babcock of Grand Rapids mandated the consolidation of the schools of Immaculate Conception and Saint Francis Parishes. Thus was born the Grand Traverse Area Catholic Schools. Under this arrangement each parish contributed funds based on the number of students in the school. This created some hardship for Immaculate Conception parish. Immaculate Conception parish was debt free in 1969; Saint Francis was not. That meant the debt for the new Saint Francis High School was also assumed by Immaculate Conception Parish. Both parishes were having financial difficulties in 1971. That led to the decision to charge tuition for the grade school students. That same year the Grand Traverse Educational Foundation was established to provide grants-scholarships for students as well as grants for improvements.

Father Louis VanBergen succeeded Father Kohler; he served until he left in 1973. His successor was Father Raymond Mulka. When Father Mulka arrived, construction began again. Throughout the tenure of Father Kohler, the 1889 church building started to show the signs of age and became too small for the growing population. Father Kohler and his advisors considered building a new church. The property on Union Street was acquired and funds were set aside. Father Kohler died before a new church could be built. In the estate of Father Kohler there was $80,000 bequeathed to the parish for a new church building.

After Father Mulka's arrival the acceptable options were explored. Should the 1889 church building be restored and expanded on the existing site (southwest corner of Tenth and Cass Streets)? Should the building be moved to the Union Street site and expanded there? Should a new church be built, and if so, where? A survey was taken to see what the parishioners wanted and the total needs and assets of the parish were analyzed. Finally at a parish open forum, February 22, 1976, the parishioners of Saint Francis voted to build a new church on the Union Street property. Richard Drury was chosen as the architect. The choice of Richard Drury of Traverse City was the first of many decisions that reflected the deliberate effort to utilize local talent as much as possible in the construction of the new church. These decisions included artisans and artists.

Ground was broken September 26, 1976 on the site, the southeast corner of Fourteenth and Union Streets. By the time of the ground breaking, $834,000 was already pledged by over 900 parishioners. The new Saint Francis Church was dedicated by Bishop Edmund C. Szoka of Gaylord, Sunday, November 6, 1977.

With the dedication of the new church, that left only the rectory and the old convent on the corner of Tenth and Cass Streets that were not replaced or renovated. A new rectory was built by the successor of Father Mulka; the old convent was demolished and removed in 1993.

Father Thomas Neis succeeded Father Mulka in 1980. He served as pastor of Saint Francis Church for nine years. While Father Neis served Saint Francis, two new parishes for the Traverse City area were established. Saint Patrick Church started on West Silver Lake Road north of Grawn when Father Francis Murphy arrived in August of 1984. By December of 1986, their building was completed; the first Mass was Christmas. March 17, 1987, Saint Patrick Church was dedicated by Bishop Robert Rose. Christ the King Church in Acme was supposed to begin at the same time as Saint Patrick. Father R. Dale Magoon, the first pastor, became ill and the beginning of Christ the King Parish waited until Father Edwin Thome became pastor August 13, 1985. Construction of the church building began in the spring of 1988. The church building was dedicated December 11, 1988.

Father Ronald Gronowski succeeded Father Neis and served for six years. In January of 1993, Father James Gardiner became the pastor of Saint Francis Church. He is a Traverse City native and his home parish was Immaculate Conception Parish. He attended Immaculate Conception and Saint Francis elementary schools. He is the present pastor of Saint Francis Catholic Church. ■

Holy Childhood School in Harbor Springs

exemplified the spirit of the 19th Century missionaries

The following account of the early years of the Holy Childhood Missionary School in Harbor Springs was written in 1924 by an unidentified author for a special edition of "The Catholic Vigil" newspaper published in Grand Rapids.

In the early 19th century Indian schools were formed at various locations throughout northwestern Michigan, but it was not until 1885 when the Franciscan fathers from the province of the Sacred Heart from Saint Louis, Missouri, took charge of the missions that their dreams of an Indian school became a reality.

It was the day after the feast of Saint Francis, October 5, 1885, that Father Servatius Altmicks opened a day school for the children of his new mission. The pupils, we are told, numbered 36 and it is recorded that Brother Novatius was the first teacher.

But a day school was not the full dream of Fathers Baraga and Dejean who then worked among the Ottawas at L'Arbre Croche, nor was it all that the good Franciscans planned. They planned to open, as much as possible, a boarding school, since experience told them that such a school alone would bring lasting results.

Accordingly, in spite of poverty and many other obstacles, a building was erected the next year which even to the present time forms part of Holy Childhood school. Although the building was constructed for the school, the teachers did not arrive until November when three School Sisters of Notre Dame arrived from Milwaukee, Wisconsin, to take charge of this school. It was formally opened on December 1 with only three students. By the end of the year, however, the number had increased to 64. One of these brave nuns who braved the wilderness, the inclement climate and the indifference of her charges to take up this apostolic labor in L'Arbre Croche was the venerable Mother M. Wilfreda. She has been at Harbor Springs ever since and if anyone's heart and soul were ever in the apostolic work it is the heart and soul of this great nun and splendid educator.

It is true perhaps that some educators receive all the credit that is due them in praise and gratitude of their students and in the acclaim of the public, but this is not true of the nun. She gives up the world, indeed, for she even gives up the just appreciation that should come to her for her sacrifices and patience in teaching children.

It would lead us too far if we were to describe in detail the great difficulties that were experienced by the sister during the first years of the school's existence. These difficulties are common enough in every religious foundation in the pioneer countries. It is enough to say that the good sisters never faltered in the struggle. That they kept ever increasing the efficiency of their work as their students grew.

They educated the children not only in the branches of a common school education but they also endeavored to train them in what was more difficult: attention to domestic needs. From half past three in the morning until late at night every hour had its allotted task. All the clothes for the boys and girls in the school had to be made by the sisters for, as a rule, children usually came to school in a neglected condition, bringing no clothing except what they wore. Yet these early days had many joyful moments for the sisters. Indeed, to hear them talk one would think there is no joy in the world like that of starting an Indian school in a neglected corner of the world.

In the course of time, as the pupils increased the buildings were rebuilt and remodeled. In 1893 the old Globe Hotel in Harbor Springs was bought and converted into a dormitory for the smaller boys, a laundry and several workshops. Later additions were made to this building and various trades were introduced and taught by competent teachers such as shoemaking, carpentering and printing.

In 1907, the present quarters for the boys were erected, steam heat was installed and other improvements made. This building was made possible largely through the generosity of friends. During the first two years of its existence, the school was conducted at the expense of missionaries and the sisters, the Indians paying nothing.

Holy Childhood students in native dress.

In 1888 the government made a contract by which it agreed to pay $108 per child a year for the education, clothing and boarding of 75 children. These appropriations were continued until 1896 when, owing to anti-Catholic influence, they were cut in half. Since 1900, when all incomes from this source was taken away, the school has existed on the charity of friends, notably that of Mother Catherine Drexel.

In spite of the hardships caused by lack of means, we learn from an article in the *Franciscan Herald* that the missionaries and the Sisters have, since 1886, educated, clothed and boarded about 3,549 children of the Ottawa, Chippewa and Potawatomie tribes. That is, on average, about 135 children a year.

Besides these, about 900 pupils, mostly whites, attended the schools. The course of studies is the same as that of the common schools, fads and frills, of course, being wisely omitted. The pupils of Holy Childhood School may safely challenge competition with children of the same age and grade in any of the public and district schools.

They receive, besides, a thorough instruction in the truths of our holy religion. As was mentioned above, the boys are also given opportunities of learning various trades. The girls are taught everything a good housewife should know. Hence general housework, plain and fancy needlework, dressmaking, rug and carpet weaving and baking are prominent features. Thus Holy Childhood Mission School can look back with a feeling of joy and gratitude to the good accomplished for the welfare of the children of the red race during the 28 years of its existence.

The indomitable courage of its founders and directors, based on an unwavering confidence in God and a genuine Christian charity, overcame all obstacles and made light of hardships and privations, and succeeded in building up a school which has been for so many a source of untold blessings.

Having fun at a sledding party.

Holy Childhood Catholic School in the early years.

In May, 1914, occurred the solemn dedication of the substantial new central building of the mission school. This building was designed by Brother Leonard of the Franciscan order and was dedicated by the Right Reverend Bishop Richter with special services. The work of the Franciscan missionary at Harbor Springs and of the good sisters who educated and cared for these Indian children certainly commends to a very tender place in the hearts of Michigan people.

While most of us are looking only for our own pleasure, the sisters have given up every pleasure to bring happiness into the hearts of these little Indians who are now strangers and aliens in what was once their own country. A visit to Holy Childhood school cannot help but convince one that here quietly and with no sound of trumpets a great work of Christian charity is being carried on. ■

Sacramentine Monastery

and Augustine Center Retreat House

Mother Mary Augustine entered the Sacramentine Monastery in Yonkers, New York, in 1918. In 1951 at the request of Bishop Francis Haas who desired to have a group of contemplatives in the northern part of his diocese, Mother Mary Augustine was chosen to found a Monastery in Petoskey, Michigan. She along with Sisters Rose Mary Burns, Mary Helene Steubenrough, Mary Francis Finn, Mary Matthew Harding, Mary Rosalie Smith, and Emmanual Fusco arrived at 918 Howard Street in early October, 1951, continuing a 300-plus year tradition of ceaseless prayer and adoration. Among the young women who joined these Sisters as religious in those beginning years were Sisters Marie McCormack, Mildred Kiefer, and Anne Maries Wellington. At the Bishop's suggestion Mother Mary Augustine purchased the house next door for a retreat house; Bethany Retreat House opened in 1953.

As the retreat movement flourished and Bethany House proved inadequate for the growing numbers of retreatants, the Sisters were advised by Bishop Allen Babcock to find a location "on the highway." Mother's complete trust and confidence in providence was rewarded by a gift of property on U.S.Highway 31, five miles north of Petoskey.

On July 1, 1960, Mother Mary Augustine led a motorcade procession with the Blessed Sacrament to the Blessed Sacrament Retreat House, Conway, for a 7:00 a.m. Mass of Thanksgiving. Mother exemplified tremendous foresight in planning a retreat house that would well serve retreatant needs of the diocese and beyond even into the third millennium. Mother brought to fruition the vision and mission of the Sacramentine Sisters that they "established the second Sacramentine Monastery of Perpetual Adoration in the United States at Conway, giving northern Michigan people a permanent retreat house."

The qualities for which her Sisters still fondly remember Mother are her truly virtuous life of selflessness, her beautiful spirit and dedication to the work of the Church, her continuous encouragement for great love and fidelity. She was a staunch woman! Edmund Cardinal Szoka probably best summed up the person of Mother Mary Augustine in his eulogy at her death: "Mother was always a gracious lady...a lady of faith, dedicated to the ideals of her community. She was a person of strong character and yet in all the years I knew her, she was perhaps one of the most gentle people I've ever met...very gentle, very humble, but very strong."

Sister Rose Mary Burns was one of the founding Sisters of the Sacramentine Monastery in Petoskey, Michigan, and is one of the most familiar Sisters to the people of the area. Sister spent hours in adoration of the Blessed Sacrament and served as Directress of Novices, yet had time for untold outside contacts with the people. Sister organized regularly-scheduled retreats for teenagers in the diocese and worked with the priest-directors on these weekends. Her talents were many including making vestments, overseeing lay workers and volunteers at the Monastery, and consoling people in need through correspondence and telephone calls. She is probably best remembered for touching the lives of many young people through her patient teaching of piano lessons. One of the most frequent and endearing comments heard when a person meets Sister Rose Mary today is, "Sister, do you remember me? You gave me piano lessons." To this day expressions of admiration and gratitude are on the lips of her former pupils. In those early years sister's two-fold ministry of sewing vestments and teaching piano were the major sources of revenue for the Sisters and the retreat house. An additional source of revenue in those early days was from the making and distribution of altar breads, selling paintings done by Sisters, and printing and engraving.

Sister Rose Mary will long be remembered as one of the cornerstones of the Blessed Sacrament Retreat House. From helping construction workers on the job...to

serving meals to volunteers at the Monastery...to sewing vestments...to working with young women who served as Guard of Honor...to teaching piano...to praying as a Eucharistic Adorer, sister always manifested indefatigable love, gentleness, patience and generosity.

Another cornerstone of the Sacramentine Monastery in Michigan was Sister Mary Matthew Harding, an extern sister, who was the principal contact with the local community. Sister exuded a charisma among the people when visiting in nursing homes or the hospital; she brought peace and joy to the sick and home bound with the promise of prayers of all the Sisters. Her genuine concern for individuals and families endeared her to many; truly she represented the Sisters who remained in the cloister. Through her many gracious contacts Sister Mary Matthew provided awareness of the Sacramentine Sisters, won the admiration of the public, and gained for the Monastery many benefactors.

The first Sacramentine Monastery.

As the retreat movement broadened in scope and demanded more attention and as vocations diminished, the Sacramentine Sisters decided to look beyond their ranks for an administrator of the retreat house, thus enabling them to live more fully their commitment to Eucharistic prayer.

In August, 1986, Barbara Hubeny, O.P., a Sinsinawa Dominican, was named Executive Director of the retreat center. On October 16, 1986, Bishop Robert Rose dedicated the Blessed Sacrament Retreat House as the Augustine Center in honor of Mother Mary Augustine Donovan, foundress of the Sacramentine Sisters in Michigan.

The Sacramentine Sisters continue to be a prayer source to encourage and support this ministry together with Bishop Patrick Cooney, our present Ordinary, as did Edmund Cardinal Szoka and Bishop Robert Rose during their administrative terms in the Diocese of Gaylord.

Through use of her many talents and her hospitality Sister Barbara has transformed the retreat house into a "center for growth" by offering and hosting programs of education, ongoing formation and spirituality. The Center is a "place set apart" where one can come to know the Lord better; to know his teachings more fully; to utilize that know-ledge as a practical foundation of one's life; and to place one's personal gifts at the service of God and God's people.

Under Sister Barbara's direction the Center has encouraged programs that focus on spiritual and human growth and development. Individuals and groups come to the Augustine Center from throughout the Diocese of Gaylord, the state of Michigan, the Midwest, and from Canada for retreats, leadership training, parish ministry, ongoing formation, in-service educational programs, ecumenical working retreats, seminars, Bible study, renewal days, clergy enrichment days, Religious Community Chapter deliberations, as well as private retreats.

Through her openness to the expanding needs of retreatants and her creative use of space, Sister Barbara has supervised the renovation of parts of the Monastery to accommodate the ever changing and growing needs without infringing on the cloister of the sisters.

Her ready smile, her gift of hospitality, her openness to learning new things, her love of ministering to people striving to deepen their relationship with God, her call to serving others, her administrative ability and her commitment to the continuing vision and mission of the Sacramentine Sisters that gave to the people of northern Michigan "a permanent retreat house" are the hallmarks Sister Barbara manifests in her ministry at the Augustine Center.

Under the leadership of Sister Barbara, the Augustine Center will be a dynamic influence on peoples' lives as they endeavor "to praise, to love, to adore" our Eucharistic God...the ongoing life of the Sacramentine Sisters...into the third millennium. ■

Overseeing construction of the new retreat center.

Dedication of the center by Bishop Robert Rose.

Today the center hosts groups from throughout the Midwest.

St. Vincent De Paul Society

has had a long, meaningful presence in the diocese

By Father Gerald F. Micketti

The St. Vincent De Paul Society is world wide organization of Christians of all ages and backgrounds who strive to bring social justice and the friendship of true charity to people in need.

The work of the Society is living the words of Jesus in the gospel: "I was hungry, I was thirsty, I was a stranger, I was naked, I was sick, I was in prison."

The work of St. Vincent De Paul Societies is the result of Frederic Ozanam, a student in Paris, who decided to put into practice what he preached. He and some fellow students started in 1833 to seek out and visit the poor in Paris. On their visits they would bring bread and clothes, along with their friendship and caring. This group took as their patron the French priest Vincent De Paul who alerted the world to social problems. The activities of Frederic Ozanam and others began to spread and eventually reached the United States.

In northern Michigan, the St. Vincent De Paul Society began as the result of a Cursillo. About 50 men of the six parishes of the Alpena Deanery of the Saginaw Diocese came together for an organization meeting at St. Bernard Parish in February, 1967. Information was presented by five members of the District Council of Lansing.

The result of that initial meeting was the formation of the Alpena Conference of the St. Vincent De Paul Society with members from the parishes of St. Anne, St. Bernard, St. John the Baptist and St. Mary in Alpena and St. Catherine parish of Ossineke. After forming the conference, the first store opened in April on Second Avenue in Alpena. This store was the location of the Society until 1973 when property was purchased on Chisholm Street.

Nine years later, the former Kotwicki Clothing Store building also on Chisholm Street became available. This is the present location of the Society store. The house on Chisholm Street is used for low income tenants and an office for crisis pregnancy intervention.

Stanley Robel, who was instrumental in starting the Alpena Conference, moved to East Tawas after retiring. He began to initiate a St. Vincent De Paul Society in the Tawas area. He started working from his home and garage. Eventually a conference was formed in 1983 in the Tawas area that included the parishes of Immaculate Heart of Mary, Tawas City (now part of merged Holy Family Parish,) Sacred Heart in Oscoda, St. Pius in Hale, St. Stephen in Skidway Lake and St. Raphael in Mikado.

The St. Raphael Parish Society activities warranted forming their own conference which was established in 1989. Other parishes have been involved and are still involved in the ministry of St. Vincent De Paul Societies - St. Paul in Onaway, St. Augustine in Hillman and the parishes in Roscommon County.

Years before the Alpena Conference started, St. Vincent De Paul Society was active in the Traverse City area, beginning in the 1940s. Some of the older parishioners of Immaculate Conception and St. Francis remember a store on Front Street during the 1950s. The store was closed in the 60s.

About 30 years later, a group of people met to unite all 15 Traverse Bay Area Catholic Parishes in an effort to assist those in need. By December, 1990 the St. Vincent De Paul Society was once again a reality in Traverse City. The Society store opened in April, 1991 and continues to meet the needs of people. ■

Bishop Ignatius Mrak

Bishop Ignatius Mrak,
Peacemaker

By Father Stanley A. Bur

About the year 1885, after the successes of the great Indian Chief Sitting Bull in the Territory of Montana and Wyoming, the Indians of Michigan became restless.

Two couriers from the camp of Sitting Bull had come to Traverse City to meet with all the tribes to declare war on the white man in this region who had invaded Indian hunting territory. Chief Petoskey and Chief Agosha, Chief Blackbird and Chief Redbird, all came with their braves. From Beaver Island came John Cornstalk and from Kewadin came John Ginsway. Even from as far as Cross Village and Little Traverse Bay came Joe Greenleaf and some braves.

They paraded down Traverse City's Sawdust Trail, now known as Union Street, past the stores and settlers' homes, marching in all of their colored and feathered Council of War costumes. They marched past the newly-established Saint Francis convent of the Dominican Sisters out to Boot Lake near the south end of what is now Union Street where the Indians had encamped.

The two tall couriers of Chief Sitting Bull, wearing their eagle feathers, were the center of all the excitement. Fear and panic stalked the community as the smoke of the council fires at the encampment burned and smoldered throughout the day.

A central figure of appeasement in their solemn and stately gathering was a little wiry man who had lived among the Indians of Upper Michigan for nearly 40 years. The chiefs present had experienced Christianity already for several generations and so the influence of Bishop Ignatius Mrak prevailed.

Peace remained as it should among good Christians and the couriers of Sitting Bull, disappointed and bewildered by the peace-loving attitude of their eastern allies, returned to the west. Bishop Mrak had saved the village and the whole settlement of the Grand Traverse area from war and complete destruction by an Indian uprising which never occurred. ■

Father Weikamp of Cross Village

and the "Benevolent, Charitable and Religious Society of Saint Francis"

By Father Albert Langheim, OFM

A determined and charismatic figure came to Cross Village in 1855 to dominate its religious history for over 35 years. Father John Bernard Weikamp was born in Bocholt, Prussia on April 5, 1818, the son of John Bernard and Johanna Margareta Do'ink Weikamp.

He first tried a career as an actor, but later in his life decided to become a priest. He was ordained in Rome by Pope Pius IX on June 21, 1849 and was assigned to work as a missionary among the native North Americans.

He emigrated to America and first came to Chicago where he built a church on the city's west side. After five years he became involved in a dispute with Bishop O'Regan and was suspended, whereupon he sold the church, kept the money and came to northern Michigan.

He arrived in Little Traverse Bay by boat in 1854, accompanied by a few Brothers. He first bought Harbor Point in Harbor Springs for $100 but, seeing it was too small, he resold it and purchased 2,000 acres northeast of Cross Village. A man named Louis Sifferath loaned him part of the money for the purchase.

In 1855 Father Weikamp and his followers moved to Cross Village and began to construct a large wooden building known as the Cross Village Convent. Father Weikamp supervised the work but most of the manual labor was done by Native Americans. The structure was completed in January, 1856. Several other Brothers and Sisters were added to the small congregation named "The Benevolent Charitable and Religious Society of Saint Francis."

Father John B. Weikamp

Bishop Frederic Baraga, bishop of the region at the time, had been informed by Bishop O'Regan of the departure of Father Weikamp from Chicago and had been advised by O'Regan not to accept him without proper credentials. After much thought and negotiation, Bishop Baraga realized that Father Weikamp could be of great service to the Native Americans in the priest-short Diocese of Sault Ste. Marie/Marquette and finally accepted him, blessing the convent and its cemetery on June 1, 1858.

In 1861, however, he suspended Father Weikamp as pastor of Cross Village. No reason was recorded.

In an 1858 letter, Father Edward Jacker described Weikamp's convent. The 160-foot by 80-foot structure had 108 bedrooms, with a male religious wing on the north side and a wing for female religious and widows on the south, separated by a chapel running down the middle from the front door.

Contrary to church regulations, Father Weikamp admitted both Brothers and Sisters to the convent. He had the chapel and buildings so arranged that the Sisters could live their lives without catching sight of the Brothers and vice versa. Even in the chapel, he had the altar and pulpit elevated above walled seating areas so that each sex could see the priest from their separate sides without seeing each other.

There were great skills among the first Brothers and

Sisters as they managed large herds of cattle, farmed many acres, and operated a saw mill, carpenter shop, grist mill, granary and a blacksmith shop which is still standing. They made a living by selling wooden shoes, currant wine, square iron nails, locks, keys and furniture. Crop yields from their fields were outstanding.

A parochial school for Native American and orphan children was opened in 1859. A hospital was built and it operated through the duration of the convent. A public school was built with lumber from the saw mill. Income from all the convent operations was enough to pay for free schooling and hospital care for all in the community, and to members of the Odawa tribe in the area.

Father Weikamp took seriously the biblical injunction to care for the widows and orphans (Timothy 5:5-16). He took in the truly destitute to room, board and educate them.

Father Weikamp was also an eccentric man. He built his own coffin and kept it in his room. He built a crypt for his own grave and would enter it every day to meditate. He had a meditation board before which he prayed each day. Despite his austerity he loved to smoke his long stem ceramic pipes. His enemies claimed he liked his currant wine and stored some in his grave to refresh himself each afternoon.

He was kind to visitors but strict to his convent community. He ruled with an iron hand and his word was law. He worked the Brothers and Sisters long hours. At its peak the convent housed 46 Brothers and Sisters and many more widows and orphans. For 35 years Father Weikamp was monarch of his little domain and over that period he did immeasurable good.

His end came quicker than anyone expected. On March 17, 1889 he was riding in a sulky inspecting the fields when his horse shied, throwing him on the reins and dragging him. Dr. C. Schneider of Cross Village and Dr. Levi Gardners of Harbor Springs came to care for him but to no avail. He died early the next morning, March 18, 1889 and was buried on March 19 in the grave he had dug and maintained.

In his last days he seemed to realize his work was crumbling. His will made provisions for the dissolution of the convent and the financing for the Brothers and Sisters to enter other convents and care centers.

The dissolution of the Society was a long, slow and painful process as it steadily declined in numbers. The administrators were of the opinion that the purpose should be more religious and less a large farm. They looked far and wide for some way to maintain the convent. The Notre Dame Sisters in Milwaukee were approached but, after investigating, declined to take it over. The Franciscans of the Sacred Heart Province in Saint Louis were asked to take it over but that request was also denied.

By 1894 the convent had but 32 Sisters. One remaining Brother joined the Sacred Heart Province and left. Some Sisters left to get jobs or marry, the rest eventually transferred to other convents. In agreement with Father Weikamp's will, the furnishings of his convent were sold at public auction to finance all the transfers.

The parochial school was sold to Cross Village, sawed

The altar of the Cross Village Convent chapel, elevated above separate wall seating areas for Sisters and Brothers.

Father Weikamp's coffin.

The reinterment ceremony at Father Weikamp's crypt on April 21, 1948.

into ten-foot sections and moved downtown where it is still used today as a Village Hall. Some convent timbers were used to build houses. The hospital was abandoned and the doctors and druggists left. The institution fell into disrepair and was abandoned in 1896.

In 1906 what was left of the convent was struck by lightning and burned.

The hospital also eventually burned, and the last section of the barn finally caved in about 1990. Only the blacksmith shop still stands today, empty. All the land was sold and is in private hands.

Even Father Weikamp's crypt was not to remain where he dug it. The site became private property and fear of vandals and abandonment in the 1940s dictated that Father Weikamp's remains be reinterred, along with those of several Sisters and Brothers, in the Indian Cemetery in Cross Village. The cemetery was so old that it already had graves placed on top of one another. For the reinterment, Father Bertram Mitchell had loads of dirt hauled in and graded to accommodate a third layer of bodies.

On April 21, 1948 a solemn procession carried Father Weikamp, seven Sisters, two Brothers and three unknowns to their new resting place. ■

Antrim County's Bohemian settlers

drew upon the church for their sense of community

By Lucy Lercel

"All we do is work, work, work, and we still have nothing of our own. Let's go to America like our relatives. They also work hard but someday they will have their own land."

That was the feeling held by many natives of Bohemia as they made the decision in the latter part of the 19th century to go to the "New Country." Most of the people who came to America from Czechoslovakia had worked for land owners in their home country. For their labor they were given a portion of the harvest, a portion that was typically harvested after the land owner's share, usually very late at night or in the rain.

Those who decided to leave left behind family, friends and a familiar way of life. They were prompted by letters from daring friends and relatives who had already immigrated to the United States. Advertisements by railroad companies in the newspapers also spurred them on.

James Svager and John Pesek were among the first of these immigrants to come to Antrim County in northern Michigan. When they first arrived, they worked for the Antrim City lumber companies for very little pay. After eight years, Svager and Pesek decided to make a claim on some free land offered by the Homestead Act and carved a place out of the wilderness with no close neighbors.

The two families worked hard to make a shelter, clear the land and find food to live. Life was very hard for the pioneers, but they were driven by the hope for a better life for their children.

As more of them came to the area, the Bohemian settlers would gather together and help each other. They built houses, barns and cleared the land for farming. Members of this close-knit neighborhood were there for each other in happy times as well as tragic times.

One thing many had in common was their Catholic faith. In the earliest days of the settlement there was no church so they would gather at one of the homes and James Svager would lead them in prayer and song. The budding congregation eventually wrote to Harbor Springs where a missionary was located and petitioned for a priest to come and say Mass for them.

It was a day for rejoicing and celebration when a Catholic priest, Father Zorn, came to visit. Father Zorn advised them to build a school before a church, saying, "Church services can be held anywhere, but it is very important to educate the children."

A log school was built in 1877 on land donated by the Grand Rapids and Indiana Railroad Company. Frank Severance was the first teacher to educate the settlers' children in the new schoolhouse. The money from the sale

of the land of every 16th section in the township was set aside for the school system. To encourage settling of the land, every even-numbered section was put up for homesteading by the federal government. All odd-numbered sections were acquired by the railroads to encourage rail transportation.

The log school remained until 1887 when a new frame school was built. The school operated until 1945 when it was consolidated with the East Jordan school system. The building still stands today at the corner of M-32 and Saint John Road across from the stone church.

The Bohemian community continued to grow as more and more people came to the United States. The homes soon became too small for the devoted Catholics to gather for weekly prayer and for Mass when a priest visited. Even the Josifek's home, built with an extra large parlor specifically for that purpose, was too small. Thus it became necessary to build a church.

Saint John Nepomucene Church as it looked originally.

An acre of land was donated by John Votruba and in May of 1885 the pioneers happily began building their church. They were accustomed to working together but this was an exceptionally joyful task; the sound of native Bohemian songs rang out as they worked.

By the fall of 1885 they had a roof on the church and the structure was blessed by a Father Graf as Saint John Nepomucene Catholic Church. Saint John Nepomucene was a tenth century Bohemian cleric who was confessor to the queen of Czechoslovakia at the time. Enemies of the queen tried to force Nepomucene to renounce her but he refused and had his tongue torn out. Thus the statue of Saint John Nepomucene that stands in the little stone church today is of the saint holding a finger to his lips.

John Votruba, Jr., and Frances Swoboda were the first couple to be married in the church. Once the roof was on, however, progress slowed on the construction somewhat as parishioners worked on it whenever they could. The rickety platform was remembered by many before the steps were finished.

The tiny church stood there, three windows to a side, no steeple, no bell, unfinished on the inside until 1893. With the encouragement of Father Bruno Torka, Francis Kolin erected a steeple and a bell. This bell, dedicated to Saint Aloysius, is still there today. The bell has been tolled for warnings of disasters, victory at war and the death of many parishioners.

The Bohemian settlement experienced its greatest development during the first decade of the twentieth century. The settlement and Saint John Nepomucene Catholic Church were practically synonymous. In 1907 the church was enlarged, and sleeping quarters for visiting priests were added. The priests would come by rail to Boyne Falls, and

The church after receiving its fieldstone veneer in 1924.

one of the settlers would meet him there with horse and buggy for the last leg of the trip to Saint John.

Eventually the invention of the automobile and better roads made the sleeping quarters obsolete. In 1924, under the direction of Father Drinnan, the church was remodeled to its present form. A sanctuary and a partial basement were added. Tom Jensen, a stonemason, was hired to add the fieldstone veneer. This unusual veneer is one of the reasons Saint John Nepomucene Church was accepted to the Michigan Historical Commission in February 1993.

The church's altar and statues of Saint John Nepomucene and the Blessed Virgin Mary have been in place since 1894. The hard work of these early pioneers can still be felt in the landscape and in the caring family traditions that survive among their descendants. ■

First quadriplegic priest
ordained in Diocese of Gaylord

By Father Albert J. Courtier

E*verything had to work out just right, but when it did, I, Albert J. Couturier, was ordained a priest for the Diocese of Gaylord on May 14, 1988.*

Just what had to work out just right? Well, it was nigh unheard of that a severely-handicapped individual could be ordained. In fact, there was a Church law against it. That form of prejudice probably went clear back to King David's time when it galled David to be told that even the blind and lame could hold Jerusalem against any invader. So when the temple was built, the handicapped were on the outside looking in.

Without the changes of Vatican II (1962-1965), I would not have been ordained, somehow classified as either abnormal or incomplete. But with Vatican II there came a new outlook at what handicap means in regards human dignity.

Bishop Edmund C. Szoka became bishop of the Gaylord Diocese in 1971. Several years later I asked him whether or not I might resume my studies for priesthood — studies that had been interrupted back in 1956 due to an accident in which I broke my neck at the end of my two years of philosophy at Seminaire de Philosophie in Montreal, Canada. His answer was that I not interfere with the comfort and happiness that I was enjoying as part of a loving family.

And that was that. I was fully satisfied with his answer, seeing as how I thought he would be bishop of Gaylord Diocese till I was old and gray. I had tried to answer what I thought was God's call and the bishop had given his answer. I thought he would probably outlive me. . . but, lo and behold, Bishop Szoka was moved on to greater things — Archbishop of Detroit and then Cardinal assigned to Rome.

Then, along came Bishop Rose. Again the Spirit called and I responded. As soon as I heard a change had been made, I sent a letter asking him to resume my studies for the priesthood. His response was most encouraging: he would try to work something out with the help of Father Bob Bissot, vocations director. That was in 1981. In 1983, with the coming-out of the new Code of Canon Law, I began my studies in theology.

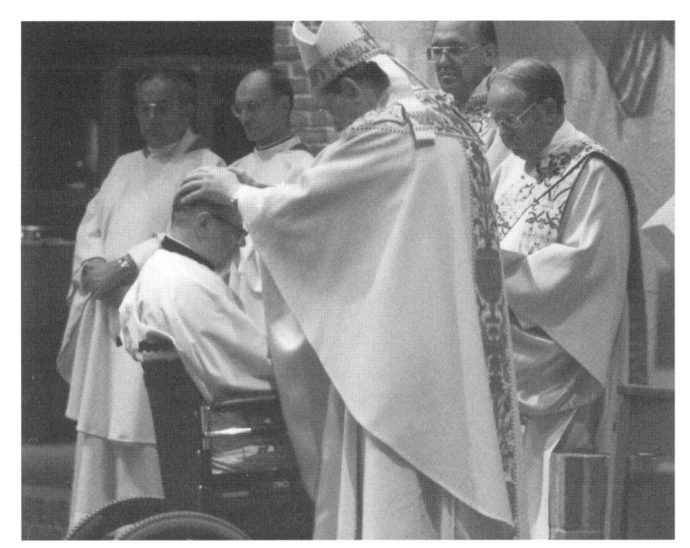

Father Courtier being ordained by Bishop Rose.

How would I be accepted by the clergy of the diocese? I just never imagined that this might be a consideration. And any reservations were unfounded — I hoped.

Bishop Rose ordained me to the priesthood on May 14, 1988, the feast of Saint Matthias, the apostle chosen by lot to fill the vacant seat left by Judas' betrayal. Then, after getting me settled at Saint Francis of Assisi in Traverse City with a particular ministry to the hospitals, nursing homes and senior citizen centers, Bishop Rose was appointed bishop of Grand Rapids.

Into the breach stepped Bishop Patrick Cooney in 1991. With his coming came a new assignment for me... pastor of Saint Helen in Saint Helen, Michigan. There the people welcomed me as the first full-time pastor of the parish. Hopefully, I can serve until the year 2004...at least. ■

Madonna House in Alpena

is one of only six in the country

By Father Gerald F. Micketti

Bishop Robert Rose invited Madonna House Apostolate to open a foundation in the Gaylord Diocese in 1984. The mandate was to provide a facility for prayer and listening.

As there was not a house of prayer at that time on the east side of the diocese, Alpena was chosen as site of the foundation. Rev. Robert Bissot was asked to become the liaison and to assist in finding suitable housing. Rejeanne George was sent from Combermere, Ontario, in April of the same year to open the house. She was followed by another member in August.

Bishop Rose formally blessed the new foundation in March, 1986 at its current location on Lockwood Street in Alpena.

Madonna House is an international apostolate of lay men and women and priests. It was founded by Catherine De Hueck Doherty in 1930. Members make promises of poverty, chastity and obedience. After seven years of living this life, these promises are made for life. There are 20 mission houses throughout the world. Six of these are in the United States, two in Michigan: Alpena and Muskegon Heights.

The Madonna House community is supported entirely by donations. The Alpena Madonna House contains a broad collection of books and tapes available for use by the public, a chapel for prayer, rooms for visiting, and facilities for retreat in the poustinia tradition of prayer and fasting. Various groups and students in religious formation and Christian education classes are welcome for retreat.

Passing on the faith tradition and customs of the liturgical year is an important element of the ministry of Madonna House Alpena. ■

Indian River Catholic Shrine
is a Michigan landmark

The largest crucifix in the world.

For the world's largest crucifix to rise out of the gentle woods of northern Michigan, the faith of the families who built the Cross in the Woods Parish at Indian River had to be nearly as great as the giant redwood from which the cross is hewn.

To the thousands of tourists who visit annually, the Cross in the Woods is a revered attraction, a picturesque shrine where Mass may be celebrated on a summer's vacation. To families of the parish, founded as Saint Augustine's in 1946, the Cross in the Woods is a home of faith.

When Father Charles D. Brophy was assigned to the new parish and its mission church, Saint Monica of Afton, he counted only 12 Catholic families and summer residents among his faithful.

They began worshiping in the township hall until Brophy and parishioner James J. Harrington were able to persuade the State of Michigan Conservation Commission to part with land that was once a portion of the Burt Lake State Park. It was their plan for a church and shrine, the latter dedicated to Indian maiden, the Blessed Kateri Tekakwitha, and the promise they would attract tourists from across the Midwest and Canada that convinced the state to give up the land.

Father Brophy started a "Buy a Block" campaign to raise funds for the shrine.

Through fundraisers, including a "Buy a Block to Help us Build" campaign, monies were collected to undertake the construction of a distinctive church. Designed by Alden Dow, the long low lines of the building followed the natural bluff of the property and blended the church into the woodland site. Five large picture windows gave a commanding view of Burt Lake and, eventually, the cross.

Ground was broken for the new church May 30, 1948. Parishioners from Indian River and Saint Monica worked to clear the land. Through the summer Masses were celebrated around an outdoor altar and on September 5, 1948, a cornerstone ceremony was held. As work continued through the winter, members returned to the township hall for Masses.

Raising the cross.

Preparing the figure.

Securing the base.

Raising the figure.

Final touch-ups.

Mass under the cross.

Finally, on May 29, 1949, Father Brophy and his parishioners, seated on folding chairs and gathered around a temporary altar, celebrated their first Mass inside Saint Augustine. The church was finished: The vision, however, was not yet complete.

In July 1952, construction began on Calvary Hill, an earthen knoll from which a giant crucifix would rise: The Cross in the Woods. Father Brophy brought soil from Kateri Tekakwitha's grave and buried it at the mound at the foot of the cross.

In July of 1953, a 2,000-year-old giant redwood was felled in Oregon. After months of seasoning, it was sanded and polished by Roy DeWitt of the Pioneer Log Cabin Company of Roscommon and encased in an iron jacket to be fastened to the concrete and steel foundation buried on Calvary Hill.

On August 5, 1954, hundreds gathered to watch the two pieces of redwood hoisted by crane onto its base.

"The cross looks like an empty house without the figure of Christ upon it," Bishop Allen J. Babcock said in his speech at the cross's dedication.

Sculptor Marshall Fredericks had been commissioned to design the figure of Christ to be put on the cross. With permission from the Vatican to omit the crown of thorns and the spear wound on Christ's side, Fredericks worked to portray Jesus in a way that "would give the face an expression of real peace and strength" and offer encouragement to people who viewed the cross.

It took six days to lift and attach the 28-foot-long bronze figure to the cross and on August 16, thousands gathered for the blessing of the cross.

Through the years, with leadership from pastors like Fathers Decker, Jendrasiak, Dominiak and Gronowski, the parish continued to grow and thrive on the theme of hospitality, grounds of the shrine were adorned with more sculptures, including a larger-than-life laminated redwood figure of Kateri Tekakwitha, sculpted by Gerald Bonnette. In addition, a family center was added to serve the growing needs of the Cross in the Woods.

The parish, now served by Franciscan Friars, continues to grow in faith, grace and numbers. In the summer of 1996, the Cross in the Woods celebrated its 50th anniversary with many who were present at the beginning of the parish. ■

Father Lenzen of Klacking Creek:

The impact of a priest

By Thomas D. Kulczynski

I go back 61 years and when my family and I used to come up north during the 1940s we used to attend Mass at Saint Joseph as it was closer to Shady Shores Park than either Mio or West Branch. The original church was small and had a coal or wood furnace for heat. Needless to say, Mass was a cold experience as fall and winter approached.

The good father's name was Reverend Godfrey Lenzen and it was his custom to come out from the sacristy into the sanctuary with a Big Ben clock which he wound in front of everyone as he surveyed the attendees. It was placed on the altar during Mass and it could be *heard*. The next part was that, having been a priest for many, many years, he was able to recite the Mass by heart without opening his eyes or the missal which was on the altar. Even though I was about ten or so at the time, I still can remember this shepherd after all these years. Father was here for a while but, upon returning the next summer, there was another older priest. I think his name was Schneider. In the 1950s I was drafted into the army and hardly ever got back to Saint Joseph's. Later it was changed to Holy Family.

This church sits on a hill overlooking the countryside and a long-dead town of Klacking Creek is just down the road.

Holy Family Parish, Klacking Creek

A mission, a parish, a fire, a new name. . .such is the history of the parish of Holy Family Church at Klacking Creek. The year 1880 witnessed the arrival of a missionary

priest to the area called Campbell's Corners. He was Francis X. Shulak, a Jesuit missionary from Chicago, who came and celebrated Holy Mass once or twice a year in the old William Mier home. When this home became too small for the needs of the Catholics, the adjoining property with a public school building was purchased for $250. After an addition was constructed to the building, Saint Joseph Church was blessed by Bishop Henry Joseph Richter of the Diocese of Grand Rapids. The small piece of land in back of the church was converted into a cemetery, and the wife of Joseph Stephens was the first one to be buried in this new cemetery.

After working for the welfare and growth of the congregation for about seven years, Father Shulak was succeeded by Father Aloysius Webbler from Cheboygan as first pastor at West Branch on February 24, 1888. It was while Father Webbler was pastor that a parish church and rectory were built in the neighboring parish of West Branch. From there the pastor could better attend to the growing flock around Campbell's Corners.

Father Webbler remained at West Branch for 12 years. He was succeeded by Father Godfrey Guthausen. To help Father Guthausen care for the missions attached to West Branch, the bishop assigned Father John Reiss as the assistant in July 1903. One result of this assignment was that a larger church was necessary for the Catholics around Campbell's Corners.

A new site was found for the church two miles from Campbell's Corners. Five acres were purchased from Conrad Meir for $125. Thanks to the work of Father Reiss and the good will of the people, the cornerstone was laid in 1904. The location of the new church building was called Klacking Creek. John Klacking, together with Christopher Reetz, were the first settlers of the area. The stream running through the property, which John Klacking homesteaded, was called Klacking Creek.

After the church was completed, Father Reiss was transferred to Grayling, Michigan. Father William J. Schueller succeeded Father Reiss as the assistant of Father Guthausen at West Branch in 1908. Later Father Anthony Eickelmann succeeded Father Guthausen as pastor of West Branch with Saint Joseph Church, Klacking Creek, attached as a mission.

The mission status was not to remain long. Saint Joseph Church became a parish on May 15, 1909, with Father William J. Schueller as its first pastor. In the spring of the following year, on April 1, 1910, ground was broken for the building of a parish rectory. While construction was in progress Father Schueller boarded for a while at the home of one of the parishioners and later moved into the Fulmer home near Klacking Creek.

Father John Abel followed Father Schueller as the pastor on January 1, 1914, and served until he was succeeded by Father Urban Miller in 1921. Father Godfrey Lenzen came to Klacking Creek in 1928 and remained for almost 22 years. During this time Saint Mary Church, Mio, became a mission to Saint Joseph Church starting in February of 1922. This arrangement continued until Father Hubert Rakowski, O.F.M., became pastor of Saint Mary Church in Mio in 1945. Also during this time the parish became part of the new Diocese of Saginaw.

Father Lenzen arrived at a time of great financial difficulty for the community. This distress was compounded three years later by a fire. On April 3 during Tre Ore Devotion on Good Friday, the wooden shingle roof of the church caught fire. It spread rapidly and was beyond control when the West Branch fire department arrived. According to the letter Father Lenzen sent to Bishop Joseph G. Pinten of Grand Rapids, the best the people could do was to save some of the contents of the church. The main altar, the sacred vessels, vestments, the stations of the Cross "and half of the pews were carried out and within an hour the church was a big heap of smoldering embers." One 12-year-old altar boy remembers that it took six men to carry the altar out of the church; it was the last thing carried out. Compounding the calamity was the fact that there was still a debt in the parish of $500 when the church burned. The plans for the new church approved by Bishop Pinten required $12,000 and the old church had been insured for only $8,000. Therefore, $4,500 had to be collected. Many of the parishioners were heavily in debt and in danger of losing their farms. So they were very discouraged. Since Father Lenzen also celebrated Mass in Mio, some of the parishioners traveled to Saint Mary Church in Mio for the Mass. Mass was also celebrated in the Grossman hall by Klacking Creek on the corner of Peters Road and Campbell Road.

After the debris of the old church was removed, the parishioners began the difficult task of rebuilding. By October of the same year the new church was under roof, although finished only on the outside. A new church bell was donated by Mrs. Victoria Housten; the bell was named "Mary Victoria." With the help of the parishioners giving of their time, talent and treasure, and a donation of $1,000, the parish had a new church and was out of debt. The new Saint Joseph Church was blessed by Bishop William Murphy of Saginaw May 14, 1942.

After Father Lenzen died on April 12, 1950, at Mercy Hospital, in Bay City following a short illness, Father George Artman was installed as pastor. He remained until September 1951, when he was transferred to Sacred Heart Parish, Gladwin. During his short stay as pastor, Father Artman took a census, instructed many converts, renovated the main altar, the church hall, and the cemetery, and refinished the pews with the help of the parishioners.

Father George W. Flanagan succeeded Father Artman as pastor on September 12, 1951. He resigned on May 5, 1956, due to failing health, and was appointed chaplain of Saint Vincent's Home, Saginaw. He died on November 28, 1957, at Saint Mary's

Hospital, Saginaw.

On June 15, 1956, Father Edward Trombley was installed as the seventh pastor. While he was pastor Saint Joseph parish celebrated its golden jubilee on June 21, 1959. After consultation with the parishioners in 1966, Father Trombley requested that the parish name be changed. In the letter to Bishop Stephen S. Woznicki, Father Trombley wrote about the confusion caused by the fact that both Saint Joseph Parish, West Branch, and Saint Joseph Parish, Klacking Creek used the postal address. The name Holy Family was chosen and the parish was dedicated to the Holy Family of Jesus, Mary and Joseph.

Father John Gentner succeeded Father Trombley in 1968. After the Diocese of Gaylord was established in 1971, Father Louis Gula became the pastor in October. He was succeeded in the following years by Fathers Robert Bissot, Walter Marek, Gordon Garske, Louis VanBergen and Zygmunt Gaj. Then Sister Ruth Adamites, O.P., was appointed the pastoral administrator serving from 1987 to 1994. She was succeeded by Fathers Herbert Silko, O.F.M., and James Krasman, O.F.M. Presently Father Miro Wiese, O.F.M., is the pastor. ■

This account is about an old country (Germany) priest who came to be a pastor at Saint Joseph Church at Klacking Creek, later to be known Holy Family Church.

Father Francis Pierz

Another remarkable missionary

By Kay Hughes

Fr. Francis Pierz came on the scene at Cross Village in 1835. He was nearly 50 years old when he heard the Lord's call to leave Slovenia and come to the Great Northwest. He stayed 40 some years before he returned to his native country and died at the age of 92.

Father Pierz was a well known horticulturist and taught his Indian charges much about gardening and farming. Because of all his activities in northern Minnesota, the town Pierz is named after him.

In one correspondence, Pierz described the agricultural practices of the time: "Farming is still in a state of slumbering infancy: except for potatoes and maize no field or garden products are known: therefore the natives regard the seeds and fruit kernels which I brought along as a great benefaction. The only farm or garden implements known here are the shovel, which sells for $2, and the axe, costing $4. I have seen a few head of cattle, that can be milked only in summer, and some horses, which are used only for riding. All livestock must shift for itself, without ever seeing a stable, and during the winter must get along on bark and the sprouts of shrubbery. Vast stretches of soil of the very best quality lie untouched and fallow because the people do not know how to make use of it."

Writing to Rev. Augustine Sluga back in Slovenia, Pierz documented the seasonal harshness of northern Michigan: "Winter, extremely severe, yielded to spring only a week ago, and even now Lake Michigan still carries a covering of ice a fathom thick. While during preceding winter violent winds caused such terrible storms on the lake that 47 ships were wrecked in this locality entailing the loss of many lives and of large cargoes. Last winter was marked by such dreadful cold that many animals and human beings met death by freezing. The ground froze to a depth of six feet and as late as March, the extra wine froze in the chalice while I was reading Mass."

One winter, Father Pierz became lost while walking back on the ice from an island on Lake Michigan. After spending two days and a night on the ice, he found his way home and to his joy found two girls requesting baptism.

Father Pierz transferred to L'Arbre Croche in 1839 and stayed until 1852. As those who preceded him, he was always in need of money. He also cared for five other missions including La Croix and Grand Traverse. Some of the people from Cross Village were so ardent in the faith, they would walk the 13 miles from Cross Village to Harbor Springs for Sunday Mass.

There seemed to be a lot of activity in 1844. At Middletown the Indians had built a new schoolhouse and a room for the priest for when he came to the mission. The Indians at LaCroix were also building a house for the schoolmaster and a room for the priest.

Between 1838 and 1855 there were several efforts by white settlers to evict the Ottawa from Little Traverse. In 1839, and 1840, rumors grew that the federal government would send the army to Little Traverse to force the Indians to leave their towns and move west. They had already evicted Potawatomi from their homes in southern Michigan.

Some of the leaders packed everything in their canoes and moved to Manitoulin Island, including 150 from Little Traverse led by Assikinac, plus 47 led by Kemewan, 49 from Cross Village, and 62 from Burt Lake followed Chingassimo.

Father Francis Pierz

Father Pierz was a champion for the Indians in helping them acquire their land before the whites could steal it. He also encouraged his bishop to purchase all the land being used by the various parishes.

In November, 1844, Pierz sent his bishop another letter of lamentation, repeating his earlier requests for monetary assistance: "My cook, an old Indian woman from Mackinac, is going to leave me because I cannot provide her with tea according to her custom. She was hired for $24 and sufficient food for the year.

"Mad. Ficher will spend another couple of months translating my large catechism: I cannot give her family of four persons any food other than my chicken and vegetables from my l'Arbre Croche garden in return for the translations. If I could content her, I would need her for even a longer time till spring or later, for her excellent translations, for, after having finished my Catechism, I plan to compose another good book of prayers for the Indians, since Baraga's book has run out and contains too few prayers."

He ended his supplication with the following sentence: "Since I do not have one cent cash I cannot pay postage on my letter, so put down one shilling and a half to my account as being deductible from my salary."

In September, 1848, Father Pierz wrote some alarming news from L'Arbre Croche: "At the beginning of this month there arrived in our bay a Government gunboat, with some commissioners aboard, to inspect the place.

"They set me many questions about the Indians and all the details of this place in such a way that I have no doubt that Petittraverse (Little Traverse) will very soon become a military station and an American town. I think that at payment time this winter we shall have a declaration from the Government on this subject.

"I would very much like Monseigneur to give me some instructions beforehand as to how I should act in this case with regard to the mission, and our poor Indians, who would have to give up the place. In this case I think that not only the Indians of Petittraverse would have to move out, but also for the others it would not be good to be stationed near a military fort."

In May, 1849, Pierz wrote the bishop of the new church the Indians at Little Traverse were building. He also wrote of a more serious matter: "Our Indians are very much afraid of the cholera since we have the sad news that this terrible malady has already caused ravages at Cleveland and Chicago. At Mackinac and Manitou Islands there is pernicious smallpox. For this reason I am busy at present vaccinating the children and all those who are not yet immunized with this remedy against this smallpox which is so harmful to the Indians. I am being asked by letter from a Chief to leave tomorrow for Grand Traverse so as to vaccinate the Indians."

This intrepid warrior attempted to vaccinate all in his missions. He wrote Bishop Rese when he arrived back at L'Arbre Croche from this journeys: "With the help of God I arrived here yesterday, very tired and having a heavy cold. During those days I risked my life often in the greatest rolling and pitching on the Lake, and I lay down twelve times on the beach in heavy storms of wind, rain and cold without sleeping. At times I could feel the cholera pains through my body, but with my medication I was always able to prevent the full force of the malady."

Father Pierz bemoaned the fact that Government monies were sent to schools according to denomination and not to number of students. By September 26, 1850 there were 3,000 Catholics while the Protestant Presbyterians, Methodists and Anabaptists in five missions had only 300 Christians. He also wrote the President as merchants had been trying to persuade the Indian chiefs to sign a petition to the Government so as to pay some large sums of debts with money from the Indian nation as they demand.

It seems that the missionary always had some occasion of puzzlement to write his bishop, such as: "Just as I have so much spiritual consolation in my branch-missions, I also

have as much sorrow caused me by the bad behavior of some malicious inhabitants of L'Arbre Croche. While I was absent another scandalous case cropped up. A Pedasige boy named Michael came to Father Pamel to be married to a newly-baptized girl from Grande Traverse, but another girl here declared she had been seduced by this same boy and that she was pregnant. The priest asked the erring boy to marry the latter girl whom he had seduced, or sign a paper whereby he would pay her fifty dollars. The boy did not deny having seduced her, but wished neither to marry nor pay her. He went off to Mackinac and got married before a Magistrate to the Grande Traverse girl, which caused much sensation and scandal. His father accompanied him to Mackinac. This boy is also a follower of the Protestant school.

"After my arrival, Pedasige senior came to ask me to marry his son properly. I answered him that he was a great scandal to all the congregation, and that for this I forbade his son Michael and his new wife any entry to the Church, that they are both excommunicated and can receive no Sacrament until after they have performed a great public penance, that I would first of all report this affair to Monseigneur the Bishop and that his reply and decision to write as to how I should act in this case so as to satisfy the Church and the common good of our religion and make a salutary impression on the Indians here."

The answer to this missive has not been found.

Father Pierz was always looking out for the welfare of his Indians, watching to see that the traders did not cheat them, that land speculators did not take property that belonged to the Indians, that traders did not give them too much alcohol, etc. He was truly a champion for their welfare.

While he was at L'Arbre Croche, Father Pierz saw that a new church was built. In the Baptismal Registry at Holy Childhood is written: "The church of Arbre Croche, lately built by the Indians alone, was lawfully blessed by me, the undersigned, missionary of this place, on the 25th of May 1851, in virtue of episcopal delegation, in honor of Our Lord Jesus Christ as youth in the temple. Francis Pierz, Roman Catholic Missionary. Wherefore this mission shall be called here after 'Mission S.S.Adolescentiae Jesu.'"

In 1852, Father Pierz officially left this diocese for that of Bishop Cretin in Minnesota whom he felt had much more need of priests. ■

The history of All Faiths Chapel
at Traverse City Regional Hospital

By Father Edwin Frederick

Do these names sound familiar: Dr. Baker (Scenic Council Boy Scouts), Jim Pound, Dr. Sommerness, John Parsons, Dr. Loomis, Arnell Engstrom, Ken Haven, Reverend Dominiak, Father Frederick and Mrs. Kimmet?

They are names of people who were alive in 1960-61 when an idea for a chapel on the Traverse City Regional State Hospital grounds began to grow.

Because Dr. Sommerness believed that religion, a person's faith and the practice thereof, was an integral part to a person's recovery from mental illness, he asked why not build a chapel for "our people?" (In the early 1960s there were 3,000 patients at the hospital.)

The patients, seemingly dressed like poor, forlorn souls in cotton clothes, baggy pants and other cast off clothing, were separated from their homes and communities. If there was a God, where was He? Those lost souls were not welcome in the community churches. They looked different, acted differently and dressed differently.

From what? I don't know but on top of being hospitalized at the State Hospital, they were shunned by the townspeople. The latter moved away from them, even in church. And mind you, some unfortunates had a deep, deep faith and a wonderful relationship with Jesus.

It was thus resolved that, if the patients couldn't worship with the brethren, then they would have to have their own chapel. The employees backed the idea because they were a caring bunch; a bunch devoted to better living conditions of the patients. Each employee pledged the most

they could. The $300,000 goal seemed way out of sight for some folks. It was a lot of money but Tom Miller, campaign manager, devised a plan so that everyone could contribute and live comfortably with their pledge.

Employees pledged a dollar a month for three years. A couple of big firms, like Continental Motors in Muskegon, had their employees allow the payroll department to deduct the money from the pay. Muskegon, Saginaw (Saginaw Steering, Wickes) Bay City and Alpena (Besser Block Corporation) were big contributors to the chapel.

Every one of the 39 counties, employers and churches of all faiths, were determined to see the chapel at the State Hospital become a reality.

The architect designed the facility with the advice of the two chaplains who said there should be three distinct sanctuaries. Respecting a person's desire to worship God in his or her own atmosphere, the building committee agreed to three distinct sanctuaries under one roof with a huge narthex in the middle for the congregations of all faiths to meet.

There was no concern about whether a patient would get lost in the facility. The chapels were marked "Catholic," "Jewish," and "Protestant" and each was distinguishable by its age-old custom of decor. If some non-Catholic strayed into the Catholic chapel where there was evidence of Catholicity, *e.g.* statues and kneelers, he quickly decided he was in the wrong place.

The decision made the person feel like a human being, worthwhile, useful and sane. As a consequence, the patient made greater progress toward getting out of the hospital and returning to the community.

The Protestant and Catholic chapels were marked with beautiful stained glass windows, created and installed by Paul Welch of Traverse City. The Jewish synagogue was clearly identifiable by the Ark. Had there been enough money we would have obtained a Torah, too.

The non-denominational All Faith Chapel, above, featured a Catholic chapel, below, for regular Mass.

The hospital chapel, built with support from communities in 39 counties, finally became a reality. In 1964, during dedication ceremonies, the building committee decided to pay off any debts incurred during the campaign.

It was a success. In three years the entire complex was free and clear of debt, due to the hard-working people who made pledges or donations. The patients even offered their nickels and dimes. In the early 1960s when this came about, be mindful that patients did not get Social Security Insurance, Social Security and all the benefits they get now.

They were poor then, forgotten and sick. Thank God for the employees of the State Hospital who loved and cared for them and directed them.The patients regarded the chapel as their own. They respected it, took part in cleaning it, mopping the floors, washing the windows, polishing the pews. All these works of love prompted them to get better faster. And with the weekly Sunday services, and later with daily services, patients grew to fall deeply in love with that House of God and with their God.

"I am with you all days," Jesus said. That made lots of sense to the patients who were separated from their families and friends.

Now the patients had their chapel. They were pleased when the towns people began coming onto the grounds and celebrating the liturgies with them. Patients began to grow, spiritually and psychologically. They loved the babies and kids who came with visitors. Patients had to adjust their own worlds to the realities of the real world.

God was really working through the chapel, taking care of his poor people and teaching others to care more for each other. The chapel and God did a lot to erase the stigma of mental illness. It began to be a privilege to say "I attend All Faiths," "All Faiths is my parish" and "I feel at home there."

The chapel became known as a refuge, a source for hope, for food, for warmth, for milk to feed the little children, for fuel, clothes and anything else that we fortunate people take for granted. ■

The Wild Rose of Omena

A story of love and Christian purpose

By Father Stanley Bur

To witness the Scripture passage of "a little child shall lead them," we shall briefly tell the story of *the Wild Rose of Omena*. This is derived from "The First Protestant Mission in the Grand Traverse Region," published in 1935 by Ruth Cracker.

It seems a young French couple of some royal blood had become separated shortly after they started their life together in France. The wife had come to America to find her husband along the Great Lakes. Some Indians had found the beautiful young French lady and brought her to the priest at Peshawbestown where he offered his meager house of two rooms as a temporary shelter.

His Indian cook prepared a meal and he provided some French wine. But, knowing the beautiful young lady's fear of the Indians, the priest set out for the Protestants' New Mission and asked the minister's wife if she would take in the young, refined lady who was pregnant. She accepted and the friendship between the priest and the minister was deepened, as Miss Cracker says, "In spite of the difference in their religious beliefs the two men were fast friends, drawn together by their own culture and lack of other society."

The child was born and the baby girl grew, but the mother died and is buried at Omena Point where the wild roses grow over her grave. The baby was baptized Rose Blanche by the priest. However, when the child reached the age of reason and needed religious instructions, the minister and his wife invited the priest to their home to give these lessons in religion. This was done out of respect for the religion of the dead mother.

Soon after these lessons had begun, a fine-appearing and graceful gentleman appeared one day, having come on one of the ships of the Great Lakes. He told his story and saw the dear little girl, the very image of her mother. After several weeks of friendship and acquaintance he persuaded her to return with him to his native France. He had desired that her adoptive mother, Cornelia Dougherty, the eldest daughter of the minister, should marry him and come with them. But she could not bear to do so, even though her heart drove her on, loving not only the "Wild Rose" whom she had mothered, but also the girl's father.

The minister of the story is the Reverend Dougherty and the priest is Father Mrak. The story itself is so poignant yet humanly touching that it is impossible to read it without tears of love in abundance at many passages. It gives forth the real essence of Christian love exceeding the differences of doctrine among the various brands of Christianity. Though both minister and priest were tenacious in their beliefs, this common bond of love held them to their true Christian purpose in going to the natives of a foreign and far away land, only to be drawn together by the love and compassion for a little child of noble birth. ■

The Knights of Columbus

have been championing the faith in Northern Michigan since 1900

By Father Gerald F. Micketti

In 1882 Father Michael J. McGiveney called together some men of the parish where he was serving in New Haven, Connecticut. He explained to them his idea of gathering men together as group for three primary purposes.

The first was to help men and their families remain steadfast in their Catholic faith through mutual encouragement. His second aim was to promote closer ties of fraternity among the men, and, third, to set up an elementary system of insurance so that the widows and children of the members of the group who might die would not find themselves in dire financial straits.

This was the beginning of the Knights of Columbus. The founders and first officers of the new organization chose the name Knights of Columbus because they felt that, as a Catholic group, it should relate to the Catholic discoverer of America.

This would serve to point out that it was Catholics who discovered, explored and colonized the North American continent. At the same time "Knights" would signify that the membership embodied knightly ideals of spirituality and service to Church, country and humanity.

The first Knights of Columbus council in Michigan was established in Detroit in 1898. Within two years councils were set up in Grand Rapids, Bay City and Port Huron. In 1900, Council 529 was formed in Alpena. That is the oldest council in this diocese. Since then, 31 additional Knights of Columbus councils have been established in the Diocese of Gaylord involving 12,000 members.

Over the years the Knights of Columbus have strived to live by the guiding principles set by Father McGiveney. The Knights have actively supported Catholic education, helped the widows and children of deceased Knights, set up insurance programs and retirement plans, emphasized family life, prayer and liturgy and encouraged vocations to the priesthood and religious life.

Some councils have also sponsored the Columbian Squires. The Squires program is part of the Knights of Columbus organization for young men ages 12-17. The Columbian Squires have the goals of spiritual, cultural, civic, social and physical improvement of its members and the development of leadership qualities.

Individual councils have also sponsored and supported Boy Scouts, Girl Scouts, Girl Guides, 4-H, Big Brothers, Babe Ruth or Pony League baseball, soccer and hockey. In Michigan the Knights of Columbus are very well known for their Tootsie Roll sale in the spring to raise money for mentally handicapped adults and children in Michigan. ■

Daughters of Isabella and Catholic Daughters of the Americas

provide Catholic women with vehicles to carry out Christ's work

By Father Gerald F. Micketti

In the late 1890's after the establishment of the Knights of Columbus, ladies auxiliaries to some of the Knights' councils were organized. Though the women were never absorbed as members of the Knights, some of their auxiliary organizations were active in the social life of the councils.

Two of these organizations became the Daughters of Isabella and the Catholic Daughters of the Americas.

The Daughters of Isabella was founded in 1897 in New Haven, Connecticut as an auxiliary of the Knights of Columbus. The patroness of the organization was Isabella of Castile, the Spanish queen who sponsored Christopher Columbus on his exploration of the New World.

The objectives of the Daughters of Isabella are: to render financial aid and assistance to the sick and distressed members and promote the social and intellectual growth of its members.

The Daughters of Isabella eventually became an independent organization. There are 43 circles (or groups) in various parts of Michigan with over 5700 ladies dedicated to their motto of Unity, Friendship and Charity. There are three circles of the Daughters of Isabella in the Diocese of Gaylord - Rogers City, Alpena, Cheboygan and Gaylord.

"The main objective of all Catholic Daughters is union with Christ. He is the vine; we are the branches. All that our organization is and does must center around this union with Our Lord. We imitate Mary, His Mother, who kept her heart and her eyes on Jesus from the manger in Bethlehem to the streets of Nazareth and Jerusalem, from the foot of the cross on Calvary to His glorious resurrection and ascension." These are the words of the Catholic Daughters of the Americas and are meant to motivate, inspire and challenge CDA members to live what they believe and proclaim to the world.

The Catholic Daughters began in 1903 in Utica, New York. They were incorporated originally as the National Order of the Daughters of Isabella. The purpose of the group was three-fold: to promote the social and intellectual standing of the members; for literary purposes; and for the purpose of rendering such aid and assistance among its members as shall be desirable and proper....

The charter Court Utica started with 60 members and within five there were 90 courts and over 10,000 members. The growth continues today; in 1978 the national organization formally changed its name to the Catholic Daughters of the Americas. In the Diocese of Gaylord there are two courts - Traverse City and Manistee.

On a national level the Daughters actively support such organizations as Catholic Relief Services, Covenant House, the National Catholic Education Association and Habitat for Humanity. The Daughters is the only all-women group to build houses for Habitat. The Traverse City Court supports the Capuchin Center Detroit, Right to Life, Father Fred Foundation, Pregnancy Resource Center and Morality in Media. The Manistee Court supports tuition at the Manistee Catholic Schools, missionaries to Lithuania and anti-gambling efforts. ■

The Church and Indian People
of northern Michigan

Taken from the volume *Sown on Good Ground* by Sister Alice O'Rourke, O.P., and recollections from Father Andy Buvala

The history of the Catholic Church in northern lower Michigan begins with French Jesuit missionaries. These extraordinary men ministered for more than a century to the Indian people serving the interests of French fur traders in the area. Their ministry goes back as far as 1671 when a Jesuit mission was established at Saint Ignace. The Jesuits continued their work for many years establishing missions and working hard building Christian communities and protecting Indian integrity.

Various political battles, the succession of wars between France and England, the disruption of tribal territories, shifts in political jurisdiction as the French were ousted in 1763 and the English colonies achieved their independence in 1783—all these developments prohibited the kind of settled life that was conducive to religious practices. A remnant of the Ottawa tribe remained in the L'Arbre Croche area where they were served by Father Pierre du January, S.J., until 1765. Not long after his departure, a further blow was struck when the hostility toward the Jesuits on the part of factions in France and elsewhere culminated in the universal suppression of the Society of Jesus in 1773.

At that time the Michigan area was part of the Diocese of Quebec from its establishment in 1674 until the erection by the Holy See in 1789 of the Diocese of Baltimore, headed by Bishop John Carroll, and including all of the territory under the civil jurisdiction of the United States government. In 1796 full ecclesiastical jurisdiction over all areas of the United States resided with the Bishop of Baltimore.

The pulpit of Blessed Kateri Tekakwitha Church.

Bishop Carroll, although facing extraordinary burdens in administering his far-flung diocese, did not neglect the northwestern parts. He solicited the help of the Sulpician priests who had fled France for the United States and established a parish in Detroit staffed by Fathers LaVadoux and Richard. These men were very committed to the Indian people and fought for the rights of the Indians under the various treaties negotiated between them and the United States governments. All this was accomplished in the midst of heavy responsibilities in their major sphere at Detroit.

Realizing the impossible task Bishop Carroll had in governing a diocese that covered all of the United States, the Holy See created four new dioceses in 1808—New York, Boston, Philadelphia and Bardstown. Later in 1821, the Diocese of Cincinnati was created, which included the territories of Wisconsin and Michigan. Edward Fenwick, Dominican priest and a man with missionary interests, was named the new bishop and during the eleven years of his leadership (he died of cholera on September 26, 1832) pastoral activity was again actively encouraged. It was at his invitation that Father Pierre DeJean, a Frenchman, Father Samuel Mazzuchelli, an Italian Dominican, and Father Frederic Baraga, a Slovenian, came to serve the Indians in the northern areas of Michigan.

Father Frederic Baraga, perhaps the best known of

Bishop Fenwick's proteges, arrived in the United States in 1830 and was assigned to the L'Arbre Croche mission in 1831. In addition to his ministrations at New Arbre Croche, Middle Village and Cross Village, Father Baraga visited Beaver Island and Manistique and ventured into the forests to the east, where, among various places visited, he established a mission at Burt Lake. After a short stay in the Grand River Valley, Father Baraga began his work among the Chippewa of the Lake Superior region serving until 1852. In that year he became Vicar Apostolic of Upper Michigan and in 1857, was appointed first bishop of the newly established Diocese of Sault Sainte Marie, now the Diocese of Marquette.

Indian gathering.

Meanwhile, changes had occurred in both civil and ecclesiastical jurisdiction. The Holy See erected the Diocese of Detroit in 1833, a jurisdiction encompassing the Michigan and Wisconsin Territories, to which Frederic Rese was appointed bishop. Michigan officially became a state in January 1837, and in 1843 jurisdiction in the Wisconsin Territory was divided between the Diocese of Dubuque and the newly-erected Diocese of Milwaukee. When Father Baraga was made Vicar Apostolic of Upper Michigan, he assumed responsibility for the Indian missions along the shores of upper Lake Michigan and southern Lake Superior.

The work among the Ottawas in the northwest portion of the lower peninsula was undertaken by Father Francis Xavier Pierz. He, in turn, was assisted after 1845 by Father Ignatius Mrak, a future bishop of the Marquette Diocese. At the time he assumed his pastorate, Father Pierz found the missions well-ordered and the congregations in such good moral and spiritual condition that they could well serve as model communities. In addition to his sacramental functions, Father Pierz was interested in maintaining schools for the Indians, where they would be taught religion, reading, writing, spelling, ciphering, geography, sewing, and knitting. In 1843, there were 206 children attending the schools of the missions: 69 at New Arbre Croche; 54 at Cross Village; 27 at Middle Village; 16 at Burt Lake; and 40 at Manistique.

With the departure of Father Pierz to the missions of Minnesota in 1852 and of Father Mrak a little later to the Grand Traverse Bay area, the missions at L'Arbre Croche were eventually turned over to Father John B. Weikamp who established a Franciscan community at Cross Village. By 1858, Father Weikamp had centralized the other missions at that location and his community included four Franciscan priests and twelve Franciscan sisters. In 1884, the mission of New Arbre Croche (Harbor Springs) was assigned to the Franciscan Fathers of the Saint Louis Province. Father Weikamp remained at Cross Village until his death in 1889.

The following is taken from an interview by Father Patrick Cawley with Father Andy Buvala, O.F.M., pastor of Blessed Kateri Tekakwitha and from material written by Catherine Baldwyn, a parishioner.

Today, in 1997, there are about four to five thousand Indian people in the Diocese of Gaylord. Most of these are Ottawa and Chippewa and about one thousand are Catholic. There are three federally recognized bands of Indians; i.e. the Grand Traverse Band, the Little Traverse Band and the Little River Band. Another band, the Burt Lake group, located in Emmet and Cheboygan counties, is trying to achieve federal status.

Ministry to the Indian people has been a part of the church's experience in northern lower Michigan since the recorded time of the Jesuits in 1671 up to the present. The church has learned a great deal from the Indians in spirituality and their sense of the sacramental and symbolic expressions of life and the universe. The church's honoring of the dead is very special to Indian people and their 'Ghost Suppers' and burial grounds are sacred. It is most important that these special traditions continue and are experienced by the whole church since so much of our faith is expressed by the Indian people in a unique way. A major concern is how to recover the culture of the people without their native language. Years ago there were traditional Indian songs in hymn books in their native language, many of these were written by Bishop Baraga. Some of these are still sung today at Blessed Kateri Tekakwitha Parish in Peshawbestown.

The Indian people have long been a focus of the church in northern Michigan, as

The statue of Blessed Kateri Tekakwitha at her shrine.

stated above. Over the years much has changed as both the church and the Indians have grown in faith and understanding of each other. History has taught us how the church wanted to teach the Indian people about God and his goodness and how, in turn, we learned about the Creator who is Mother and Father to us all. There is a richness in this history and we all should be proud to be a part of it and to live here, where so much of the tradition and beauty abounds.

In the Diocese of Gaylord there is a parish in Peshawbestown that now bears the name, "Blessed Kateri Tekakwitha." This parish dates back to 1849, and, prior to 1991, was Immaculate Conception. Blessed Kateri is most appropriate to be the patron of this parish located in Indian land. She is a special person and offers the whole church a unique sense of what is holy.

"At age 20, Kateri Tekakwitha left her Mohawk village in Fonda (now Auriesville, New York) to live in the Christian village of Caughnawaga (now LaPrairie, Quebec) at Saint Francis Mission. She brought along a letter from the priest in the Mohawk village to the priests of Saint Francis Mission, which read: "Kateri Tekakwitha now comes to join your community...you will soon realize what a jewel we have sent you."

"This same Kateri Tekakwitha comes to the community of Peshawbestown as the patron of the church and as a presence in the form of a shrine. The 'jewel' is within a new setting. From beneath the bough of a blue spruce she looks out on this village with her eyes focused on the east, the direction of the rising sun, as if in prayer that the Risen One might bring a life of hope, peace, and harmony to her Native American brothers and sisters in this community." ■

The Carmelite Monastery

A powerful ministry of prayer

By Father Gerald F. Micketti

When Bishop Haas learned from Reverend Mother Teresita that Carmel in Grand Rapids had been forced to turn away applicants, he had an idea. The bishop was concerned about the number of fallen away Catholics in the northern part of the Diocese of Grand Rapids. He approached Carmel in November 1948 with a request. Bishop Haas wanted the Carmelite Sisters of Grand Rapids to set up a foundation up north as soon as possible. The Chapter accepted his proposition and the search began for a suitable site. The bishop asked the sisters to consider either Petoskey or Traverse City.

By June of 1949, Father Joseph Kohler, pastor of Saint Francis Assisi Church in Traverse City, had located five possible locations. Reverend Mother Teresita and Sister Teresa Margaret had been chosen by their community to lead the foundation. They came to Traverse City on the 20th of June. One location was selected. This location required remodeling and additions. One advantage of this location was the low price. This situation soon changed when the owner of the site became aware that the prospective buyer was a Catholic institution. He doubled his price and the sisters found another site.

A large house on Peninsula Drive was purchased by Mrs. Molly Mahoney. The two nuns came with $50 to supply their immediate needs and later were given $500. The Grand Rapids Carmelite community also gave the new foundation furniture, clothes, choir books, bedding

and dishes. A miracle of sorts seemed to have happened when the Carmelite nuns came to Traverse City. The people of the two parishes in Traverse City, Saint Francis and Immaculate Conception, who had been divided, united and worked together to help the new monastery.

Since the Traverse City area relied upon cherry farming and resort businesses for income, the new foundation could not rely exclusively on alms and the donations of the residents for income. The founding Carmel generously turned over to the monastery the altar bread orders which they had been supplying to the parishes in the northern portion of the diocese. This is still a source of income for the Carmelite monastery.

The renovation of the house was aided by the donation of labor and materials or supplied at cost. The farmers of Lake Leelanau supplied 1400 cedar tress and planted them to provide an enclosure. While the renovations were in progress the two nuns stayed with the Dominican Sisters and the Mercy Sisters.

The wonderful day arrived — February 1, 1950! After a special High Mass with tears and farewells, the nuns who were to establish the foundation, left Grand Rapids accompanied by the Mayor of Traverse City, Jane Guiffre and others. When they arrived, the new community of Carmelites was greeted by friends, a luncheon and their new chaplain, Father Joseph Panavas.

The first Mass at the new monastery in 1962.

The chaplain wanted to celebrate the Mass in the new chapel. The chapel, however, was a mess, because the carpenters left tools and material everywhere. The sisters soon cleared the room and set up a table for a temporary altar. Father Panavas supervised the unpacking of the altar linens and the sacred vessels. After Mass, he departed.

The tired but happy nuns prepared for their night's sleep. Soon peals of laughter were heard. The nuns discovered that there was no way they could sleep on their new straw mattresses. Before the sisters arrived, the ladies had charitably stuffed the straw mattresses. Since they had never slept on those mattresses, they stuffed them so full that the mattresses were round instead of flat. The nuns were accustomed to flat mattresses. That night the sisters slept on their blankets.

In 1951 the sisters began the process to pronounce their solemn vows. One of the obligations was to make the enclosure permanent. The monastery itself met the requirements of Papal enclosure, but the wall of trees surrounding the enclosed yard did not. Plans were considered for the erection of a proper wall and enlarging the monastery. When this became known, the neighbors petitioned against the proposed enclosure. The petition was accepted and the sisters were forbidden to build anything over four feet high and to enlarge the monastery building. The foundation decided to look for another location of the monastery.

The second wonderful day — May 7, 1960! The nuns of the Carmelite Monastery moved from their first location to their new building on Silver Lake Road. They were transported by members of the Third Order. The sisters wanted to begin a regular life so they moved into their new monastery, a simple concrete building, with the interior partially finished. Upon arrival they were served a meal prepared by another group of women who called themselves the Society of Carmel. Mass was celebrated after the meal.

Carmelite Sisters celebrate the monastery's Silver Anniversary.

Through the generosity of friends and donations of labor and material, the walls, ceilings and floors of the interior of the monastery were completed. Construction started for the permanent chapel, nuns choir, sacristies and two other work rooms by the end of 1961. The first Mass celebrated November 19, 1962, by Monsignor Anthony Arszulowicz. The next year the enclosure wall was completed. In 1979 the monastery was completed.

Bishop Haas wanted the Carmelite Monastery in northern Michigan to set up a powerhouse of prayer to counteract the evil influences and to aid the few priests in their work of reclaiming the stray sheep. This prayer ministry and life is what the Carmelite Sisters continue to do in the Diocese of Gaylord. ■

The Diocesan Council of Catholic Women

began in the first year of the diocese

By Father Gerald F. Micketti

On the first page of the initial minutes book of the Diocesan Council of Catholic Women, somebody wrote: "It is not enough to do good; one must do it in the right way."

That is exactly what the Gaylord Diocesan Council of Catholic Women have been doing from the beginning of their organization in 1971. Over the years, through their by-laws and policies, commissions, parish and vicariate activities, they have fought and continue to fight abortion, domestic violence and pornography.

They have also collected items for layettes to be given to families in need in the Diocese of Gaylord. Through their Madonna plan they have donated money to Third World countries to help communities, villages and families develop their own sources of clean water.

At one of the annual DCCW diocesan conventions, a woman from India said she would liked to have hugged each member present because their monetary donations helped her and her community dig a new well. Prior to the project the people of her village had to walk three miles for clean water. Now, thanks to DCCW charity, they have their own well for the community.

In September, 1971, soon after the Diocese of Gaylord was established, Bishop Edmund Szoka invited 20 women to discuss organizing a Diocesan Council of Catholic Women. After Mass at St. Mary Church, they met for the discussion with Helen Quinn of Bay City to begin the process of organizing the Gaylord DCCW.

The ladies agreed and a committee was set up to initiate that process. One of the first activities of this new council of Catholic women, at the request of Bishop Szoka, was to provide Christmas gifts for the Native American children in the Holy Childhood of Jesus School at Harbor Springs.

Almost one year later, the Gaylord Diocesan Council of Catholic Women officially began. As a Diocesan organization, the DCCW is associated with the National CCW. The members of the DCCW are also members of the parishes of the diocese. What is decided by DCCW is discussed at the parish level, then at the regional or vicariate level and finally at the diocese level.

If the activity is national significance, discussion and decisions are made at that level. Every first Wednesday of May, the DCCW meets for its convention. Since their beginning the DCCW has helped the Diocese of Gaylord continue the work of the Lord as was urged upon by Bishop Szoka at their first official meeting. ■

Grand Traverse Area Catholic schools

Excellence in education, commitment to faith

The first Catholic school in Traverse City began in 1877. Father George Ziegler was the first resident pastor of Saint Francis of Assisi Church in Traverse City. He arrived in Traverse City in 1877. He requested through Father Mendel in Saint Paul Parish, Greenville, New Jersey, that the Sisters of Saint Dominic of Second Street, New York City, come to Michigan to start a school. Five sisters accompanied by Mother Aquinata arrived in Traverse City, Thursday, October 23, 1877. The sisters were Mother Camilla Madden, Mother Angela Phelan, Sister Mary Martha Mueglich, Sister Mary Boniface Hartleb and Sister Mary Borromeo Ahlmeier. The superior was Mother Angela. After a short stay in Traverse City, Mother Aquinata returned to New York.

Their first residence was a house on Union Street purchased by Father Ziegler from his own private means at a cost of $1,000. The house was furnished by the congregation for church and school purposes as well as for a sisters' residence at a cost of $600. The ground floor contained two classrooms. In one of the classrooms Mass was offered on weekdays. The second floor, the sisters' dwelling proper, had a small chapel where the Blessed Sacrament was reserved, two bedrooms, a sitting room and a kitchen. The sisters lived in this house for nearly six years. On the Monday following their arrival, school was opened with six pupils. By the end of the school year the number increased to 50.

Perry Hannah donated six lots on Tenth Street to the sisters for the purpose of erecting a convent boarding school. In May 1883, construction began. The building was completed in the beginning of September of the same year. The new Holy Angels Convent was dedicated by Bishop Henry J. Richter of Grand Rapids on the first Sunday of September. The next day school opened. Holy Angels convent was the first mother house of the province of Saint Joseph of the Sisters of Saint Dominic. In time the mother house was moved to Grand Rapids where it has remained at Marywood.

On December 5, 1883, the sisters completed the arrangements for the legal corporation of Holy Angels Academy. The Academy celebrated its first high school commencement in 1889 consisting of three young women: Anna Shane, Mary Donley, and Stacia Burden.

The convent-academy continued to benefit from civic improvements, such as the claying and graveling of Union Street in 1883, tree planting in 1886, and the installation of street lights in 1889. A brick annex, begun in April of 1911, provided a new chapel, refectory and sleeping areas. This work was completed in May of 1913. The building continued to serve as a convent for the sisters who staffed Saint Francis Schools. In 1972 the original convent-academy was demolished. Modifications were also made to the 1913 addition to improve the living areas for the sisters serving at Saint Francis and later in the Grand Traverse Area Catholic Schools. That part of the building became known as the Saint Francis Convent. On Saturday, October 24, 1993, a prayer service and reception were held in the Saint Francis Convent. Shortly after the convent was demolished — the passing of an era for Saint Francis Parish and schools.

Father Joseph Bauer was the pastor of Saint Francis Parish for 33 years. Under Father Bauer not only the church but the school also expanded. Construction for a new parish school facing Cass Street began in June 1893 and was completed the following September. There were four classrooms on the main floor and two classrooms and a larger room on the second floor. The opening enrollment was 150 students. By 1898 the school enrollment was 20 pupils in the high school and 180 in the grade school. Father Bauer also saw to the construction of a gym in 1913.

Another pastor of Saint Francis who was instrumental in the expansion of the Catholic Schools was Father Joseph Kohler. In 1952 Father Kohler began fund raising to build an elementary school and high school. In August of the next year bids were sought and contracts were signed to build a new elementary school, gymnasium and auditorium. Construction began but was slow. The structural steel was in place for the new buildings by March 15, 1954 and the remainder of the construction began after that. The new school has 14 classrooms, a study hall and other facilities. A new gymnasium and auditorium were built next to the elementary school. The gym was officially opened November 26, 1954, when the Saint Francis High School basketball team played against the Saint Mary of Lake Leelanau High School team. More than 2,000 people watched Saint Francis defeat Saint Mary 41 to 33. The students entered the new school for classes by the start of the second semester of the 1954-55 school year, January of 1955.

Local businesses outfitted the kitchen which served the school cafeteria and the gymnasium. These businesses were paid in notes with no interest. This made the gym the focal point for community gatherings and the rental of the gym helped pay the debt on the new school and gym.

A classroom visit by Bishop Rose.

The fund raising activity was started with two goals in mind — to build a new elementary school and a new high school. One of the goals was accomplished; the second goal would take a little longer.

In 1964 Father Kohler began to solicit funds for a new high school. At that time there were 700 children in the new elementary school and 400 students in the old high school. The first shovel of dirt for the new high school was turned by Father Kohler March 29, 1965; and Bishop Babcock of Grand Rapids dedicated the new Saint Francis High School the following October 16. When completed in 1966 the students moved in with books and equipment. This is the present Saint Francis High School. At this time the complex of buildings that made up Saint Francis Parish was bounded by Cass, Tenth, Eleventh and Union Streets.

Immaculate Conception Catholic School began in 1906. Bishop Henry J. Richter dedicated the new Immaculate Conception Church February 22, 1906. The first church building was a two-story structure. The first floor was the school and the upper floor was the house of worship. The pastor, Father John J. Sheehan, sought and obtained the services of the Sisters of Mercy of Farmington. The school opened with four rooms and 80 students on the first floor of the building. Three rooms were used for classes and the fourth room was used for assemblies.

Sr. Mary Edith Kneblewski RSM wrote in a 1979 letter: "When Immaculate Conception church was blessed and dedicated in 1906, I was at the ceremony with my parents. That year I attended first grade at Saint Francis school and in the fall of 1906, I transferred to second grade at Immaculate Conception. Sr. Mary Lawrence was my teacher and had primary, first and second grades. Sr. Mary Austin was the principal and taught the sixth, seventh and eighth grades. Sr. Mary DeSales taught the third, fourth and fifth grades. Saint Mary Claver was the housekeeper. They lived at 612 Third Street."

During the tenure of Msgr. Russell Passeno, an addition to the convent was completed and other repairs to the church-school building and the rectory were also completed. In 1949 the first tuition of $390 was paid for Immaculate Conception students at Saint Francis High School. Two years later Bishop Haas of Grand Rapids gave permission to build new church; the cost was $229,814. Ground was broken May 23, 1952 and construction was completed nine months later. The first Mass celebrated in the new church was Easter Sunday, April 5, 1953. The church was dedicated May 30, 1953. The old church, the second floor of the church-school building, was remodeled to add four classrooms and a principal's office in 1955. Four sisters and three lay teacher taught full time. The bell in the cupola of the old church was eventually given to Saint Patrick Church when that parish was beginning to form.

In 1956 the parish had 630 families. There were 360 students in 8 grades in 8 classrooms taught by four sisters and four lay teachers, and 60 students at Saint Francis High School. In the summer of the following year the parish Men's Club had the first outdoor carnival to raise money for a new school. The next year the parish debt was paid in full and Bishop Babcock gave permission to consider building a new school to cost around $355,000. The new school, an addition to the old school building, opened February 16, 1961.

In 1969 Bishop Babcock of Grand Rapids mandated the consolidation of the schools of Immaculate Conception and Saint Francis Parishes. Thus was born the Grand Traverse Area Catholic Schools. Under this arrangement each parish contributed funds based on the number of students in the school. This created some hardship for Immaculate Conception parish. Immaculate Conception parish was debt free in 1969; Saint Francis was not. That meant the debt for the new Saint Francis High School was also assumed by Immaculate Conception Parish. Both parishes were having financial difficulties in 1971. That led to the decision to charge tuition for the grade school students. That same year the Grand Traverse Educational Foundation was established to provide grants-scholarships for students as well as grants for improvements. ■

Office of Catholic Education

An important resource for Catholic schools in the Diocese

By Father Thomas A. Neis

This anecdotal incident has nothing to do with any particular parish history, but with the early years of the formation of the Diocese of Gaylord.

Bishop Edmund Szoka, founding bishop of the Diocese of Gaylord, often decried the church's demand for certified "experts" in the field of Canon Law, social work and religious education, but did not supply this personnel when a new diocese was created.

In the late summer of 1971, the bishop notified us that we needed to choose a diocesan Director of Catholic Education from amongst the three priests gathered in his office: Robert H. Bissot, Francis C. Partridge and myself. We had been gathered together because we three were the ones with Master's degrees, still involved in Catholic schooling administratively.

The lot fell to me to serve in this capacity, with the other two forming the nucleus of the first diocesan Board of Catholic Education. I was serving the Catholic Central Schools in Manistee; Father Partridge, the Catholic Central Schools in Cheboygan; Father Bissot, Saint Mary's School in Hannah. The first organizational meeting "for those interested in promoting Catholic Education in our new diocese" brought out some 250 adults to the October meeting at the Cathedral in Gaylord. We had expected some fifty persons to show up!

When I was transferred to Grayling the following summer to better serve the people from the center of the diocese, I set up an education office in Saint Mary's former convent. The first person hired was William (Bill) Jacobs: author, lecturer, college professor, husband, father, itinerant preacher and champion talker! He spoke at length on any topic suggested, whether it was in the classroom, on the phone, in person, or in writing, and he spoke with humor: subtle, lilting humor which was followed by a huge, boisterous guffaw.

In discussing our new diocese's educational needs, he insisted that we establish a program to help our volunteer catechists learn about the great happenings of Vatican II and how it should be presented to the children and adults in the classrooms. The program initiated was ambitious: four weeks of classes in each of the seven vicariates in the diocese! The volunteer teachers of these classes were recruited and they responded with enthusiasm that reflects any pioneer spirit. Our catechist certification program had begun.

In addition, we determined that what was most needed to help recruit new catechists on the parish level was to help them know how to formulate a lesson plan, how to share the 'good news' in an attractive, non-boring, memorable manner. We concluded that our Catholic school teachers and catechists were not products of Catholic college education, many not of Catholic high schools nor even Catholic elementary schools. We needed an annual diocesan convention, with national speakers and many, many workshops for the volunteers on every level of Catholic faith and teaching skills. It was well planned for early September, just prior to the celebration of Catechetical Sunday. With nearly 400 potential clients, what would we call this fabulous convention? Bill Jacobs came to the rescue: "How-To-Do-It Day" was born, and lived on for some six or seven additional years. It was the parent of the Diocese of Gaylord's fifth annual conference now held in late September or early October, with many of the same faces present. ■

The faith in Leelanau County
"Land of Delight"

By Father Stanley Bur

For 40 years missionary activity in the Grand Traverse area centered on the western shore of the bay in and near Peshawbestown. From there it sent its flame of love and truth to the numerous Indian clans and settlements of a vast area. Many of these were in what later became known as Leelanau County, the "Land of Delight."

But now a larger center was shaping up in new docks, mills, stores and woodworking factories at the base of the west arm of the bay.

A church had been established there already. Fathers Mrak, Herbstret and Zorn, as well as Young and Jung, had all offered Mass there, but no priest was available to live among the settlers there until the fall of 1877.

We quote from the introduction of the Silver Jubilee booklet of Saint Francis Parish of October 10, 1897:

"Twenty-seven years ago, when all was yet in the primal state, when but a few old settlers, with the roving Indians, watched on the shores of our beautiful Traverse Bay, when the stillness of undisturbed nature reposed on the same spot on which we now stand; a repose broken only by the transient rustling of the leaves or the hoot of an owl, which soon died away in the echoes of the solitary forest, where now stands our thriving little city; then, also a dedication was made that marked the first epoch in the history of Saint Francis Parish.

"Opening the Jubilee sermon with this beautiful description, the speaker graphically depicts in poetic words the condition of Traverse City 27 years before.

"Indeed, it is not to be wondered at that Traverse City, pre-eminently a favored spot of 'resorters', Traverse, so lavishly enriched with all the gifts of nature, was also selected, in the days of yore, as the favored camping ground of the children of the forest who knew and loved nature so well.

"Neither is it to be wondered at that the white men, eager of enterprise, also beheld with envious eye this golden field, so teeming with rich opportunity, this favored spot of shady bowers, where sweet repose held sway and nature reveled in luxuriant beauty.

"But this was not to last. 'Change is inevitable in a progressive country' says Disraeli, and the words found a living echo in the wonderful transformation of a few years in Traverse City and environment.

"The onward march of progress, beheld this inviting field of waving forest of the tall, stately pine, the sturdy oak; she beheld with a prophetic eye the verdant fields of ripened grain, wafting their incense from every hillside of our fertile Traverse region. Progress came, saw and conquered.

"The transformation began in the early fifties, when people of various nationalities and creeds came north in quest of work and riches. Catholics were among the first to come and share the hardships of early pioneer life. As usual, with a sturdy heart and ready hand for weal of for woe, did they link their fortunes with the rest of the small community to develop the opportunities that lay before them.

"The task indeed was great; but they knew the providence of God was still greater, and hence undaunted, they built their little log huts in the wilderness on the site where now stands our beautiful thriving city in which we justly pride and glory.

"The early pioneer life was not an easy one. They knew nothing of the luxury and convenience of our modern homes, and yet, where wants are few, contentment — the abundance of riches — fills the heart. So it was with the early settlers. Their needs were few and simple, their habits frugal and contentment dwelt in their humble homes, a peace that is often hard to find in the gilded homes of modern day luxury and abundance."

We marvel at so expressive a feeling of progress and luxury in 1897 as we contrast it to the early pioneers in their humble surroundings. Today, with men flying into space, walking on the moon and trying to control the pollution of that once beautiful scene of the Grand Traverse Bay region, we wonder at Father Henry P. Maus's description of the simple but stately homes and accomplishments of this youthful city of lumber camps and sawmills.

The zeal of the many missionary priests who walked the soil of Traverse City before 1877 inflamed the spirit of faith there that was to flourish and spread to over 20 missions in the next 25 years. ■

The Charismatic Movement

has introduced a dynamic new energy into the Catholic experience

By Father Gerald F. Micketti

To gather and praise the Lord; that is the vocation of all people, all Christians. In this diocese there are groups of people who gather often and in various parishes who do just that - they gather to praise the Lord through prayer.

The Charismatic Movement propounds no new dogmas. Instead it stresses the experiencing of the truths Catholics already accept. If there is anything novel about the Movement, it is the belief that the charisms, or gifts of the Holy Spirit, should play a larger role in the life of every Christian.

Vatican Council II opened a window for this concept when it emphasized that the manifestations of the Holy Spirit were not restricted to the age of the Apostles, but are a continuing reality.

As the Movement grows, evangelization is becoming more important. The need to bring the Word of God to the world and to those around us is one element of the Charismatic Movement that has much to offer the Catholic Church.

Father Albin Gietzen is the Liaison of the Movement in this diocese. The leadership in the Movement consists of members of the various parishes of the diocese. The diocesan charismatic renewal is associated with the All Michigan Catholic Charismatic Conference. ■

The mystery of the missing nun of Isadore

Adapted from an account by Father Stanley A. Bur

In 1907, Holy Rosary Parish in the village of Isadore, about two miles north of Cedar, had just finished rebuilding its school after it had burned down for the second time in 13 years. Before the school year could even begin, however, the struggling community was faced with yet another heartache.

On August 23 of that year the school's Superior, Sister Mary Janine, disappeared without a trace.

For 11 years the mystery went unsolved, causing much anxiety and fear among the other sisters and the people of the community. It was not until 1918 when plans were being made for a new church that the scandal behind the strange disappearance of Sister Janine began to unfold.

We begin the story in 1905 when Father Andrew Bienawski took up residence at Holy Rosary. Father Bienawski was born in Poland but we are told his parents were Chinese or Mongolian. As an infant he was adopted by a Polish couple and raised in Polish customs. The Russians controlled Poland at this time and religious freedom was unknown. Young Andrew eventually managed to escape the country and make his way to Rome. When his religious studies were completed, the bishop of Grand Rapids, Michigan, sought him out to minister to the people of Polish extraction in the diocese. He was thus appointed pastor of the heavily Polish congregation at Holy Rosary.

Father Bienawski was the last priest of the diocese who still ran the parish according to the fifth commandment of the church in the Old Baltimore Catechism which stated that "you must contribute to the support of your pastor." He considered his salary to be the collection from one Sunday each month. He conducted all the financial affairs of the parish from his pants pocket which made bookkeeping very simple.

He liked to tell the story of the fine team of horses and harness that he was accused of stealing from the parish. No matter that Father had used the team for ten years and they had become old and weary, and the leather harness had all but dropped from the horses' backs from wear. Many a trip and sick call he made with this team and he felt the parish owed him for his services. Besides, the horse he had inherited when he came was so crippled that it had to be shoved up hills when hitched to a buckboard. Still, some parishioners looked dimly on his taking the team with him when he moved on.

A great lover of all kinds of animals, Father Bienawski reportedly kept an alligator as a pet for several years. While this animal was not known to have a taste for humans, it was said to enjoy a choice morsel of duck, goose or chicken when it could be had. The pastor's alligator was not restrained by any boundaries and made frequent visits to the yards of neighbors who raised ducks and geese. One young neighbor boy decided to terminate the raids and set out a poisoned duck for what turned out to be the alligator's final banquet. Father Bienawski missed his pet when it did not return home, but never learned what became of it as the young neighbor and his brothers kept their secret for many years.

Other than the disappearance of Sister Mary Janine, Father Bienawski's tenure at Holy Rosary was a normal one. The school grew in size and the pastor boarded many boys from far away in his rectory during the winter months. He was very strict and the boys either kept in line or were severely punished. There is a feeling that the Polish-speaking Father Bienawski was not loved too dearly by the people in his mission; it seems likely the language barrier added to his stern character.

In August 1913, he was succeeded at Holy Rosary by Father Leo Oprychalski. Father Leo stayed four years before being replaced by Father Edward Podlaszewski whose morals — and those of his housekeeper — were said to be questioned by some people of the community, especially the more nosey ones seeking any excuse to downgrade the church.

By 1918, a movement was emerging to build a new, larger church as more space was needed. The first step of the plan called for demolishing a shed attached to the back of the old church. But before this could happen, something else had to be done.

The missing nun's body had been buried under the shed and it had to be moved without attracting attention. With the aid of a janitor and a lantern, the body was dug up in the dead of night and transplanted into an unmarked grave in the cemetery. But the housekeeper at the time was not happy about the situation and trouble began to brew. After a whispered story here and there and a few dropped hints, the scandal broke wide open.

Father Bienawski was recalled, charged with the sordid crime and had to stand trial. Acting as his own lawyer, he helped his case by exhibiting his brilliant mind. He was also helped by his stern demeanor which gave the impression of a sterling character. He was judged not guilty by the court, although many so called "tavern talkers" in town were not convinced of his innocence.

Father Bienawski's housekeeper was eventually found guilty and sentenced to prison for killing the nun who, it was revealed, was with child. The housekeeper served several years of her term in prison but was freed by an amnesty granted by Michigan Governor Alex Groesbeck in his last official act in office.

The real culprit in the whole case got off scot free...or did he? The medical doctor who lived in the community is said to have made frequent visits to the convent at Holy Rosary as Sister Mary Janine was not well and apparently needed continuous attention. The trouble was, she was getting the wrong kind of attention.

The doctor had a summer home on Big Glen Lake which was dug up during the scandalous trial in a futile search for evidence. Nevertheless, his health later failed, his practice dwindled and eventually he committed suicide.

Despite the stigma, Father Bienawski bore from the experience, the accused pastor went on to live to the age of 90. Many people would have been broken by the character defamation to which he was subjected, but this priest had been steeled for hardship by his boyhood trials in his adopted native country. Father Bienawski died in 1964 in Mackinaw City where he had retired in 1961 and was still saying three Masses each Sunday during the summer season.

The community of Isadore definitely suffered from the scandal. It caused the faith of many people to waver for a time, but that faith eventually returned and, when it did, it was even stronger than before. ■

Teams of Our Lady

offer a support group for Catholic families

By Father Gerald F. Micketti

Teams of Our Lady is an international Catholic couple's movement that was started in 1938 in France by Rev. Henri Caffarel and has since expanded into 52 countries. A Team consists of five to seven Catholic sacramentally married couples and a priest who meet once a month for a shared meal, prayer time, and a prepared discussion. Teams of Our Lady is a lifetime loving support group for individuals as they go through the spiritual "highs" and "lows" of family life.

Bob and Pat Verhelle moved to the Petoskey area in 1978. They had been active in Teams of Our Lady in the Detroit area prior to their move north. After they moved to Petoskey they held information meetings in their home. The first Team was started in 1981. Two more Teams were started in 1984 and 1985. Two more Teams followed. The priests of St. Francis Xavier parish became involved with the Teams and still more growth followed. Teams of Our Lady are flourishing now and providing married couples with opportunities for prayer and support. ■

Marriage Encounter

has been a strengthening influence for many couples

By Father Gerald F. Micketti

How to make a good marriage better. One Father Gabriel Calvo of Spain pondered that question in 1952 and came up with an idea.

He began by developing a series of conferences for married couples. The focus of the series was the development of an open and honest relationship within marriage and learning to live a sacramental relationship in the service of others. Each presentation ended with a question designed to encourage the couple to look at the concepts presented in terms of their own relationship.

For the next ten years the "Marriage Teams of Pope Pius XII," as the presenting teams were called, traveled throughout Spain with these conferences challenging married couples to look at their marriages.

By 1966 the movement had spread to Latin America and Spanish-speaking couples in the United States. The following year a couple and a priest presented the weekend to seven couples and few priests at the Christian Family Movement convention at University of Notre Dame. Within two years a national executive board was formed to coordinate the development of Worldwide Marriage Encounter in the U.S. and Canada.

Marriage Encounter was introduced in the Diocese of Gaylord in the mid-1970's. Sometimes the presenting teams gave two Marriage Encounter weekends a month to make the program available to all the couples who wished to experience this new way of living and loving. That dream continues and many married couples in the Diocese have found their love deepened as a result. ■

Beginning Experience

helps the healing after the loss of a spouse

By Father Gerald F. Micketti

The structure and the success of Marriage Encounter helped create spin-offs, just like successful television shows. One of the movements that modeled itself on Marriage Encounter was Beginning Experience.

When a person loses a spouse, how does that person continue to live, function, work, establish friendships, deal with the emotions of the loss? Beginning Experience is one way of dealing with such a situation. Beginning Experience is a weekend program designed to help widowed, separated and divorced persons make a "new beginning" in life through a powerful, intense and positive experience of hope.

In this diocese Beginning Experience started in early 1980 when Laura Smith, SSJ., Cathy Schmidt and Delores Duddles met to organize Beginning Experience of Northern Michigan. Following a training program, the first weekend session was held in October of the same year at Crystal Mountain in Thompsonville.

Since that time many people of different faith experience and denominations have shared, cried and laughed while talking about their hurts and pains, joys and sorrows of the loss of a spouse. Regardless of the circumstances of the marriage, there is some hurt and pain. Beginning Experience helps people deal with those emotions and begin again. ■

SECTION THREE

Our parishes

The Catholic church in Cheboygan County

From the manuscript "Untold Stories of Cheboygan" by Ellis Olson

Bishop Frederick Baraga and other missionary priests visited the Cheboygan area during the 1800s. One of these was the famous Father A.D.J. Piret, who held services in 1852, saying Mass at the home of Charles Bellant at the southwest corner of Water and Third (State) Streets. Father Piret was a missionary priest for the Indians on Mackinac Island and the surrounding area.

Reverend Piret was born in Isnes Company, Namur, Belgium, in 1804 and immigrated to the United States in 1843. He died at the residence of Reverend Charles L. DeCeuninck, the resident pastor of Saint Mary, on the 22nd of August, 1875. He is buried at the Calvary Cemetery in Cheboygan.

In 1856, the Reverend Patrick Murray, resident priest at Mackinac Island, came to Cheboygan to dedicate the chapel that had recently been erected on Peter McDonald's farm. The chapel was located a short distance from Calvary Cemetery. Other missionaries of the Roman Catholic faith that held services here were: Reverend Angelles VanPanel, an Indian missionary from Little Traverse Village; Reverend Bishop LeFevre, of Detroit who accompanied Father VanPanel on one occasion; Father N.L. Lriffrath, Father Zorn, of Mackinac Island.

Bishop Baraga administered the Sacrament of Confirmation in Saint Mary Mission Church, July 27, 1862.

In November, 1868, Saint Mary received its first resident pastor, Father Charles L. DeCeuninck. Through his efforts, the Saint Mary building project was started in 1869 and completed in 1875 on land which was donated by McArthur, Smith & Co. at the corner of Fifth (State) and "D" Streets. This large building, 55 by 100 feet had a capacity of 850 people. Thompson Smith honored Father DeCeuninck by naming one of his large steam boats after him. Father DeCeuninck was succeeded by Father John VanGennip in November 1876.

Father VanGennip built a white-frame schoolhouse in the summer of 1881 and it was first opened that fall. Father VanGennip was succeeded by Father Peter J. Desmedt in February, 1882.

The old Saint Mary School building burned July 11, 1884, and Father Desmedt erected the present brick building facing State Street. The new addition was erected in 1892. Father Desmedt died March 1, 1892, at Saint Mary.

The church edifice was moved about 1895 from the corner of State Street to the southwest corner of Fourth and "D" Streets. About the same time the Sisters of the Immaculate Heart of Mary were replaced in the school system with the Sisters of Mercy. They continue in this capacity. Under the directorship of Father Aloysius Webeler, the church building was enlarged and completely remodeled.

The new church rectory was built and presented to the parish by the late James Brown in the 1920s.

Father Hugh Michael Beahan, a past assistant pastor at Saint Mary in 1951-53, after leaving Cheboygan, became the narrator of a 15-minute television show in Grand Rapids entitled, "Fifteen With Father."

Monsignor James Maloney was pastor at Saint Mary from April 8, 1953, until his death.

Father John B.E. Magnan became the pastor March 1, 1892, when Father Desmedt died. In September of that year, Father Magnan began organizing a parish for the French speaking people of Cheboygan. An auction was held in 1893 at Saint Mary for the purpose of releasing funds from Saint Mary for the establishment of the new French Parish of Saint Charles.

Father Magnan purchased the Saint Charles site from the estate of W.S. Bartholomew and contracted Joseph Bourrie and William Moody to construct the building to be used as the school, church, and rectory of Saint Charles. The first floor was used as the rectory and grade school and the upper floor was used exclusively as a church. The school was taught by the Principal Professor Lacuyer, a French speaking teacher from Quebec assisted by Mrs. McDonald and Ella Smith. The lay teachers were replaced by the Sisters of Mercy in 1912. A temporary convent was purchased in 1925.

Saint Charles Church was constructed by William Moody in 1915 and was consecrated October 14, 1915, by Bishop Gallagher.

Father Gougeon started the first Saint Charles High School in 1945. Father Gougeon died January 8, 1948 and was succeeded by Father D.F. Albert Imbault who had a new convent constructed in November of 1948 at a cost of $48,000.

The high schools of Saint Mary and Saint Charles were combined in September 1952 and named Cheboygan Catholic Central High School. The Saint Charles School building was enlarged and renovated for this purpose at a cost of $65,000.

The first superintendent of Cheboygan Catholic Central was Father Robert Heyer, the pastor of Saint Francis Parish at Alverno. He had charge of the entire school program in Cheboygan, including the elementary school at Saint Mary.

In 1890, Father Grochowski, who had been assigned to Saint Mary to take care of the needs of the Polish speaking people in the area, petitioned Bishop Richter for the right to establish their own parish with a church, school and resident pastor. The bishop approved and the work of establishing a parish was begun. The Saint Lawrence Church building was completed in 1896 and housed the school the same year. The church was on the first floor and the school was on the second floor. The pastor responsible for the construction was Father Skory, who became the first resident pastor of the church on the corner of Cleveland Avenue and "C" Streets. The first teacher of the new school which had 50 elementary students its first year was Mr. Saremba.

In 1902, Father Stanley Sosnowski built the rectory. He was succeeded by Father Francis Piaskowski in 1913. At that time the lay teachers were replaced by the Felician Sisters. During the Great Depression, the Polish families became less numerous and the school was closed in 1931 because of lack of students. In 1967, the church was discontinued and the parishioners were transferred to Saint Charles and Saint Mary.

The first Catholic Cemetery was adjoining the chapel of 1856 on Peter McDonald's farm. This cemetery was relocated in 1874 on six acres of ground donated by Charles Bellant (three acres), Peter McDonald (two acres), and David Hudson (one acre). The people interred in the old cemetery were removed to the new cemetery (Calvary Cemetery) when it was consecrated November 15, 1874. This cemetery is south of the farm of Peter McDonald. It was blessed and dedicated by Father Piret, who died less than a year later and is interred there today. The bell from the old chapel was brought to this country by Father Patrick Murray and is now at the Bishop Baraga School.

The most outstanding program in the Cheboygan area schools was the shared-time program which involved the Catholic and public school children. The idea of shared-time started about 1949 and became a workable program in Cheboygan in 1952. Cheboygan's population was about 50 percent Catholic at that time. The academic needs of the Catholic children were primarily satisfied by the Cheboygan Catholic School System which supported one elementary-junior high and Catholic Central High School. The elementary-junior high building, formerly Saint Mary, is located on the northeast corner of State and North "E" Streets. The Catholic Central High School building was located on Bailey Street next to Saint Charles Church. Catholic Central was located on the same intersection where the old public high school building was located. The present Cheboygan Junior High occupies the old high school site. A new middle school will replace this building in 1999.

With the two high schools so close in 1952, it was convenient for the Catholic children to attend classes in the public school part of the day and still be enrolled in Catholic Central. This method of supplementing the classes which were not offered in Catholic Central and still pursue their Catholic education proved satisfactory. Some of the classes which were offered to the Catholic students were: shop, mechanical drawing, physics, chemistry, home economics, and several advanced math courses. The participating Catholic students allowed the public school to offer more courses in its curriculum and at the same time eliminate the financial burden for the Catholic Central. There were some minor problems but, for the most part, the shared-time program was conducted in a wholesome atmosphere and a congenial relationship was maintained between both school systems.

The people responsible for starting the shared-time program were Harold Witherell and John Hicks from the public schools and Father Robert Heyer from the Catholic schools. At one time, Cheboygan had the greatest percentage of Catholic students participating in a shared-time program in the United States. It was also the first such program in the country. The shared-time program worked well here because the public school system needed the Catholic vote in support of their operation and the Catholic community needed the expanded curriculum. In a friendly give-and-take manner, the two school systems worked together to provide the best educational opportunities possible for a community the size of Cheboygan.

Ironically, the main speaker at the last Catholic Central Honors Banquet, in 1986, was Ellis N. Olson, a freshman in 1952, the first year Cheboygan Catholic Central operated, and former teacher in the Catholic schools. ■

Christ the King, *Acme*

By Father Gerald F. Micketti

Our history began in the summer of 1984 when Bishop Robert Rose announced that there would be two new parishes in the Traverse City area — one to the west near Silver Lake; the other somewhere in Acme. Father Dale Magoon was assigned to the Acme area. Illness prevented Father Magoon from laying the foundation. The new parish remained in the state of limbo for a year until the arrival of Father Edwin Thome in August of 1985. The first outward sign of a new parish, called simply "Catholic Church," was the little yellow office-chapel on U.S. 31 where the present Acme Mall is now located.

For nearly two years the "little yellow office" was the only identification for a parish-family. Mass was offered there daily. There was a font for baptisms and even a marriage took place there. On Saturdays, Father Thome administered the Sacrament of Reconciliation in his back room office. On the weekends the liturgies were offered in Bertha Vos Elementary School; first in the cafeteria, then in the gymnasium. A certain crew would show up to assemble the church on Saturday afternoon. After the last Mass on Sunday almost everyone had a job to help dismantle the make-shift church. It was during this period that the congregation voted on the present title for our parish.

We remained at Bertha Vos Gym for six months. We celebrated our first Christmas there. In February of 1986 we moved to the then-empty drug store in Tom's Market. Our church took on a more permanent atmosphere, although at times, we suddenly changed from church to class space to social hall. Several baptisms and marriages took place in our much-loved temporary church.

Groundbreaking.

Because we could rent only on a month-to-month basis, our fast growing congregation of nearly 300 families was forced to make a decision; namely, to purchase property for a permanent church or risk the possibility of finding ourselves "in the street." It was a happy day in the Spring of 1987 when we were able to purchase our present eleven acres from Mrs. Kathleen Hall.

In the fall of that same year (October 18, 1987), we processed from Tom's Market to bless our new land and started to break ground although, as yet, we did not have definite plans for a permanent church. A committee of 18 men and women met on a regular basis to plan a new structure.

The evening after ground breaking, we met in the lower level of Embers Restaurant to "kick-off" our "Mini-Drive." A little over $300,000 was pledged from 300 families. The decision had to be made either to build small in keeping with the pledges or to borrow and build large enough for years to come.

We began to build in the Spring of 1988. The reasons for the decision were: 1) the purchase of the land by one family ($100,000) 2) the success of the mini-drive ($300,000) 3) the faith expressed by our Finance Council to borrow $1,100,000

from the diocese at seven percent interest and 4) the devotion of an architect.

The church was completed in December of that year. In the fall of 1989 we started a three-year "Second Mile Drive" which helped to amortize about one-half of our debt.

In the summer of 1991, knowing that the parish would have to put on a final Fund Drive, the finance committee appointed a Building Fund Committee. Assisting Father Thome as a Steering Committee were: Michael Haley, Rosemary Cook, Thomas Czerwinski and Larry Inman.

Many people gave of their time and talent. The members of the Advisory Committee for the Goal Line Drive were: Dr. Donald Piche, Bernice Kusina, Barb Allen and Mike McNulty. Others were: Priscilla Payne and Joe Kostrzewa. The name "Goal Line Drive" was selected to help everyone realize that one more successful Fund Drive would help us to retire our entire debt by 1995. ■

Holy Childhood, *Harbor Springs*

By Kay Hughes

Holy Childhood of Jesus in Harbor Springs long was known for one thing. People drove from near and far to assist in the major ministry, the boarding school for indigent Indian children which the first Franciscans and brothers established, erecting the school buildings one by one. The School Sisters of Notre Dame of Milwaukee, Wisconsin, were asked to join in the endeavor in 1886. Their contract wouldn't set very well today. These heroic women offered to take 24-hour care of the children, including teaching, for merely their room and board — no salary! They did it, too, until the last few were recalled by the motherhouse in 1996. Sometimes there were as many as 200 boarders!

The government was not too helpful, so the poor sisters had to depend on benefactors including the summer residents. Policemen would bring fresh road kill venison so that it could be canned. One gentleman yearly brought a large truck of potatoes. The sisters provided the children's clothing, making it if they had to. The older girls often helped out.

The children learned trades as well as ordinary school subjects. They even set type for several magazines and two full size books as well as several hymnals and prayer books. One room in the school was dedicated to sewing. There was a book bindery, presses, a carpenter shop and a shoe shop.

The boarding school was closed, and a day school was carried on until 1988 when it, too, was closed. Shortly before the closure of the day school, the sisters had started a child development center. Some of the second floor is used for religious education and the Northern Michigan Dyslexia Center rents space on the third. A thrift shop is in the basement. The buildings built by the brothers are still being used.

One of the reasons Holy Childhood Church seems so familiar is that it is in the background of many December calendars. Main Street takes a jog right in front of the church, so that it appears that the church is sitting the middle of Main Street. When the town Christmas tree is put up in the middle of the street, the lit spire appears behind it, reminding all of the "reason for the season."

The church is in the middle of Main Street. When the present church was in the planning stage, the city fathers asked that the church be built in a different location. The pastor and his flock of mostly Indians would have none of it, so they built the new church around the old, continued to attend Mass in the old, and when the time was right, dismantled the old and took the pieces out the front door of the new. ■

Holy Cross, *Beaver Island*

Edited by Father Patrick Cawley from the 100th anniversary booklet written by Father Francis C. Partridge, Genie Vreeland and Helen LaFreniere Pike

Beaver Island, like an emerald, lies in the blue waters of Lake Michigan. It is 32 miles northwest of Charlevoix and 22 miles from the nearest mainland point. It is part of Charlevoix County. It is the largest of the eight-island group known as the Beavers. These islands are: Hog, Garden, High, Trout, Whiskey, Squaw, Gull and Beaver. It is approximately 16 miles long and 8 miles wide. There are more than 41 miles of shoreline and seven inland lakes. There are no majestic mountains — no thundering Niagara — yet there is a quaint and quiet beauty that can be found in a solitary walk down one of the scenic paths that rival anything one has ever known.

Life on the island goes about unhurriedly. Changes are slow to come. Let us turn back the pages of history now and see what they tell us of Catholic history on Beaver Island. Mention of Beaver Island in historical documents is surprisingly early. Yet, when one considers that the Jesuits were at Sault Ste. Marie as early as 1641, it isn't too surprising.

The first unmistakable reference was made by Father Frances Xavier de Charlevoix, S.J. (1682-1761). Father Charlevoix made extensive explorations of the Great Lakes region in the early 1720s, and his accounts were later compiled into his famous work, *The History of New France*. The reference that Father Charlevoix makes to the islands is that he passed them as he proceeded south into Lake Michigan, and the island appeared very green to him. The French explorers and voyageurs referred to Beaver Island as "Ile du Castor."

Holy Cross Church & Sister House.

We now pass over about one hundred years and come to the first really concrete fact we know: in 1832, we have the first recorded Mass said on the island. This was said by Reverend Frederic Baraga who was then pastor of the parish which is today Holy Childhood Parish of Harbor Springs. This parish was founded in 1829. Father Baraga spent a considerable amount of time on the island in the spring of 1832 for the purpose of converting the pagan Indians who were living there. Baraga kept a diary or journal of all his labors throughout his long missionary career in Michigan which lasted from 1831 until his death in 1868.

After a short visit to what is now known as Manistee, Father Baraga returned to the island where the newly-converted Indians determined to erect a chapel on the northwest section of the island known as "Indian Point." Father Baraga remained at L'Arbre Croche until 1833 when he was transferred to the area where the city of Grand Rapids now stands. Here he founded a mission and remained until 1835 when he was transferred to the Upper Peninsula of Michigan, where he spent the rest of his days.

Various men succeeded Baraga at Harbor Springs, and Beaver Island was cared for by the pastors at Harbor Springs, Cross Village and Middle Village until a permanent pastor was located on the island. Among these men the most famous was the Reverend Francis Xavier Pierz who was pastor at Harbor Springs from around 1840 until 1852. In

1852 he went to work in Minnesota where he labored until 1873 when he returned to his homeland in what is Yugoslavia today. When we think of these pioneer priests who served the island, we see how blessed the parish was to have true saints of God connected with its history. Father Baraga can be considered in no other light but that of a saint, and one, who beyond doubt will be listed in the calendar of saints one day. And here we have Pierz who may also be listed in the future.

It may be well now to look in on the diocesan development of Michigan. At the time of Father Baraga's first visit to the island in 1832, all of Michigan was in the Diocese of Cincinnati. But the following year, 1833, the Diocese of Detroit was established, and this included all of Michigan. In 1853, the Upper Peninsula of Michigan was made a Vicariate Apostolic with Father Baraga appointed as Vicar Apostolic. In 1857 his Vicariate was created a full-fledged diocese, and Father Baraga became its first bishop. This diocese included only the Upper Peninsula with its adjacent islands.

It did not include Beaver Island. But because of the poor means of transportation and communication, or we might even say lack of it, the Bishop of Detroit asked Bishop Baraga to take over the administration of the northern portion of the Detroit Diocese. This included the Indian missions which stretched from about where Traverse City stands today to where Cheboygan now stands. It also included the missions of Beaver Island and Garden Island. The bishop agreed and so became administrator of our area of the state until his death in 1868. Upon his death, the administration ceased with the exception of Beaver and Garden Islands which still were under Marquette until 1871. In that year Bishop Baraga's successor, Bishop Mrak, dropped the islands from his jurisdiction and returned them to their rightful bishop, the Bishop of Detroit. This was the status quo until 1882 when the Diocese of Grand Rapids was set up and the Beaver Islands were included in its territory. On July 20, 1971, Beaver Island became part of the newly-formed Diocese of Gaylord with Edmund Szoka as its first bishop.

Many stories have been told of the trek of the early Irish settlers to Beaver Island. Some say those hearty souls selected the place because it was an island and reminded them of their homeland; others because the climate with its fogs, mists and rains was reminiscent of the land on the Irish Sea. But according to a story told by Captain Owen J. McCauley, eighty-year-old retired lighthouse-keeper, now deceased, whose parents were in that first band, it was nothing but an Irishman's temper which brought them here.

Fran Martin, writing in the *Charlevoix Courier*, tells the story of Captain McCauley. The first settlement of white men on Beaver Island dates back to the early 1800s. They worked as lumbermen and fishermen until the advent of the Mormons in the late 1840s, when most of them were driven from the island. Among a few who remained was James Cable, for whom Cable's Bay is named, who stayed to tend his lumbering interests. The United States Government also had building projects on the island in the form of two lighthouses, the Beaver-head light on the south end of the island, started in 1851, and the lighthouse on the northeast part of the island, known as the Harbor Light, started in 1856.

The story is that in 1856, the year of the assassination of the Mormon leader, King James Strang, a group of Irish men and women from the western part of Ireland decided to come to America. After fifty days sailing on a vessel bound for Quebec, the twenty families and a few single persons landed in Canada on the first lap of their journey to the land of freedom and opportunity. They took a second boat down the Saint Lawrence River and landed in Toronto where all sought employment.

One of the party named O'Donnell got a job as a foreman on a building project but his temper got the best of him, and he had "difficulties" with the workmen. Fearing bodily harm after his outburst, he left Toronto and proceeded to Buffalo, New York, where he boarded a vessel for Chicago. At Detroit, several government employees included carpenters and bricklayers boarded the boat en route to Beaver Island where they were to complete the construction of a light station which had temporarily been put into commission a few years earlier.

O'Donnell took a job with the crew and wrote his wife who was still in Toronto to join him there and to inform the others that they should come to the beautiful island to make their home. He also told them of the many vacant houses left by the Mormons where they could live.

The party made hasty preparations to join O'Donnell and in a few weeks had arrived at the island. They were a bit disappointed in the new land for it did not prove as fruitful as it had been pictured to them, but since they were there they had to make the best of the situation and see about procuring jobs. Some were engaged on the lighthouse projects, but others took jobs in the woods for Mr. Cable. Here again they ran into difficulties for none knew the art of cutting wood, for in their homeland there were few trees. These were not used for lumber and fuel.

The first winter brought many hardships for the men were paid only fifty cents a cord for cutting wood, and unskilled choppers could earn but little. Eventually they mastered the wood chopping; others turned to fishing, and still others to farming. They applied for citizenship papers so they could acquire land under the Homestead Act.

Within the next 15 years Beaver Island became populated by Irish immigrants, and the names of Gallagher, Donlevy, O'Donnell, Boyle, McDonough, McCann, McCafferty,

McCauley, Kiltey, O'Brien, Gillespie, Greene, Martin, Mooney, Burke and Bonner became as much a part of the island as they were in County Mayo and County Donegal from whence they came.

It was Bishop Baraga who finally established the permanent parish on the island and assigned the first resident pastor. In 1860, the Reverend Patrick Murray received this assignment. With much zeal and great labor he had built the first portion of the present church. The following is an excerpt from an agreement between Bishop Baraga and Alexander Guilbeault, dated July 23, 1860 (now in the Burton Historical collection), authorizing this building:

"Alexander Guilbeault agrees to build a frame church at Beaver Harbor on Beaver Island, Lake Michigan. The church shall be fifty-feet long, thirty-two-wide and fifteen-feet high inside, with one double door eight-feet high, and two windows in front, and three windows on each side. He agrees to make the door, but not the windows, except the frame of the same."

There are a number of letters extant from Bishop Baraga to Father Murray praising him for his industry and zeal among Beaver Islanders. He accomplished much good in combating the vice of intemperance among the people. He seems to have dealt strongly with them, for on the very first page of his record book he has this notion, "Those names marked by a capital "O" have not paid their dues, and those that have a double "O" are a disgrace to the church; besides many more in consequence of their bad acts I did not enter their names or take over any money from them, until a change and restitution is made, and who yet remain obstinate." Father Murray also erected a small church in honor of Saint Ignatius on the southeast end of the island, two miles north of Cables Bay on land which was the former Malloy farm. This mission lasted perhaps two years or so.

In 1864, the first nun is said to have come to the island. Father Murray makes note of this surprising fact in a curious entry which we find in his death-register:

"Sister Dympheny ... came to Beaver Island from Buffalo at the request of Bishop Timon to keep house for the priest on Beaver Island, lived here one year and eight months, at Christmas took a cold and died on Monday at two of the clock, January 16, 1865. She was from her youth an example of piety and a copy of virtue. May her soul rest in peace. She is buried at the foot of the high cross as befits a religious. She died in the forty eight years of her age."

Father Murray accepted the new pastorate and in the spring of 1866 left Beaver Island for Alpena. Bishop Baraga then appointed Father Peter Gallagher as pastor of the island, and there he remained until his death on November 18, 1898. A long pastorate indeed, of 32 years.

Father Peter Gallagher was from Ireland, but was adopted into the Marquette Diocese by Bishop Baraga and trained by one of Baraga's trusted priests. The need for priests in those days was so acute that Baraga was forced into cutting all formal training to the barest minimum. Gallagher was sent to one of the better trained priests of the diocese where he received his training in philosophy and theology, and in only a matter of about two years, was ordained and stationed on the island.

Father Rezek in his *History of the Sault Ste. Marie and Marquette* records this somewhat humorous story about Father Gallagher and the second bishop of Marquette. When Ignatius Mrak became Bishop of Marquette in 1868, he was well aware that his predecessors had ordained a few men who had very little formal training. Bishop Mrak was afraid that some of these men might not be fit for the work that they were doing, so he set about on a visitation of the diocese, and where he found such a man, he gave him a test to determine his ability. Should such a priest fail the test, he was retired. News of this reached Father Gallagher and being one of those ill-trained priests, he was a little worried about the outcome of his examination. He finally prepared the people for his possible removal.

All went well until the day that Bishop Mrak arrived on the island for the purpose of testing Father Gallagher. The people welcomed him with open arms, but waylaid the boat captain and threatened him. They told him that if he did not leave the island at once and take the bishop with him, they would burn his boat. The poor captain was completely at a loss as to what to do. He ran after the bishop and explained the situation to him. Bishop Mrak was so disgusted by the whole affair that he promptly left the island. Upon arriving back at Marquette, the first thing he did was to write off the island from his administration and lay it into the lap of its rightful ordinary, the Bishop of Detroit.

The ability of Father Gallagher was never determined, but a few old timers left say that Father Gallagher never was known to say a High Mass while he was on the island because he had never been trained to say more than a Low Mass. If this is true, Father Gallagher might have been retired from the island in 1871, had it not been for the action of the islanders.

After the death of Father Gallagher, care of the island parish fell to the lot of the Franciscan Fathers of the Sacred Heart Province. These Fathers were in charge of the Indian Mission, Holy Childhood of Jesus at Harbor Springs.

Henry J. Richter, the first Bishop of Grand Rapids, appointed Father Alexander Francis Zugelder pastor of Holy Cross Church on July 4, 1899. After serving at Saint Ann Church in Cadillac and Saint Mary, Lake Leelanau, he came to Beaver Island, where

he remained for six years.

Among the first things he did was to petition Bishop Richter for the Dominican Sisters of Marywood in Grand Rapids to come to the island and teach in the schools. In 1899, Sister Clementine was the first superior. The sisters taught in two of the grade schools, McKinley and Sunnyside. The Little Red School House continued to be taught by lay teachers until 1941, when it was closed. High School was added in 1908. The first convent was the present home of W.J. Gallagher which is next door to the parish hall.

In 1901, the original convent was completed, and the sisters moved in. It was necessary for them to be driven by horse and buggy to school each day. In 1924, the sisters acquired their first automobile.

Father Zugelder was also instrumental in getting the telephone cable to the island. It was also during his time the pastor became a weather man. The tall tower was built in the front yard, and from it by means of ropes and pulleys the priest raised storm warning flags by day and lanterns at night to warn the ships at sea. His official title was "Storm Warning Display Man." This work continued until 1937, when the tower was abandoned.

The care of the parish again reverted to the Franciscans at Harbor Springs.

A newspaper clipping found in an old book describes Father Jewell's days on the island. And what he says of himself pretty well describes the work of the other pastors; though, perhaps they were not all quite so energetic. It is captioned: "ISLAND PRIEST IS RECORD JOB HOLD OF U.S." It reads: Father Edward Jewell believes he holds more jobs than any other man in America. Here are some of his positions: Priest - Physician - Surgeon - Dentist - Librarian - Captain of the Saint James Ball team - 3rd baseman and pinch hitter - U.S. weather observer - official "bouncer" at dances - official marine signal display man - Notary Public - Agricultural expert - historian - teacher of music and dancing - emergency farm hand. The article concludes with these words of Father Jewell: "I have asked the bishop to permit me to stay among these wonderful people until I die." The last hope of Father Jewell was not realized as he was changed from the island the following year.

One cannot think of the island's history without a mention of the kindly old Russian, Feodora Protar, who was affectionately known as "the Doctor." He came to the island in 1902 and never left. In his later years he resembled an old patriarch from biblical times, with flowing white beard. He utilized his knowledge of chemistry to a wide extent — though he never claimed to be a doctor. He traveled everywhere to aid the sick. His abandoned home today is a shrine, zealously guarded by the islanders, who boast that his possessions are still intact after 60 years.

The people erected a rock tomb in his behalf with the following inscription beneath a chiseled likeness of their benefactor: "To our heaven sent friend in need, Feodora Protar, who never failed us — in imperishable gratitude and admiration — his people of Beaver Island."

The parish celebrated the centenary of Bishop Baraga's first visit to the island in 1932. The celebration began, under the direction of Father F. L. McLaughlin, with Pontifical Mass offered by the Most Reverend Joseph Pinten, of Grand Rapids.

The Order of Friars Minor Conventual took charge of the parish in 1942. Father Fabian Keenan, O.F.M.C., was appointed pastor. He was succeeded in the summer of 1948 by Father Giles Berthiaume, O.F.M.C. Father Giles had completed three years as pastor when he died suddenly, on September 25, 1951, as the result of a heart attack while on vacation in the Porcupine Mountains in the Upper Peninsula. He was buried in the Order's cemetery at Mount Saint Francis, Indiana.

For a number of years, talk of moving the church to town had occupied the minds of the people. It was during the pastorate of Father Joseph Herp, O.F.M.C. that action was taken in this regard. Property extending from the Medical Center to the corner across from the parish hall had been donated to the church by the Gallagher Estate through the generous instrumentality of Father Bernard Schied, of Chicago, and formerly of Beaver Island.

In November 1957, work on moving the church began. A moving concern from the mainland was engaged for the work and the owner of the *Mackinaw Islander*, a freight boat plying these northern waters carried the heavy equipment over to the island free of charge over operating expenses.

The church was cut in two just beyond the second window from the front and each section was moved separately. It was noticed that the foundation beams under the 97-year-old section were pretty far gone and as that part was raised up on a dolly the old church really looked her age. But with fervent prayers and much luck it made the trip to town. During the period of moving, services were held in the parish hall. The Catholic Church Extension Society granted $5,000 toward the project of moving the church. The church in its new site presents a pleasant sight as one comes into the harbor aboard the *Beaver Islander*. The new convent and rectory were built alongside the relocated church and across from Holy Cross Parish Hall, making a church complex of which the parishioners are proud.

Tourism is now Beaver Island's main industry. Construction is of major importance, too, because of the hundreds of cottages and homes that have been built, especially in the last 25 years. The island is still amazingly beautiful and unspoiled, with miles of

sand beaches and seven inland lakes. It is a haven for deer, partridge, rabbits and other small game. The surrounding shoals and islands, with their small-mouth bass, perch and pike encourage visits from avid anglers. Summer finds the marina filled with pleasure craft and boating enthusiasts.

So...Holy Cross Church is now celebrating 125 years of loving and living. What joys and sorrows of the island people it has witnessed: its walls echoed to infant cries as proud parents brought their babies to be baptized; the overwhelming joy when they saw their little ones march solemnly to the altar to receive their first Holy Communion; the tears of joy and gladness that were shed as parents gave their sons and daughters away in marriage; and the tears of grief and heartbreak as a loved one was taken to the church for the Requiem Mass. Yes, we may well exclaim the words of Jacob as he awoke from his dream and cried out: "How awe-inspiring is this place! This in no other but the house of God and the gate of heaven." (Genesis 28:17)

Over the years the wants and needs of Holy Cross Church have been generously aided by donations from the Beaver Island Clubs of Chicago, Grand Rapids and Ludington. These clubs have underwritten individual projects and have encouraged others to join in their efforts. Special gifts of great beauty and spiritual enhancement have been made by families and friends in memory of loved ones. ■

Holy Cross, *Cross Village*

By Kay Hughes

Cross Village Second Church built in 1841 by Father Francis Pierz, named Saint Anthony, dismantled in 1898.

Holy Cross Parish celebrated its 300th anniversary in 1996, although Sebastian Rasle spent the entire winter of 1691 here and reported that there was a Jesuit in Cross Village. Father Du Jaunay pastored the church from 1741 until 1765. He also pastored Saint Anne de Michilimackinac. For some time he was helped by Father Le Franc. During their stay a church was built on the bluff next to the cross. This cross has long been kept on the bluff, replaced many times, a real navigational aid as well as a spiritual aid. In 1840, Father Ignatius Mrak was sent to assist Father Pierz and they built a frame-church attached to the old church. In 1855, a very colorful figure came to Cross Village, Father John Bernard Weikamp.

Cross Village has traditionally been peopled by Indians and Polish immigrants. Until the last few years, one of the popular summertime experiences was the annual pow-wow. Colorful dancing, bingo, good food, including golombki, and games, all contributed to a fun day for those who came from near and far. The pow-wow is no longer, but an annual homecoming has replaced it with many of the amenities of the original.

There is more than one mystery about the parish. One is the legend surrounding

a statue of an angel, it bears no resemblance to the usual statues of particular angels. Some theorize that it is the angel Moroni, the one who delivered the tablets to the Mormon founder and that when the Mormons were forced off Beaver Island, someone hid it under the church at Cross Village.

In 1918, during a killing wind, a fire started in downtown Cross Village. It raged the length of main street, destroying five large businesses, the post office, the Presbyterian church, and twenty five homes, before driving its way toward Holy Cross Church. Everyone was encouraged to pray and to pray hard! Their prayers were heard. The wind died and the fire stopped just short of the church!

Another tradition at Holy Cross has been the ancient celebration of Corpus Christi — with outside booths. Holy Cross carried on this beautiful tradition long after many parishes stopped.

For 300 years the Light of Christ has shown from the cross on the bluff in Cross Village. ■

Holy Family, *Nessen City*
Saint Raphael, *Copemish*

By Father Gerald F. Micketti

Holy Family Parish started as a mission attached to Saint Francis Parish in Traverse City. At the time of the parish founding, the little community of Colfax was located about 35 miles southwest of Traverse City on the Michigan and Northeast Railroad. Father Zorn visited the area in the 1870s to minister to the spiritual needs of the Catholic families in the area. He offered Mass in the houses of John Hickey and Patrick Dwyer. In 1883, the family of Ludwig Doneth settled in the area. The Doneths along with J.H. Obermeyer, John Hyde, Dave Smith, Dave Hickey and John Rebman formed the first parish. When more room was required to accommodate the increasing numbers in the mission, someone in the vicinity of Colfax built a barn in which an altar was erected on the threshing floor. The priest came all the way from Traverse City for the Mass. Thus the parish was started. Mass was offered periodically, presumably whenever the priest could get to Colfax. The first day there were several baptisms including Ellen Dwyer Monold, Margaret Coughlin Finan, Lyda Coyne and Anne Coyne Bolton. Some of the early members of the parish included the families with names of Carl, Doyle, Egan, Rebman, Smith, Hickey, Hannabal, Daugherty and Coyne. Later Colfax became known as Nessen City.

Father George Ziegler, pastor of Saint Francis Parish, served the mission from 1877 to 1885. He was followed by Father Theophile Nyssen, serving from 1885 to 1889. At stated times they traveled to Nessen City to offer the Mass. Sometime later the administration of the mission was transferred to Guardian Angels Parish in Manistee.

In the year 1890, a neat little church was built. The structure was about 32 by 60 with a tower added later. The property of one acre was donated by David Smith. The enthusiasm of the parishioners led them to build the church under the supervision of the first church committee — J.H. Obermeyer, John Hyde, David Smith and David Hickey. Donations were also received from members of the parish. Holy Mass was offered for the first time in the new church by Father Grimme in January 1890. Sometime later Father Grimme died and Holy Family Parish was served by Father Joseph Steffes

then-pastor of Guardian Angels Parish in Manistee. When Father Prud'homme arrived in Traverse City in 1895, he assumed the care of Holy Family Parish. Father Prud'homme was assigned as an assistant to Father Bauer of Saint Francis Church in Traverse City. His activity was to care for the mission churches attached to Saint Francis Church. He was transferred to Saint Ann in Cadillac in August of 1895. Father H.P. Maus was his successor. January 14, 1895, is the date registered for the first regular Sunday Mass at Nessen City. Father H.P. Maus offered Mass on the first Sunday of every month.

During this period, Holy Family Parish consisted of 60 families who came from the little towns of Copemish, Thompsonville, and Marilla. Some names of the families included Barry, Naud, Flynn, Crimmin, Finan, Coughlin, Gleason, Prevost, McGrant, Currie and Hyde. A number of parish organizations were formed such as the Altar Society, the Men's Building Society and the Father Marquette Literary Club. To house the activities of these various groups, the need for a hall was determined. Mr. J.H. Obermeyer offered a generous proposal. If the members would assist in erecting the building, he would furnish the lumber. There was no lack of positive response. In a short time a large spacious hall of two stories, 24 ft. by 60 ft., stood near the church. It became the center for a number of community affairs such as Thanksgiving dinner, New Year's festivities and Saint Patrick Day celebration.

The parish choir was under the direction of Mr. Obermeyer with Miss Bina Hickey as the organist. Mr. Henry Wilkins, who was not a member of the Catholic Church, did most of the repair work on the buildings when called upon to do so.

Father James Golden was the first resident priest; he was transferred after seven years serving the community. He was succeeded by Father F.X. Downs who also served seven years. Then Nessen City became a mission of Saint Ann of Frankfort where Father Arthur Flajole was the pastor. He served both parishes until 1916, when Father Timothy O'Connell arrived. When he departed is not certain. About this time the lumber mills were gone; the number of families in the parish diminished. Eventually the mission residence was closed and Mass was offered by Father McGinn of Elk Rapids.

On May 31, 1930, the church and residence were destroyed by fire. The cause of the fire was attributed to a lit cigarette thrown in the grass after a funeral service. After the fire, members of the parish went to Saint Joseph Church in Onekama.

In July of 1930, members of parish traveled to Saint Ann, Frankfort, to discuss with Bishop Pinten the construction of a new church building in Nessen City. He assured them they would get a new church.

Bishop Pinten also sent Father Joseph Bocek from Bannister to Nessen City to do missionary work in the area; this was in July of 1931. He was also in charge of Saint Joseph Church in Karlin. For three months Father Bocek labored diligently, gathering people who formerly had worshiped at Holy Family Church. He offered Masses at the home of David Connelly in Copemish because that was the central locality for the Catholic families to gather for the Mass. There was no attempt to rebuild the church in Nessen City after the fire. He instructed the children in their religious duties and on September 27 of that year celebrated First Communion with 60 children. On November 1, Father Bocek was transferred to Immaculate Conception Church in Traverse City. He still had the care the missions of Karlin and Copemish. He would offer Mass at the missions once a month, usually on a Saturday.

The building used in Copemish for the gathering of the church was too small to accommodate the crowd that wanted to attend. On October 3, 1931, Bishop Pinten came to Copemish to celebrate Confirmation. At that time, a decision was made to buy the house and lot then being used. The house was to be demolished and the land used for the location of the new church building. The demolishing of the house and the construction of new church did not start until the spring of the following year. Father Bocek, meanwhile, had been transferred and he was succeeded by Father James Bryant.

The new church building in Copemish was modeled after an old Franciscan mission church. The church seated about 250 people. The altar and statues, saved from Holy Family Church in Nessen City, were refinished and installed in the new church of Saint Raphael. The estimated cost of the church was $5,000. Expenses were met by a contribution from Bishop Pinten, the insurance money from the loss of Holy Family Church in Nessen City, and the parishioners who sponsored parties, dinners and other activities to earn money for the new building.

While Father Bryant was pastor of Immaculate Conception Church, he came to Saint Raphael Church on weekdays. Then the parish became a mission of Saint Joseph Church at Onekama with Father Leo Zielinski as pastor. Father Bernard Sikorski succeeded Father Zielinski. While Father Sikorski was pastor, the Altar Society purchased for $900 the Millarch store building to be remodeled as the parish hall. The priests who followed Father Sikorski included Fathers Edward Kubiak, Joseph Dunphy, William Reitz and Thomas Schiller.

During the tenure of Father Schiller, due to the influx of tourists and summer visitors, the need for a larger facility became apparent. A ten-acre parcel of land at the corner of highway M-115 and County Road 604 was purchased. With the help of parishioners such as John Napora, John Romsek, Joseph Pawlak, Henry Chandler and George Milliron, the new and present church structure was built. The first Mass offered in the new building was on November 13, 1966. The hall and kitchen were included in the new building plans. The old church and hall were sold.

Father Schiller remained as the pastor until April 18, 1971. He was succeeded by Father Casimir "Casey" Zawacki. Father Zawacki was the pastor of Saint Joseph Parish, Onekama and Saint Raphael, Copemish. He served Saint Raphael Church until his transfer in October of 1982. He was succeeded by Father James Gardiner, who served there for four years. His successor was Father Richard Sitar who served for three years. He was followed in 1989 by Father John Ladd. August 9, 1995, Father Michael Conner became the pastor of Saint Joseph Church in Onekama and Father Richard Kosterman was appointed resident pastor of Saint Raphael and presently serves the community of Saint Raphael Church. ■

Holy Family, *Tawas City*

By Father Gerald F. Micketti

The newspaper article reported that "Tuesday [July 1, 1997] will mark the beginning of Holy Family Catholic Church in the Tawases." Bishop Cooney came to the parish and celebrated with the community their new parish and new identity and installed as pastor Father Ron Gronowski. This new parish is the result of a merger of two parishes — Saint Joseph in East Tawas and Immaculate Heart of Mary in Tawas City — both of which had their own lives.

Saint Joseph Parish started in 1869 as a mission cared for by the pastor of the Sacred Heart Parish in AuSable, now Oscoda. The pastor came once a month to celebrate the Mass. Five years later the first church was built and named Saint Joseph. The first resident pastor, Father William Nevin, was appointed in 1883. He was followed by Fathers J. Brooks, William Kinney, Anthony Bogacki, Edward Kinney. Under Father Edward Kinney the first school was built but it remained empty for several years due to a lack of funds. More pastors followed and so did the sisters. The present church was dedicated in 1954 and the present school was opened in 1957 with an enrollment of 180 students.

Immaculate Heart of Mary Parish is a newcomer to the Tawas area, commencing in the year 1952. Due to the growing population and the influx of tourists, the people of Tawas City voted to form a second parish. Bishop Woznicki of Saginaw agreed and the IHM was established. The first pastor was Father Bernard Kirchman. Since there was no church building, the community leased the Bay Theatre in Tawas City and renovated the interior for a worship space. The first Mass was said September 7, 1952, and 135 families were registered as members of the parish. Eventually a pledge drive was instituted to construct a church and the new church was dedicated August 18, 1957. ■

Holy Rosary, *Cedar*

By Father Edward Boucher

The history of Holy Rosary Parish began with the arrival of immigrants from Poland around 1880. The first families to arrive were members of Stephen Miemczynski, Adam Popa, George Cichocki, Anthony Dziendzielski, Adam Cerkowski, Felix Kelenski, Frank and Thomas Fleis and Jacob Rosinski.

As there was no church in the community named Isadore, Mass was offered in homes of the families. After much consideration, a committee decided to erect a church on land donated by John Szudrowicz, the site of Holy Rosary Community to this day.

From 1883 to 1892, Holy Rosary was serviced by priests from Manistee and the surrounding area. Father Nowakowski worked zealously from 1892-1900. Since there was no rectory, he resided in the house of Michael Gatzke.

Father Nowakowski was succeeded by Father Bienawski 1900-1913. Father Oprychalski and Podloszewski served in the year 1913-1917. Father Stephen Narlock ministered from 1919-1926. Father Narlock was instrumental in the construction of the present church. He was followed by Father Piaskowski 1926-1938.

From 1938 to 1953, Father John Klonowski pastored the families of Holy Rosary. He was truly a dedicated and priestly pastor. He enhanced the parish and school before being transferred to Saint John Vianney Parish in Grand Rapids.

Since 1953, Holy Rosary has been pastored by many priests, namely: Father John F. Grzybowski, 1953-1955; Father Herman L. Kolenda, 1955-1958; Father Aloysius U. Ulanowicz, 1958-1971; Father Benjamin Marciulionis, 1971-1972; Father Arthur Mulka, 1972-1978; Father Ronald Gronowski, 1978-1979; Father Anthony Machcinski 1979-1981; Father James L. Holtz, 1981-1986; Father Albin J. Gietzen, 1986-1994. It was during the pastorate of Father Gietzen that Holy Rosary Parish was united with Saint Rita's Parish of Maple City and Saint Joseph's Parish Bohemian Center. In 1994, Father Charles Zeeb was pastor, followed in 1995 by Father Martin Schaub, who, in turn, was followed by Father Edward F. Boucher, the present administrator.

Holy Rosary School

Holy Rosary Parish, almost from its beginning, has dedicated itself to spiritual and intellectual formation of its family. From 1892, Father Stephen Kawokowski served Holy Rosary Parish, living in Traverse City. By 1898, the area was flourishing with growth in population, due to the completion of the North Eastern & Manistee Railroad. In that same year, the Felician sisters operated a school with 73 students present.

Prior to 1898, there is a scanty history of a school back to 1892. In 1894, the school building burned down. Records show that in March of 1895, there was a financial board formed to collect money for a new school. This collection process continued for the completion of Holy Rosary School in 1898.

In August of 1898, the Felician Sisters arrived there with a combined salary of $50 a month. The first sisters were Sister M. Wenceslaus, Sister M. Paula, Sister M. Jadwiga. Sister M. Bibiana was in charge of domestic work. Both Polish and English were taught.

In 1904, the school-convent burned down. The sisters escaped with Sister Regina receiving serious burns. In 1906, the new school was ready for classes with an enrollment of 175-200. The school continued with a steady enrollment up to 1933.

In September of 1933, a unique situation rose in the Centerville Township public school enrollment. The public school had only eight students, so the public school board had its students enroll at Holy Rosary. The arrangement lasted until 1938.

In 1938, Father John Klonowski became the seventh pastor. This same year, an unusual experiment was begun at Holy Rosary School and proved successful for almost a decade. In August 1928, Holy Rosary School became Holy Rosary Consolidated

Public Schools and opened the ninth grade, thus beginning a high school.

This consolidation was caused by a lack of school buildings in Centerville Township. All went well until 1947 when non-Catholic parents demanded the removal of religious icons and wanted to forbid the buildings to be used for religious instruction. Unable to acquiesce to these demands, Holy Rosary reverted to its own Holy Rosary School.

From 1938 to the present, the school has a rich history of instilling Christian values within the community. The high school discontinued in 1961, due to low enrollment.

The educational programs have been most instrumental in promoting vocations to the religious life and also establishing Christian values in the families of the parish. In its history, Holy Rosary has fostered over 46 vocations, seven to the priesthood and 39 to sisterhood (33 Felicians, three Dominicans, one Mercy, and two Franciscans).

Stained Glass Windows

On December 21, 1923, Bishop Kelly of the Diocese of Grand Rapids blessed the present structure of Holy Rosary Church. It was over two years in the making. The church cost about $40,000. The building was erected on a hill in the countryside, standing uniquely for the world to observe.

The church is blessed with special stained glass windows depicting the life of Jesus. They were manufactured in Munich, Germany, by the F.X. Zettler Co.

The 13 windows are set on lead and are 3/16 of an inch thick. Ten windows are 7,000 square inches, two are 4,860 square inches and another 3,888 square inches. The glass was hand painted and was fired in a kiln.

Each window depicts a scene from Christ's life, with rare details, including the nativity scene with a backdrop of the City of Jerusalem. The company went to the "Nth degree" in manufacturing the windows. It is awe-inspiring, with perfect blends of rose, lavenders, and blue colors.

The windows were ordered in 1921 for $1,500 each. The window makers did not have the $1,500 windows so they sent windows valued at $2,500 at no extra cost. They were actually made during World War I, but the Zettler Company protected them until they could be delivered to Holy Rosary.

To our knowledge, only two other buildings in Michigan have Zettler windows. They are Saint Andrew Cathedral in Grand Rapids and Saint Francis Hospital in Escanaba. Today the windows are valued at about $150,000 each, but realistically, they are irreplaceable.

The parishioners know they possess a special and priceless possession. Over the years, special protection has been added to preserve the windows and their quality. In fact, in the spring of 1997, the parish council contacted a firm to update the protection factor of the windows. ■

Immaculate Conception, *Traverse City*

By Dorothy Walt

By 1902, the only parish in Traverse City, Saint Francis Parish, had already served the Catholic Community for 15 years. The Catholics on the west side of the city were finding the long walk to Saint Francis quite difficult, especially the little school children and the elderly who wished to attend daily Mass. Besides, Saint Francis Church was becoming quite inadequate because of the increased Catholic population.

And so, on April 30, 1902, Bishop Richter looked favorably on the westsider's request to form a separate congregation with their own church. "To promote the religious interests of the Catholics in the Western part of Traverse City, and, at the same time, to relieve crowded conditions at Saint Francis Church," stated Bishop Richter in his informal decree giving permission that a new Catholic parish be organized on the West Side.

Reverend Thaddeus Krakowski was appointed pastor. He lived with Father Joseph Bauer, pastor of Saint Francis Parish. Father Krakowski had no more than completed the census of 100 families who were to form the new Immaculate Conception Parish when Reverend Cornelius Emperor was appointed by the Bishop to take his place.

Father Emperor immediately assumed the responsibility of laying the foundation of the new school-church building. It was a formidable task, but made much easier by the generosity and support of his parishioners. Many farmers, including some grandfathers of present day parishioners, came with their teams and scoops to excavate for the foundation of the new building to be erected at the corner of North Division and Second Streets. What a scene that must have been with all those teams and scoops getting deeper and deeper in the hole! It was not beyond Father Emperor to work as a common laborer on the foundation, in addition to his priestly duties. He became overworked, took ill and died on January 5, 1905.

Immaculate Conception Church decorated for Christmas in 1939.

On February 15, 1905, Bishop Richter issued a formal decree giving the new parish canonical existence and marking its boundaries. Father John Sheehan was appointed as its new pastor and he worked hard to complete the new church-school building which was blessed and dedicated by Bishop Richter on February 22, 1906. The school was opened in September 1906, with the Sisters of Mercy in charge and an enrollment of 80 students.

Father Sheehan was transferred in 1914 and Father John Yeager became pastor of Immaculate Conception. He endeared himself to his flock during the 17 years of tenure, but was also known at times to tell his parishioners: "If the shoe fits, put it on" when it came to explaining what was allowed or not allowed in church doctrine. For students unable to attend the Catholic School, he would travel to a parishioner's home for group catechism instruction, something he felt very important. In his own Catholic School Father Yeager would often give the students a half day off on an especially hot day, much to the consternation of Sister Boniface, the principal. She felt there were too few days to fill those little skulls. Some of her former students remember her well!

The church was on the second floor of the building with the four rooms on the ground floor housing the school. Some present-day parishioners especially remember the seating arrangement for school students at Sunday Mass. The front pew on the far right of the church was always reserved for the sisters. The grade school students were required to sit in the pews reserved for them. These pews were graduated in size to comfortably fit students in grades 1-8, but they were directly in front of the sisters' pew at right angles, so woe to any child that misbehaved!

I recall the story of my parents' wedding on June 7, 1916, at Immaculate Conception Church. Everyone traveled by horse and buggy in those days, so, naturally the church building was surrounded by hitching posts to which the horses were tied during Mass. Henry Ford had begun his assembly line of Ford cars just three years earlier and a close neighbor of the bride-to-be had very recently purchased a new Ford, the first automobile in the surrounding region. So, the young couple successfully persuaded the owner (for a fee) to drive them to the church on their wedding day, while their guests all came by horse and buggy! It certainly helped to make their wedding day very special. (As a side note, care had to be taken so the car did not get too close to a horse as the horse became spooked by the sound of the car.)

The people of the parish for the most part were poor and often times their jobs were very demanding. Sister Generose Kubesh, R.S.M., tells about her parents' wedding day in 1924 at Immaculate Conception. George and Mary were married very early in the morning. George had to leave his bride at home and go to work as he was in charge of the cattle herd at the state hospital and it was his duty to feed and weigh the prize cow at very precise times each day.

The church, being on the second floor, created some special problems. People with heart problems often had to stand at the top of the first landing for a while before beginning the climb to the second landing. Esther Kohler's mother, in her nineties and unable to climb, but determined to attend Mass, would stand at the bottom of the stairway and listen to the Mass being celebrated. What faith! The climb was also especially difficult for pallbearers carrying the casket into church.

And everyone remembers the days of pew rent at $12 a year. That was a lot of money in those days and sometimes it was rather embarrassing if you had to retreat from a pew that was not yours. Seats were assigned with the name placed on a metal plate fastened to the end of the pew. Times were hard and it is said by some present day parishioners that Father Yeager, on many occasions, was able to pay only the interest on the building debt.

Reverend Joseph Bocek was appointed pastor on November 1, 1931, which by this time included the missions at Copemish and Karlin. The new pastor was a very soft spoken man and was considered to be very holy. He was often seen praying his rosary while walking the parish grounds. He truly loved his flock, especially the little children at the time of their First Communion. In his quest to help the financial situation of the parish he often went from house to house gathering chickens, potatoes, pies—whatever was needed to make the parish chicken dinners a success.

Father James Bryant, 1936-1940, became the parish's fourth pastor. He truly possessed an ability of building good will and making converts. His mother and father lived with him at the rectory, with his mother serving as the housekeeper and his father working at Parsons Manufacturing plant on the Grand Traverse Bay just a couple blocks from the rectory. Father Hugh King became the first assistant pastor in 1940.

It was under Father Roman Kosnik, pastor from 1940-48, that a large building fund drive was undertaken to purchase a square block for the eventual site of the new church. Father loved baseball and was instrumental in organizing city-wide teams. He not only organized the teams but was a very active player himself. Another love of his was the Immaculate Conception School Marching Band that performed, among other events, in the Cherry Festival Parade. This was the youngest marching band in the city. The Festival parade route always went by the school building on Division Street. (The route was changed years later when Division Street became a state highway.) It was an unwritten law that the top landing of the school steps was reserved for the older people with their folding chairs. It was a great experience for the band students and a source of community pride.

The church-school building did not have a fire escape from the second floor church part. To rectify this unsafe situation, Father enlisted the help of Frank Rokos, Jr., a parishioner and blacksmith by trade. A suitable metal escape was purchased and installed by Frank. It remains on the building today.

The assistant pastor, Father Ceslaus Klimowicz, well aware of the financial need of the parish and also the need for sociability of its people, sought and obtained permission from Father Kosnik to start a parish bingo with the help of a parishioner, Louie Kohler. The agreement was that the first bingo had to show a profit or the pastor would cancel the whole thing. Chickens, which served as prizes, were strung on a wire across the social hall. It proved to be an enjoyable event for everyone but the final tally showed they were $3.00 in the

hole after paying the expenses. So, Louie took $3.50 out of his pocket and gave it to Father Klimowicz. Now there was 50¢ profit! Father Klimowicz did not want to take it but Louie insisted. When questioned by the pastor as to how they did, Father Klimowicz replied, "we made 50¢ profit," and so permission was given for future games.

Father Kosnik was succeeded by Right Reverend Russell Passeno in 1948. At the time of his arrival the parish finances were in such bad shape that Monsignor Passeno declared during his second homily: "If we don't get $250 a week this parish is going under." It was a huge task, but every parishioner was expected to do their utmost to help the parish get out of debt and move forward with the building of the new church.

The 21-year pastorate of Monsignor Passeno saw many changes: the new church was built and dedicated on May 30, 1952; the old church was renovated to four additional classrooms; a new eight classroom school was built in 1961 immediately adjacent to the old school; additional land was purchased for a future new rectory.

The Holy Family and Holy Name Societies worked hard for the parish. Eventually Monsignor replaced the Holy Family Society with circles whose primary purpose was sociability and fundraising. It must be stated here that Louie Sleder's wife, Marge, ran card parties in the basement of their home for thirty years with all the proceeds going to the parish. Every Circle worked hard with fundraising, including among others, serving breakfast after the Sunday Masses in Lucille Zoulek's backyard, located close to the church.

One of Monsignor Passeno's proudest days was the ordination day of Father James Gardiner, the first priest from Immaculate Conception Parish. Monsignor had been instrumental in getting Father Jim to go to the seminary. Father Jim's first Mass at Immaculate Conception was very special with a most beautiful liturgy, the angelic-like choir, and the beautiful tenor voice of Father Jim made the day very memorable.

To facilitate the school children to attend every First Friday Mass and Communion (fasting rules were different then), Monsignor always served breakfast to the students consisting of scrambled eggs, sweet rolls and milk. Not only did he feed the students, but he also fed the pigeons on a daily basis. The parish grounds were flooded with pigeons and everything that goes with pigeons.

Monsignor Passeno was a superb musician and used his abilities to organize and direct a beautiful male choir at the parish. He had several organists but Mrs. Walter Hittle served in this capacity for 25 years. The choir eventually became a mixed choir with the addition of women. He also organized, directed and played all the music for a yearly operetta put on by the seventh graders. The students couldn't wait to become seventh graders so they could be in Monsignor's operetta! What wonderful productions they were, complete with costumes and stage scenery!

During the 1950s community support helped make possible the spacious gym, kitchen, auditorium erected at the adjoining parish, Saint Francis. It provided the space and good will for many Catholic and community-sponsored events.

The parish and the school continued to grow through the years. Monsignor Passeno left the parish in 1969 and was succeeded by Father Edwin Thome. Father Thome built the new rectory and occupied it in August of 1971. (It might be noted here that Father Thome also got rid of the pigeons.)

Reverend Dennis Stilwell was also assigned to the parish. After the formation of the Diocese of Gaylord, Deacon Stilwell was ordained at Immaculate Conception Church by Bishop Edmund C. Szoka on December 19, 1971. Bishop Szoka was the first Bishop of the Diocese of Gaylord.

Another event of great importance occurred in 1969. Bishop Babcock of Grand Rapids ordered the consolidation of the Catholic elementary schools and high school. Thus was born the Grand Traverse Area Catholic Schools. Each parish contributed funds according to the number of students attending the Catholic schools. Immaculate Conception parish, which was debt free in 1969, found itself with a debt, having to help pay for Saint Francis High School which was built in 1965. Both parishes were having financial difficulties in 1971. That led to the decision to charge tuition for the grade school students. That same year, the Grand Traverse Educational Foundation was established to provide grants-scholarships for students as well as grants for improvements.

During the tenure of Father Thome a new rectory was completed and occupied in August 1971. Immaculate Conception School, in the consolidation, became a middle school housing grades five through eight the next year. The elementary grades were consolidated in the Saint Francis Elementary School. In 1972 Father Thome was transferred and he was succeeded by Monsignor Victor Gallagher. He served as pastor for two years. He was followed by Father Ronald Gronowski; Father William Rabior served with Father Gronowski as associate.

In 1977, members of the Capuchins, of the Franciscan Order, began tenure as pastor and assistants. Father Eugene Tuller was assigned as pastor to succeed Father Gronowski. The last of the Capuchins assigned to serve as pastor was Father James Mausolf; this was in 1982. He and Father John McCracken, then the associate with Father Mausolf, transferred from their order and joined with the Diocese of Gaylord in 1984. In 1985, Father Dennis Stilwell was installed as the pastor of Immaculate Conception Church and served for 12 years. The associates serving with him included Fathers Gerald Micketti, Kenneth Stachnik, David Agee, Gerard Hunko and Chad Zielinski. Starting in August of 1997 James Hayden became the pastor of Immaculate Conception Church. ■

Jesus the Good Shepherd, *Atlanta*

By Father Gerald F. Micketti

Jesus the Good Shepherd Parish is relatively new in the Diocese of Gaylord. Located on highway M-32 between Gaylord on the west and Alpena on the east, Atlanta was merely a fishing and hunting area prior to 1950. The lumber had been cleared long ago and very little industry remained. During the 1950s there were no more than a dozen Catholic families living in the area. These families traveled to Lewiston or Hillman to attend Sunday Mass.

The 1970s witnessed an influx of Catholic families from downstate and these new Atlanta residents wanted a parish of their own. There were many, small, non-Catholic churches where their friends and neighbors came together to worship the Lord each week. A small but determined group of people set out to make their hopes and dreams of their own church a reality. Word of this endeavor spread throughout the community and a census of area Catholics was taken. Undaunted by the small number of Catholic families found through the census, this core group went to the pastor at Lewiston seeking his help to begin a parish in Atlanta. While the Lewiston pastor was willing to cooperate, he was unable to offer any financial assistance since Saint Francis Parish was in the midst of its own building program. For several years the idea of a Catholic parish at Atlanta remained dormant.

Another attempt was made in the fall of 1971 when a group of Catholics approached Father Arthur Mulka, pastor of Saint Augustine Parish in Hillman. He agreed to work with them. This attempt ended after short work when Father Mulka was transferred. Again the idea remained dormant since the next two pastors at Hillman made no efforts to establish a parish in Atlanta. Father Robert Nalley was installed as pastor in 1978. The group requested his assistance. He agreed to work with them. The group also requested assistance of Bishop Szoka. He promised to help them.

When Father Terrence Donnelly was assigned as pastor of Saint Paul Parish in Onaway, the picture began to change. He met with the residents of Atlanta. With no church building of their own, the Atlanta parishioners rented facilities as the fairgrounds for their meetings and Masses. One hundred fifty people attended the first Mass that was celebrated October 18, 1979. This is considered the founding date of Jesus the Good Shepherd Parish. ■

The Catholic church in Manistee

An historical perspective

By Monsignor Gerard Guszkowski

The year is 1900. It is a Sunday morning. Members of three worshiping congregations gather to meet their God. These are the Catholics of Manistee, most of them blessed or burdened with the baggage of their Old World culture as, sometimes painfully, they weave their lives into the kaleidoscopic fabric of a New World.

A half-generation ago, these worshipers would have met at an upstairs wooden church which was hardly large enough to accommodate one congregation. This was Saint Mary Church, home since the Civil War to the French Canadians from the Montreal area imported here to ply the logging trade. In the 1870s, the advent of the Irish and German immigrants who largely engaged in the service occupations and, more recently, the large number of Polish peasants from the Poznan area, who sought refuge from the ethnic cleansing of Bismarck and his fellow overlords, made worship space uncomfortably confining to say the least. The church building was cramped far beyond its capacity; this plus the irritations of cultural differences led the Poles to obtain permission to establish their own (Saint Joseph) parish in 1884. Emboldened by the example of the Poles, the German and Irish Catholics petitioned successfully for their own parish church (Guardian Angels) in 1888.

For some worshipers, in this year of 1900, it's a climb up 42 rickety steps to the nave of Saint Mary Church; for others a frantic search for space in Saint Joseph Church which, as large and expansive as it is, still means wall-to-

On August 15, 1911 the original Saint Mary Church caught fire.

After the fire, parishioners gathered to survey the damage.

Guardian Angels Catholic Church as it looks today.

The interior of Guardian Angels Church.

While under construction on Nov. 17, 1961, the beams of new Saint Mary of Mount Carmel Church were toppled by a storm.

The present Saint Mary of Mount Carmel Church was completed in 1962.

wall people; for others still there's the smell of newness in Guardian Angels Church, not yet ten years old. They had come to remember, and to celebrate God's love for them as this new century dawned. Here are ladies whose flowing skirts swish almost to the floor; men straight-jacketed in what was still their Sunday best; and children, fancied and frilled in testament to their parents' pride.

Most of these people came from homes of modest means. From these families had come the faith and generosity shining through meager livelihoods and giving expression through the building of two magnificent worship structures, the maintenance of three parochial schools (with well over 1,000 youngsters in attendance!), and the maintenance of fit ancillary buildings to meet parish needs.

These were people whose faith and generosity kept shining through storms weathered. These storms were many and were severe. Among these: the trauma of Saint Mary parish losing two-thirds of its base and support due to the establishment of the two additional parishes; the painful confrontation of ten years previous that had pitted the pastor of Saint Joseph against a strong partisan group of dissidents which led to physical violence, lawsuits, a riot and the imposition of an interdict by the Bishop. Earlier still had been the painful experience of Saint Joseph parishioners forced to reconstruct the church building shattered by a devastating storm on the eve of its intended completion; and, in more recent times, the fire that destroyed their school. Pain, too, came to Guardian Angels people in the untimely death of their founding pastor even before their church building was completed.

Their homes, in comfort and convenience, modest at best, were blessed with an abundance of faith and generosity. These were the nurturing grounds then and in the time ahead for 21 vocations to the priesthood and 70 to religious life.

Standing on the threshold of a new century, could they have imagined how, in time, many things in the Catholic way of life would change? Among the "unimaginables:" the impact of Papal and Conciliar decrees affecting their worship life; the expansion of ministry roles in the Church; the incorporation into a new diocese; mobility bringing newcomers to the area with their unique expressions of faith and generosity; substantial changes in religious education as programs kept reaching out beyond the limits of parochial school; the near dissolution of Saint Mary Parish and its dramatic resuscitation; the economic and social changes hastening the demise of church oriented mutual aid and burial societies; closure of the hospital and sanatorium directed by the Sisters of Mercy; major expansion of Mount Carmel Cemetery to meet the needs of the three congregations to entrust to hallowed ground the mortal remains of loved ones to await the dawn of Resurrection Day; and last, but not least, the mutual acceptance by priests and people alike of foibles, faults and failings in a spirit of faith and generosity spilling over from the outreach of the Lord's forgiving hand.

What was imagined, inexorably, in God's providence, gave way to reality; and, reality's promise is that the faith and generosity of a stolid people yet remain the rich legacy that will ennoble the hearts and homes and worship centers of generations yet to come. ■

Saint Ann:
The radiance of faith from Cadillac

By Father Patrick Cawley

Traveling north on U.S. 131 into the Diocese of Gaylord, the first parish is Saint Ann in Cadillac. This parish and the faith of the people located on the southern edge of the diocese has a special history worth looking at. Saint Ann's location serves as the entrance to the new diocese after having been in the center of its old diocese, Grand Rapids, since 1882 when the Diocese of Grand Rapids was formed.

As the Michigan population grew during the second half of the 19th century, more Catholic churches began to appear throughout the western part of the state as well as elsewhere in the lower peninsula. Father McGee, in his book, *The Catholic Church in the Grand River Valley*, mentions the cluster of churches and mission stations which flowered along the Grand River in Kent, Ionia and Ottawa counties and later in towns farther north, among them Newaygo, Big Rapids, Ludington, Manistee, Cadillac and Traverse City.

In 1878, the Reverend Andrew Herbstret, a Precious Blood Father and pastor of Saint Mary Parish in Big Rapids and its 15 surrounding missions, invited a small and struggling community of Sisters of Mercy at Grand Rapids to come to Big Rapids to open a hospital in his city. Mother Joseph Lynch, mother superior of the community which had run into financial difficulty while operating an academy in Grand Rapids, readily accepted the offer. The sisters moved to Big Rapids, began a school there and at the same time started planning for the hospital which Father Herbstret knew was so urgently needed to care for injured lumberjacks.

Right Reverend Monsignor James A. Callahan

With the help of lumber camp operators and by means of $5 tickets sold to men in the lumber camps to insure their hospital treatment if injured, the sisters opened Mercy Hospital in Big Rapids in 1879. That was the beginning of the hospital work of the Sisters of Mercy in the Grand Rapids Diocese. The sisters opened and operated another hospital in Cadillac in 1908 and later one in Grayling, both now in the Diocese of Gaylord.

Cadillac, previously known as the Village of Clam Lake, became incorporated as a city in 1877. At that time the spiritual needs of the Catholics in the area were attended by priests from Traverse City or Big Rapids who offered Mass in a private home in the section of the city referred to as Frenchtown. The first Catholic Church to be erected in Wexford County began in 1880 under the management of a Father Ziegler. This was just prior to the establishment of the Diocese of Grand Rapids in 1882 and when the entire lower peninsula of Michigan was the Diocese of Detroit.

Father Zugelder, a few years after Father Ziegler, was appointed to take care of Saint Ann but to take up residence in Reed City. However having fallen asleep on the train he continued on to Cadillac and decided to take up residence there.

Reverend Henry Joseph Richter, D.D., pastor of Saint Lawrence Church in Cincinnati, was named by Pope

Leo XIII as the first bishop of the new Diocese of Grand Rapids.

With Bishop Richter's encouragement, Catholic churches were built in Lake City in 1896 and in Jennings in 1903, and in 1912, a small Christian Reformed Church was purchased in McBain to become a house of worship for the small Catholic congregation in that community. Saint Ann can be called the mother church of the Catholic faith in a broad area of northwestern Lower Michigan. Over the years, with the support and encouragement of their Cadillac parishioners, priests at Saint Ann have reached out to serve at least a dozen mission congregations in seven counties.

In *The View from Courthouse Hill*, Circuit Judge William R. Peterson writes that in 1882, "the new Saint Anns Church marked the southeast corner of the settlement. A small Catholic congregation had been served irregularly by visiting priests, meeting in a private home in Frenchtown from 1875 on. In 1880 a building was put up and enclosed along the Whaley trail in the southeast corner of the village, and it was completed in 1882 except for the spire, which was added in 1889."

Frenchtown was a settlement on the north side of Cadillac and they were outnumbered by settlers of other nationalities in other parts of the community. In fact, Catholics have always been a minority among Cadillac's residents, despite the city's French Catholic namesake. Saint Ann has been its only Catholic church, other than the small chapel in Mercy Hospital. It remains today the only Catholic church in Wexford County with a resident pastor.

The old Saint Ann Church was demolished in August, 1987.

"Saint Ann began in 1880 with 40 families as a parish in the Detroit Diocese. On April 22, 1883, it came under the ecclesiastical jurisdiction of the Right Reverend Henry Joseph Richter when he was installed as the first bishop of the Grand Rapids diocese. On July 29, 1971, with the creation of the Diocese of Gaylord in northern lower Michigan and the installation of the Most Reverend Edmund C. Szoka as its first bishop, Saint Ann became part of the new Gaylord Diocese. It had then grown to around 500 families. By 1982 with 800 families on the parish registry Saint Ann ranked among the largest parishes in the new diocese." *(Taken from A Heritage Of Faith, The Catholic Church in Missaukee County and Northwestern Lower Michigan by Willard M. J. Baird and The Catholic Church in the Grand River Valley by Father John McGee.)*

From the time the Village of Clam Lake became incorporated as a city in 1877 and was given the name "Cadillac," the Catholic faith was celebrated in private homes in a section of the city referred to as Frenchtown. From there it would grow, as did the area, and be served by many loyal and dedicated priests and religious women. From the time of the first church building in Cadillac just prior to 1880, under the management of Father Ziegler when the entire State of Michigan comprised the Diocese of Detroit to the present pastorate of Father Francis Murphy the parish of Saint Ann has been salt and light to all her parishioners and to the many travelers and passersby.

Over the years Saint Ann has served the mission churches of Saint Stephen in Lake City, Saint Ambrose in Jennings, Saint Rita in McBain, Saint Philip Neri in Reed City, Sacred Heart in Evart, Saint Agnes in Marion, Saint Ann in Frankfort, Saint Aloysius in Fife Lake, Saint Ignatius in Luther, Saint Edward in Harrietta and Saint Theresa in Manton as well as an early mission station at Temple in Clare County. Some of these missions are now parishes and some belong to the Grand Rapids Diocese but all received nurturing and strength from their once mother church, Saint Ann in Cadillac.

This leads me to a little aside or sidebar as we have come to know the term. My name is Father Patrick T. Cawley and I was born and raised in Cadillac. I am the only one to come from Cadillac and be ordained a priest. This happened in 1970 when Cadillac was part of the Diocese of Grand Rapids. My little story goes back to my upbringing and influence of Saint Ann on my life and vocation.

The first priest to die in the new Diocese of Gaylord was Monsignor James Calla-

han, pastor of Saint Ann in Cadillac from 1947 until his death in December, 1971. Monsignor Callahan represented a church from the past and his passing ushered in the new church. Those of us who grew up under his pastorate were not aware of any other church but Saint Ann. Monsignor Callahan was a giant of a man and he represented authority, leadership, strength and faith. He was the church and we listened to him and often trembled in his presence. He was an old time Irish priest whose bark was much bigger than his bite. He ran the parish, lived in a large rectory, had a large Irish setter, a kind housekeeper, went through assistant priests like they were just passing through town on their way somewhere else, that is until Father John Tamulis came and faithfully served Monsignor Callahan for 18 years and served as administrator for a year after his death until Father Thome was appointed pastor in 1972.

The Mass was in Latin back then and Monsignor's sermons weren't much to speak of. They were just a few jokes and a word or two about doing good for others. His Mass took about forty minutes and we were on our way. Going to confession to Monsignor was frightening because of the mystery of it and the very size of the man. Of course he couldn't see who was on the other side of the screen but you always suspected he knew. The one constant was that no matter what you did, even if you thought it was the worst thing in the world, your penance was always three Hail Marys. Monsignor never gave many words of advice so, if you had something to confess that you were sort of embarrassed about, you could save it until the end and while you stopped to catch your breath Monsignor would most likely jump in and say: "Say three Hail Marys for your penance." Then he would slide the panel shut and you were on your way.

In the early 1950s we few Catholics attended Saint Ann grade school. This small four-room, eight-grade school house, directly across from the rectory, was a place of great formation to say the least. There were two classes to a room and one teacher, a Sister of Mercy, controlling both grades with total authority and dominion. Everything you have ever heard about Catholic schools went on in that four-room school house but I don't think we suffered because of it. Speaking for myself I believe it was the best formation possible and has served me well over the years.

Father Edwin Thome breaks ground for the new St. Ann's Catholic Church.

The education we received was first rate. When we left the Catholic grade school and went to the high school we were always well prepared and often ahead of the other schools. This was not because we were brighter but the sisters made sure we got the message and the lessons. There was some rough treatment from some of the sisters and certainly this would not be tolerated today but back then it was accepted and, I must admit, often justified. We developed a certain pride being Catholic in a small town of mostly non-Catholics. We played sports against the other public schools and quite often they ended in fights or at least disruptions. I remember one year a young assistant priest named Father Hugh Michael Beahan came to referee all our games and he ended up keeping the peace most of the time.

The impression left by Monsignor Callahan and the many assistants was strong and vivid. Saint Ann was the whole church and we were a part of it. Not going to Mass on Sunday morning was never even considered no matter what you did Saturday evening or how late you were out or if you had to work on Sunday. That was part of your faith and you did not question it or try to explain it. This was part of being a Catholic and it was a part of you and, in a real way, it made you proud.

This parish of Saint Ann, now of considerable size and part of the Diocese of Gaylord, has been the source of inspiration and faith to many, many people over the years. Several priests have served the parish and made their impact. The faith of the people has been shaped and tempered over the years but it has grown in size and stature.

Following Monsignor Callahan's death in 1971 and a brief administration by Father John Tamulis, Father Ed Thome assumed the pastorate of Saint Ann from 1972 until 1984. This was a difficult time in many respects. Following Monsignor Callahan in itself would be a real adjustment but this, along with identifying with the new diocese, the need to renovate the rectory and church and eventually build new ones on a different site were major tasks. There was also serious economic concerns in Cadillac in the late 1970s when there were public school bond rejections and even a pay-to-play sports program in the city. Yet, in the midst of this, Father Thome and the people of Saint Ann came together and raised the money to build the new church, hall and rectory at a new location on the north end of town. This was no small commitment and much credit is due Father Thome for his ability to motivate and enflame the pride of the parishioners. Father Thome was transferred to Traverse City after his pastorate in Cadillac and Father Robert Bissot was assigned until his transfer to West Branch in the summer of 1997.

Traveling north on U.S. 131 the first parish you come to is Saint Ann in Cadillac. It is a holy place and has been the source of strength and God's presence to many people over many years. From here the faith has spread and flourished. People have been baptized, married and buried from the old church and the new. There have been many changes in priests, people, practices and facilities but the one constant is that the Catholic faith in Cadillac is alive and well. It is a joy to behold. ■

Saint Ann, *Frankfort*

For many years, before Saint Ann Parish had a church building or the status of a mission church attached to any neighboring established parish, the Catholic families of the Frankfort area were served by priests from Nessen City or Cadillac, perhaps even Big Rapids. A descendant of one of the oldest families of Saint Ann remembered his grandfather speaking of having Mass said only a few times a year in private homes or in store buildings. Among the priests who served the Catholic families in Frankfort were Fathers Guthausen, Eickelmann, Kettmann, Golden, McDonald and Williams.

In 1895 Bishop Joseph Richter of Grand Rapids gave permission to build a church building. The building committee included L.W. Crane, Edward Goethals, D.G.F. Warner, George Morency, Thomas Rudelt and Fred Kern. At that time Father J.G. Hudon of Manistee was ministering to the needs of the people.

The original Saint Ann Church erected in 1895.

Ground was broken on May 14, 1895, and on the following July 15, the grounds were consecrated, the cornerstone laid and the church named for Saint Ann.

The document in the cornerstone read: "The cornerstone of this church was laid on July 15, 1895, by Most Reverend Joseph Richter, Bishop of Grand Rapids, in the presence of Rev. J.G. Hudon of Manistee, who took care of this congregation, and Rev. Jos. Steffe of Manistee. During the happy reign of Pope Leo XIII and Grover Cleveland, President of the United States."

After many difficulties and delays, the church was finally bricked in by the autumn of 1901. Father L.M. Prud'homme served the needs of the congregation from 1901 to 1906 at a time when Saint Ann was still a mission of Saint Mary in Manistee. Father L.A. Golden was his assistant.

A grandson of Ed Goethals remembered his grandfather walking regularly to Nessen City to take the parish report to the

pastor. Goethals would often preside at the funerals of parishioners when it was impossible for the pastor to come to Frankfort due to the bad weather or distance.

On July 15, 1911 Saint Ann was established as a separate parish with Father John A. Yeager as pastor. The following year the church rectory was completed.

In 1941, under the direction of Father Earl Denay, a 66-foot lot on M-22 was bought, the Altar Society established and the outdoor Marian Shrine built.

In 1958, the original church building was demolished and the present structure constructed. Father Paul Kerjes was the pastor at that time. Altars from the old church were given to the parishes of Saint Anthony of Padua in Mancelona, Saint Rita in Maple City and Saint Phillip Neri in Empire. The first Mass in the new Saint Ann Church was celebrated on Christmas Day, 1958.

For the first time, the parishioners of Saint Ann had their own place to hold bazaars, dinners, youth and social activities. Between 1963 and 1969, Father Harold Feltman had the large assembly room, CCD office and ground floor classrooms built, and outdoor stations installed. ■

Built on culture, sustained on faith:

Saint Anne, Alpena and the parishes of Northeast Michigan

by Betty Werth Westrope

Imagine...it was only about 125 years ago, but the new world of 19th century northeastern Michigan was foreign, bare, cold and best suited to the brave. The Catholic immigrants who found their way to this northern forest, mostly by boat, had to have come ashore clutching hopes in one hand, fears in the other, surveying with trepidation whatever small village they had chosen, no more than a cluster of shacks, lumber yards, and wood-frame houses along a street or two of sawdust and muck.

In 1870-80 in northeast Michigan, they were many hard miles from anything resembling urban white civilization, and they were carrying in their bags all they would have to build upon in a land that offered them little but lumber, dirt, river, and rock.

Imagine what they must have thought as they unpacked those bags in Alpena or Rogers City or Hillman. Imagine how important it must have been, knowing there was no quick "going back," to have held onto what was familiar, what was enduring, what had been handed down through generations in the "old world" to this generation in the new. What they took out of their bags to furnish their new surroundings were their traditions, their culture and, inseparably bound with those, their religion. It was a time when "being Catholic" meant being "Irish Catholic" or "Polish Catholic" or "French Catholic," and for many, living by one's cultural creed was indivisible from living by one's faith.

Imagine how important it must have been to have kept alive the culture/religion they'd brought with them.

With no common language, no broadly dominant culture in many of these small towns, ethnic neighborhoods sprang up—one for the French, another for the German, others for the Polish, Irish, English, Swedish, Norwegian. The people would live with their own kind, as they had lived before. It was key to their survival. Their cultural identity was all they had to build upon, and part of that identity was to worship as they had worshiped before, in churches where the French praised God in the French tradition, the Polish in the Polish tradition, the Irish as they had for centuries.

Imagine, then, the need, not for one priest to serve a community like Alpena, but a French one to serve the French, a son of the "Auld Sod" to serve the Irish, a Pole to serve the Poles. One big Catholic church wouldn't do. It wasn't a time, in what was then the Diocese of Grand Rapids, to quibble about "human resources" or "financial feasibility." If the French, Irish, and Polish were to remain Catholic, the bishop understood, it would only be if they could be French Catholic (he sent them Father Winter), Irish Catholic (he sent them Father Flannery), Polish Catholic (he sent them Father Kozlowski).

Imagine what it was like to be in on the ground floor of establishing your own culture/religion in a new place in a new church in the new world. At Saint Anne, the French church, they lined up before Father Winter for baptism, and the records tell the tale: Prieur, LaMarre, Sabourin, Couture, LeBlanc, Desourmeaux, Brousseau, Pomerleau, Cousineau, Chabot, Sylvester, Desroshers, Brunet, Saint Charles, Lemieux, Berriault, and many more, all French Canadians.

Imagine how important it was to have a Father Winter, and a Saint Anne Church, when they lined up for burials of their beloved French children: In the first weeks of 1884, right after Father Winter's arrival, the Record of Interments shows Napoleon Masse, age 12 days; Joseph Rivet, age 6 years; Anne Menard, age 12 days; Leberge twins, at birth; Joseph Rheaume, 3 months; Modeste Robert, aged 4 months. From Father Winter's beginnings in January 1884, through the next five years, Saint Anne Parish buried 186, and 129 of them were children younger than 10 years! Imagine what a hard life it was.

Imagine the struggle—and the exhilaration—of building a "parish family" and keeping it together through its infancy and childhood. After Father Winter at Saint Anne came Father Letellier, then Father Hudon, then Father Blais—all, of necessity, French; all short-term. Then came the gently powerful Father Charles DeQuoy, a man who took the Saint Anne parish from childhood to adolescence and into young adulthood in 26 years of remarkable service. As the turn of the century approached, the French church continued in its French ways (Father DeQuoy heard confessions and gave his sermons in French), and each ethnic neighborhood clung tightly to its cultural heritage, yet the community as a whole suffered and prospered in common. In 1895 telephone service arrived; in 1897 the whole town was quarantined because of a diphtheria epidemic; in 1898 the Alpena Business college opened. Imagine how "modern" life seemed!

Imagine how crushed the Saint Anne parishioners were when their church home burned to the ground in August 1907, just a week after the final payment had been made. Like so many other young congregations, Catholic, Lutheran, Baptist, they'd sacrificed and struggled and succeeded—and then suffered terrible loss. And then, undefeated, regrouped and rebuilt—grander than before!

Under the long-term tutelage of two other priests—Father Bouchard (1919-1944) and Monsignor Simon (1944-67)—the parish of Saint Anne, the Alpena home for French Catholics, blossomed like a sturdy French lily. It survived two World Wars and the Depression and had grown from 300 families to upward of 800! Imagine how proud these French Canadians were!

And then, in 1968, the parish home of the Gilberts and the Roussins and the Cadieux and the LaMarres suffered terrible culture shock. The list of pastors, which up until then had read like the roster of the Montreal Canadiens, was now to include a Mikulski—a priest who many thought more properly belonged in the line begun by Father Kozlowski at that Polish church across the river.

Imagine how wrong they were. Like any parish, any congregation, any people, any person, they could only see where they'd been, not where they were going. And where they were going was into another era, this one as full of hope and fear as the one into which their ancestors had stepped when they came ashore in the 20 and 30 years before the turn of the century. With the reforms of Vatican II after 1965, and the formation of the Diocese of Gaylord in 1971, it was another new world, in the same place as the old but with the ground (and the ground rules) rearranged.

Without any obvious point of demarcation, the parishioners at Saint Anne had stepped away from being French Catholic to being just Catholic, and if a much-respected Father Mikulski at their head forced them at last to notice it, their faith was no longer bound to their ethnic heritage. Who knew when it had happened, but clearly it was no longer necessary to have a French priest for the French church, or an Irish one for the Irish church, or a Polish one for the Polish church. They were all Americans now, and as the ethnic and political and religious walls that had shaped the early churches began to fall, parishioners saw more clearly what they had always had in common.

The common point, of course, was faith. If culture and tradition had helped foster it, fine. But what had once been considered inseparable had separated, culture and

tradition had fallen back, and faith stepped forward, strong enough to stand on its own.

Imagine now what it would be like if northeastern Michigan were divided into ethnic parishes. Where would you fit? If you are like most Americans, probably seven or eight places...or none.

Instead, we're in an era when a church home is a matter of choice, built around proximity or comfort or family background. As Catholics, we're welcome at any parish, anywhere, and that's progress. It's faith we have in common, and if we stand with no little trepidation as we prepare to step ashore in the 21st century, that's what we carry with us. That's what we have in our bags, ready to unpack; that's what we'll have to build upon. Imagine how important it will be, knowing there is no "going back," to hold onto what is familiar, what is enduring, what has been handed down through generations in the old millennium to this generation in the new. Imagine what we have in store! ■

Saint Anne, *Harrisville*

By Father Gerald F. Micketti

Bishop LeFevre wrote to Reverend Patrick Murray of Alpena in February 1868, giving him missionary faculties (after the death of Bishop Baraga) requesting: "Please be so kind as to visit occasionally Harrisville and the Catholics living in adjacent places." So Father Murray did. That same year, a site was chosen for a church; the land was donated by Francis LaChapelle on South State Street. During that same a year a church 24 feet x 40 feet was built. The site was chosen on a hill overlooking the settlement on the lake.

With the rapid development of the lumbering industry came an influx of people of French, Irish and Scottish extraction, which necessitated the enlargement of the church. In 1874 Father Nevin, pastor of Sacred Heart Church, AuSable, who had the care of Saint Anne mission at Harrisville, put an addition onto the church. By 1900, Saint Anne Church had been built and was enlarged several times.

When lumbering ceased to be as important in Alcona County, some of the men who followed the forests decided to stay behind and farmed to feed their families. The cut-over land was cleared of stumps. They needed spiritual help and Saint Anne Parish provided that. Many of the parishioners lived in Barton City, Lincoln, Greenbush and other areas. They came to Saint Anne Church by horse and buggy, sleighs, stage coach, boat and walking. A pioneer, Mrs. Clare LaFave of Barton City, recalled that her parents, Mr. and Mrs. Alex Joseph, would leave by horse and buggy at midnight in order to get to Mass in Harrisville at 8:00 a.m. At other times, the family home near Barton City was used by Father Bouchard to say Mass periodically. All the Catholics would gather there (15 miles from Harrisville) for baptisms, first communions and Mass. The Kane Family lived in Greenbush five miles from the church. Mr. Kane was a station agent for the Detroit and Mackinac Railroad. Mr. Kane had permission from the railroad to use the hand car. When there were enough people to pump the car the five miles up a long hill, they came to Mass.

From 1884 to 1889, Saint Anne Church was attended by Father Roche and Father C.P.A. Winter. In October 1889, Father F.H. Ruessmann was appointed the first pastor. He purchased the so-called C.P. Renolds house, next to the church, but never resided there. In 1892 and 1893, either Father J. Mahar of Sacred Heart, AuSable, or his assistant, Father Edward LeFevre, took care of Saint Anne Parish. Father Julien Doucet of AuSable took care of the parish 1893 to 1895. Father Joseph L. Poulin was appointed the first resident pastor in February 1895, with the missions of Saint Gabriel, Black River and Saint Raphael, Mikado. Father Poulin finished the construction of Saint Raphael Church in Mikado.

Father Louis Bouchard succeeded Father Poulin in February 1905. After the fire in 1910 in AuSable destroyed Sacred Heart Church building, Oscoda was attached to Saint Anne Church as a mission. Father Bouchard also had the missions of Mikado, Black River and Nicholson Hill. His parish and missions covered parts of four counties. His 1911 Buick helped him cover all that territory. Father Arthur Houle came in October 1913. He died of influenza February 19, 1919. He was succeeded in March by Father Fred W. Ryan. Father Ryan served for five years and was succeeded by Father Joseph W. Delehanty. During the tenure of Father Delehanty the rectory burned and was rebuilt (1926) and the church was completely renovated (1930). In the fall of 1934, Nicholson Hill (Ossineke) was given a pastor and the mission of Saint Gabriel, Black River, was transferred to Nicholson Hill. Father Delehanty was succeeded by Father Julian Moleski in August 1937, who served for one year and four months.

On January 13, 1938, Father Adalbert Narloch was appointed the pastor of Saint Anne Church with Saint Raphael, Mikado and Sacred Heart Church, Oscoda, as missions. On June 26, 1950, Sacred Heart Church became a parish with a resident pastor. The mission of Saint Raphael was transferred to Sacred Heart at this time. Saint Anne Parish grew spiritually as Father Narloch devoted many hours to religious instruction. There is a long list of persons who joined the Catholic Church during his tenure as pastor.

After World War II, tourists began pouring into Alcona County. With the progressively greater influx of summer visitors in the northern part of lower Michigan, the need for a new and larger church building became evident. Sunday Masses were so crowded in the summer that many people stood outside on the lawn. Father Narloch began planning for a new church. By the time he left for Rogers City, $22,000 had been accumulated for a new church.

Father Narloch left Harrisville for Rogers City at the end of 1952. He was succeeded by Father Raymond Mulka. Under Father Mulka a new church building was planned, built and dedicated. In 1955 the Albert Noyes' home and property just south of the old church was purchased as the site for the new church. Preliminary plans were presented to Bishop Woznicki of Saginaw in 1959. The following year the plans were approved and ground was broken July 10, 1960. The church was dedicated August 12, 1962.

Father Vernon J. Sierminski came to Saint Anne as pastor in 1963. His first task was the completion of the new church building and the reduction of the debt on the new church. Maria Hall was built during his tenure at Saint Anne. He was followed by Father Charles Klingshirn in 1970. He served for two years before being transferred to Saint Mary in Alpena. Father David Gemuend served for six months as administrator. Father Gemuend helped the parishioners with changes of Vatican Council II especially in the area of liturgy. Father Gemuend was succeeded by Father Lionginas Dieninis (Father Leo). Father Leo also had the mission of Glennie. While he was pastor, the church building at Glennie was built. He retired in 1985 because of poor health. He was followed by Father Clarence Smolinski. Father Smolinski retired in 1994 and was followed by Father Lawrence Boks, who is the present pastor. ■

Saint Anthony, *Mancelona*

The history of Saint Anthony Parish begins in 1881 when Franciscan Priests from Petoskey served Catholics in this area, with Mass being available only at intermittent intervals. As the town and congregation grew, the need for a church was obvious and an acre of land was donated by D.P. McGuirk near Antrim where the Catholic Cemetery is now located. Work was started on the building in 1887.

The first Mass was celebrated in the new church on Saint Anthony's Day, June 13, 1888, and on July 4, 1888, Bishop Henry Joseph Richter of the Diocese of Grand Rapids dedicated the new church in honor of Saint Anthony of Padua, a 12th century priest born in Lisbon, Portugal. Saint Anthony devoted himself to spreading the faith among the African people and preaching in France and Italy. His sermons were notable for their learning and gentleness. He died at Padua in 1231.

In 1889, new bells were purchased for the church and these same bells ring from the tower of the present church.

The Franciscan priests from Petoskey continued to serve the church on a missionary basis with Mass celebrated only once a month until 1904, when the growing congregation made it feasible to have Mass celebrated twice a month. The church building was moved from the Antrim site to its present location in 1910. In 1929, diocesan priests replaced the Franciscans in the care of Saint Anthony.

On February 25, 1955, fire of undetermined origin extensively damaged the church and the parish made plans for building a new church. Ground breaking ceremonies were held on May 5, 1957, and the cornerstone was laid on September 15, 1957. Bishop Allen J. Babcock of the Diocese of Grand Rapids dedicated the church on October 21, 1957, and the first Mass was celebrated in it on November 10, 1957. The total cost of the church was $71,000.

Saint Anthony Church in 1938.

The altar of the old church.

With the liturgical reforms mandated by the Second Vatican Council, some slight modifications were made. However, in the summer of 1977, because of a significant amount of money that had come to the parish, planning was begun to restore, beautify and renovate the church in a manner in keeping with both the letter and the spirit of the Vatican II liturgical renewal.

Plagens Studios of West Bloomfield, Michigan, was selected to design and complete the renovation. A parish committee of 15 worked with the pastor and Mr. Cass J. Plagens for seven months on the project. Work was begun in January, 1978, with the total cost being $73,000.

In keeping with Catholic Church tradition, when a new altar is installed in a church, it is dedicated by the bishop and, after extensive renovation, the church itself is rededicated. The Most Reverend Edmund C. Szoka, first bishop of the Diocese of Gaylord, dedicated the new altar and rededicated Saint Anthony Church in 1978. ■

Saint Anthony, *Mackinaw City*

By Father Gerald F. Micketti

In the year 1857 the land of Old Mackinaw was in the hands of owners such as Mr. Edgar Conkling and other people who resided outside of Michigan. During the summer of 1857, Mr. Conkling had the land adjoining old Fort Michilimackinac surveyed and platted for a town. For 13 years that land remained unoccupied. In 1870, Mr. Conkling had a dock built. His dream was that his town would become a great town, the Detroit of the north due to its access to the Great Lakes and the direct routes to the south when the railroads arrived.

The group of people to hold religious services in what became Mackinaw City were the Catholics. While Mr. Conkling's dock was under construction, a priest came from Cheboygan and offered Mass for the benefit of the workmen. The first Mass was celebrated in the boardinghouse of Patrick Manion. Fifty men, ten women and children were in attendance. The priest preached in English and French.

The priests from Cheboygan continued to care for the needs of the Catholic families in Mackinaw City through the remaining decades of the 19th century and into the 20th century. Prior to the construction of a church building for worship and instruction, Masses were offered in private homes. In 1905, Bishop Richter gave permission for the erection of a church building. He did stipulate, however, that no debt may be incurred. That was the green light for the parishioners to begin the fund raising. The fruit of their efforts was seen five years later. July 2, 1910, Bishop Richter blessed the new building and placed the parish under the patronage of Saint Anthony of Padua. The priest serving the needs of the people at that time was Father John McDonald. Four years later a rectory was constructed.

Father George L. Nye was appointed the first pastor of Saint Anthony Parish in December of 1914. He also had served the missions of Saint Aloysius in Wolverine and Saint Monica in Afton. There was a feeling that the church and rectory were built "out of town." This feeling was also felt by Bishop Kelly. He directed that a new location be selected so that the church would be in the confines of the town. In 1920, land was purchased. The next year the church building and rectory were moved to the new location. That same year, Father Hanskneckt succeeded Father Nye as pastor.

After the 1930s and the war years, Mackinaw City was growing and tourism was increasing. The need for a larger building became apparent. Also the building was old and in need of repairs. At this time the pastor was Father Bieniawski. Ground breaking ceremonies were held in later November of 1958. The following July 3, the first Mass was offered in the new Saint Anthony Church. ■

Saint Augustine, *Hillman*

By Father Gerald F. Micketti

The people of eastern Montmorency County and western Alpena County were Catholic and almost exclusively French-Canadian in heritage. They came from the Quebec and Ontario Provinces, having been enticed here by the good wages paid in the lumber camps. In the 1880s the Catholics in the Hillman area had their spiritual needs met by Father Winter of Saint Anne Church and Father Flannery of Saint Bernard Church, both churches located in Alpena. They would come to the lumber camps periodically and celebrate the sacraments with the men who were Catholic, as well as the needs of the Catholic families in the area. Father Flannery offered Mass in the home of Mr. and Mrs. John Butler in Long Rapids. The families living north of the present village of Hillman had to travel eastward along the rough, narrow and heavily wooded long Swamp Road. Usually two or more families made the trip together in a buggy or wagon. The Mass at the Butler home took place only once or twice a year. Later, Mr. E.O. Avery gave consent to have the Mass offered at his farm home where Mr. and Mrs. John Forrest were caretakers. Father Blais and Father Charles DeQuoy, Saint Anne Church, also met the sacramental needs of the residents until the church was built. At one time 23 babies were baptized in the living room of the Avery home.

During the 1890s Mass was offered at the farm home of Mr. and Mrs. Napoleon LaFave. Their farm was located one-and-one-half miles north of the village of Hillman. Father DeQuoy was the first priest to offer Mass at that home. The LaFave family had a small altar built against the wall of the living room. The families of the area met there not only for Mass but also to pray the rosary during Lent. The first lay catechist was Mrs. William Carter. She taught children religion in her own home north of Hillman; she also taught a few adults who decided to become Catholic. She continued to teach for a few years even after the church was constructed. The members of some of those first catechism classes had to go to Alpena to receive their first communion.

Land for the church building was donated by Judge Frank Emerick of Alpena and located at the south end of the village on a hill. The first church building was built through the volunteer labor of men of the community — Romeo Gamache, Alfred DeLoge, Napoleon LaFave, John Forrest, Alfred Sabourin, James Hubert, Napoleon LeFleche, Adolph Amelotte, Joseph LaFranier, John Morrow, Alfred LePine, Joseph Chartrand and Cleophas Cadieux. It was built entirely of work bees in 1889 under the direction of Fred DeLoge. All the men in the parish helped with the excavation, cement and carpentry work. There was little money among the early settlers but there was a great willingness to work and a strong desire to have a church building of their own. What a beautiful sight it was to those parishioners! The solemn blessing and dedication was held in 1900 with Bishop Henry J. Richter of Grand Rapids. The name chosen for the parish was Saint Augustine.

One amusing incident is still remembered by the old timers. The floor at that time was not completely finished and wide cracks allowed people to look down into the hole under the building. (This hole later became the basement.) The benches were nothing more than boards set up on blocks. They often slid one way or the other unexpectedly if the people were not careful about sitting down. Three ladies of the parish were kneeling by one of the temporary benches praying during the Mass. While these ladies were praying they noticed through the floor boards a number of the neighboring cows were standing under the church contentedly chewing their cud. When the ladies rose from their kneeling position and were just about to sit on the benches, their bench slid backwards and all three ladies found themselves on the floor. The cows, disturbed by such noise, let out loud snorts and ran from beneath the building to seek their solitude elsewhere.

Even with a new building, however, the congregation of Hillman seldom had Sunday Mass during the winter months. Poor roads and bitter cold conditions made offering of Mass in the winter difficult. Originally, the church was heated by an old wood-fired box stove which stood in the middle of the nave. It was one of the old two-lid camp style stoves made of iron with a door in the front. Wood was piled high in the summer both beneath and inside the church.

The first recorded baptism was Mary Olive LePine, daughter of Alfred LePine and Alvina Arneald, on December 12, 1897. The first recorded marriage was between William Villeneuve and Amelia Sheff witnessed by Father O'Connell May 25, 1898. The earliest First Communion class was composed of 11 children and took place July 11, 1905.

The first priest who regularly covered Saint Augustine Church was Father Godfrey Lenzen. He was appointed pastor October 1, 1897, of Saint Rose of Herron with a mission of Saint Augustine, Hillman. He resided at Saint Anne Church in Alpena until a rectory was built at Herron. The priests who served Hillman continued to live at Herron for over 50 years. That meant Saint Augustine Church was locked during the week and no Blessed Sacrament was reserved there. Father Lenzen either rode a horse or a bicycle to Hillman once a month for Mass, except in the winter months.

Father Thomas W. Albin succeeded Father Lenzen in 1903 and served Saint Augustine mission for three years. He had been a medical doctor for 12 years prior to deciding to study for the priesthood. He practiced medicine in Cheboygan where he met Father Edward Caldwell who encouraged him to consider becoming a priest. Father Albin was a very good speaker. Through his efforts a number of people decided to join the Catholic Church.

Father William Schueller followed Father Albin in 1906. He was one of the first priests in the area to drive an automobile — a Model T Ford. He delighted the boys in the parish with his ability to shoot crows. Under Father Schueller, new pews were purchased as well as a large outdoor bell. Napoleon LeFleche, Cleophas Cadieux and John Forrest were responsible for transporting the pews and the bell from Alpena to Hillman.

After two years serving Herron and Hillman, Father Schueller was succeeded by Father Patrick O'Toole. He also built a new church at Indian Reserve in western Alpena County. He began a new Sunday Mass schedule which included two Masses per month at Saint Augustine; an increase from one Mass per month. He also was responsible for changing the heating system in the church. By this time, three wood stoves were in use during the winter months. He replaced all three with a coal furnace. Also, the parish cemetery was purchased and consecrated as well as a new altar was installed in the sanctuary.

Father J.A. Camirand followed Father O'Toole in 1917. During his tenure, the Holy Name Society was begun and a definite Sunday was set aside each month as Communion Sunday. Father Camirand also gave instructions for those who wished to join the Catholic Church. He left in 1921 for Carrollton and died soon afterwards.

Father George Gougeon was the next pastor. He was known as a musician, missionary and builder. He was accustomed to playing at the graduations and other festive events throughout the region. He liked to play the piano for children and sing with them. He served for six years and was followed by Father William Fraser who served until 1934. He served during the difficult years of the Depression. Annual chicken dinners and card parties were held just to meet ordinary expenses.

He is remembered for his care of the sick. After his transfer to Cadillac, Father Fraser was succeeded by Father Lucien Bourget. He had three places to cover — Herron, Hillman and Indian Reserve. He began a Mass schedule that allowed each of the three parishes to celebrate Mass each Sunday. This schedule was wonderful for the parishioners but Father Bourget was traveling fast between each Mass to be on time for the next Mass, thus the title, "The Flying Frenchman." During his tenure, the church was lifted so that additional excavating could be done to build a new basement. A new foundation for the church was completed, the church set on the foundation and the parish hall, the basement, was completed. Father Bourget served until 1950.

His successor was Father Harry Hart. He was responsible for beautification of the property and the sanctuary. He also was responsible for the Felician Sisters of Saint Mary Church, Alpena, to come to Hillman every Sunday during the school year to teach catechism to the grade school children. With the money of the parish, the home of the late Charles O'Farrell in the village of Hillman was purchased with the intention of converting it into a temporary rectory. The conversion was completed during the summer of 1951.

ith a view to the future, eight acres of land were purchased in the southeast section of the village. The old church was situated on less than an acre and it was not possible to purchase land adjacent to the church. Father Hart decided, without diocesan approval, that he would make his residence at Hillman, since Saint Augustine Parish was twice the size of Saint Rose Parish at Herron. In the middle of the night on October 5, 1951, he packed his car and moved to Hillman, thus changing the status of Saint Augustine from mission to parish and he became the first resident pastor.

Father Hart left Hillman in January of 1953 and was succeeded by Father Francis Lang. He remained less than a month due to ill health

and was followed in February by Father Joseph Branigan. His first change was to give Saint Augustine two permanent Masses with one Mass at Saint Rose. Saint Mary Church at Indian Reserve was closed prior to 1950. The new Mass schedule brought an increase of tourists attending the Masses at Hillman. As a temporary measure to handle the crowds during the summer months and the rifle deer hunting season in November, Mass was offered at the Hillman Town Hall. A larger church was needed.

To change the situation, two additional acres were purchased adjoining the original eight already owned by the parish. The land was situated on Highway M-32. To get the land it was necessary to exchange properties with the local VFW post which owned a basement building on the two acres. The old church was exchanged for the VFW building with the understanding that the parish could use the old church until a new one was erected. The parish had saved $65,000 and permission was received to hire an architect. After the plans were completed, bids were accepted July 26, 1957. Actual construction began the following August 16. Through the late summer, fall and winter of 1958, construction progressed to the point that the first Mass was offered Saturday, June 14, 1958. The first Mass was a wedding for John Altman and Muriel Stamm. During the next two years interior and exterior work was completed. This work was funded through donations from summer visitors. The new church was dedicated July 3, 1960, by Bishop Stephen Woznicki, Bishop of Saginaw. A banquet at the Hillman Town Hall followed.

Father Branigan left the parish in July of 1967. He was a shy and quiet man; he requested a transfer. The stress and problems of building the new church, together with personal problems with some parishioners, caused the pastor to put all the parish books in order and quietly leave the parish. His accomplishments included a new church building and laying the foundation for successful religious education program in the parish. The Felician Sisters of Saint Mary Church, Alpena, continued to teach at Saint Augustine after the Sunday Masses. Father Branigan also taught the high school students in the rectory basement.

Father Branigan's successor was Father Patrick E. O'Reilly. He remained for six months. He was followed by Father Richard Seifferly who also served for only six months. Father Robert Davey succeeded Father Seifferly. Saint Augustine was his first assignment as pastor. He was the Superintendent of Catholic Central High School in Alpena, living at Saint Bernard Church during the week and offering Mass on weekends at Hillman. He began an Ushers Club and worked extensively with the young people of the parish. Father Davey served until 1971.

Father Arthur Mulka became the pastor of Saint Augustine Parish during July, 1971. Quiet and reserved, he remained for one year. He was known for riding his bicycle and evangelizing activity as well as spending time with the kids on the playground.

Father Mulka's successor was Father Ben Marciulionis, arriving in August of 1972. He was one of the displaced persons in Europe following World War II. He and his older brother escaped when the rest of his family was killed by the Communists. Under Father Marciulionis' administration the James Cronk property next to the church was put up for sale. Prior to this time, the pastors lived in the rectory on Third Street in the village of Hillman, no short distance from the church. Father Ben proposed that the parish purchase the Cronk home and adjacent property since it was located next to the church. Alas, this was not an easy proposition. The parish was torn into factions that either supported the proposal or were not in favor of it. A vote was held and the property was purchased. One of the casualties of the situation was the health of Father Ben. His health began to deteriorate from that time on. He left the parish in July of 1977.

His successor was Monsignor Victor Gallagher. He, too, was of ill health and remained one year. He continued to make the liturgical changes following Vatican Council II. He was followed by Father Robert Nalley. Father Nalley remained at Hillman for five years. He also served on the Diocesan Tribunal which took him to Gaylord several days each week. He was interested in ecumenical issues and joined with area Christian churches for special services throughout the year. He worked for a strong family-oriented religious education program. Under his administration major renovations of the church took place such as new entrances, the former entrance became a beautiful chapel, the stained glass windows were removed and replaced with energy saving windows. There was also a debt of $82,000.

Father Raymond Pilarski succeeded Father Nalley in August 1983. An immediate need was a new roof for the rectory. With a donation, the roof was replaced in time for the first snow fall. Repairs were made to the parish hall by Stanley Wojciechowski, John Stamm and Father Pilarski. The rectory also required attention. The rooms in the basement were reconstructed during the winter of 1984.

In June of 1984, the parish pastoral and finance councils developed a master plan for the next ten years. The plan included landscaping of the parish grounds, building a religious education center, replacing the rectory windows, insulating and installing new siding on the rectory, building a new garage to house the parish equipment, painting the interior of the church, installing new lighting in the church, sandblasting the exterior of the church, refinishing the exterior of the church and resurfacing the church parking lot. Father Pilarski presented the plan to the parish asking for the cooperation of all of the parishioners. During the following years, each of the goals of the master plan were completed and then some other projects, too. One of the hardest and most active volunteers for those projects was Father Raymond Pilarski.

Father Pilarski once said that the Knights of Columbus were always second in his heart next to the parish. He certainly showed that at Alpena and also at Hillman. The council was started in 1982, prior to his arrival as pastor of Saint Augustine Parish. The Knights of Columbus of Hillman are very active in the community of Hillman and their parish. Father Pilarski, of course, is their council chaplain. Father Pilarski was also chosen to be the State Knights of Columbus Chaplain for the year 1986 and 1987. ■

Saint Bernard, *Alpena*

By Sylvia L. Owens, Pastoral Minister

In 1861, Bishop Frederic Baraga trod through snow and icy waters from Sault Ste Marie to Alpena where he founded a Catholic Church. However, it was not until 1866 that Father Patrick Murray became the first resident pastor of the church dedicated to and named for Saint Bernard.

Father Murray was instrumental in the building of the first church structure, which was located almost directly opposite the current edifice. The foundation of the stone structure was laid in 1880. Three years later the church split into three parishes. The French parish, which kept the original structure, became Saint Anne; the Polish became Saint Mary; and the Irish retained the Saint Bernard name and records. This structure, completed by the Irish in 1884, houses the oldest Catholic parish between Bay City and Cheboygan.

Inside Saint Bernard Church.

It is hard to imagine what this lumbering settlement was like in its early years. It had changed its name from Fremont a short time before and seemed to exist in a no man's land between the Dioceses of Marquette and Detroit on the north Huron shore. Streets were made of sawdust, drinking water came from barrels filled at the lake, wash water in winter came from melted snow, and the most common form of entertainment was enjoyed at the abundance of saloons in the community.

In 1870, Saint Bernard School began with 100 pupils, taught by lay teachers. In 1876 there were 250 pupils and three Sisters of Charity came from Cincinnati, Ohio, to run the school. (This order kept the school supplied with teachers for 65 years, to 1939.) Then it was staffed by members of the Dominican Order based in Adrian, Michigan, until closing of the parish school in 1974.

Father Patrick Murray, who had acquired the church, school, rectory and Catholic cemetery, left in 1871. The next pastor was Father William Taaken, a stern and determined Hollander, followed by Father VanGennip who so concentrated his efforts on strengthening the spiritual life of his people that they called him "the Saint."

Short pastorates followed with Father E.M. Dekiere, Father Francis X. Shulak, and Father Thomas Muer. Then came young Father Robert Doman of Bay City, newly ordained. He performed his first baptism here July 14, 1878, and launched the construction of the church. The issue of the *Alpena Argus* of September 29, 1880, reported that "the foundations are being laid for the erection of a new Saint Bernard Church."

On November 22, 1883, the Right Reverend Monsignor Thomas Dowd Flannery arrived as pastor and remained firmly in charge until the day of his death, January 4, 1921 — a regime of more than 37 years. This physically and spiritually powerful native of County Sligo, Ireland, spent his youth through Ireland's troubled years and arrived in the United States in 1873 at the age of 21. One of his jobs was to divide the families of Saint Bernard into three parishes. He was to lead the English-speaking families, predominately of Irish extraction. He was admirably fitted for this task by his personality, his physical presence, and his love of the "old sod" that gave him birth. It's a fair bet that Alpena's attention to Saint Patrick's Day each March 17 is traceable to him.

Alpena's division into three parishes left Saint Bernard with a greatly reduced number of parish members, but there was consistent progress under Father Flannery's leadership. The new church was completed in 1884. In 1890, the 3,000-pound bell was blessed. Its inscription card reads, "My name is Bernard Joseph. I will call the members of Saint Bernards to praise God, I will arouse the slothful and I will bewail the dead." In 1891, Father Flannery laid the cornerstone of a three-story school building, which functioned until 1963 when a new school was completed.

A view of Saint Bernard Church in the 1920s.

The nuns of Saint Bernard shown at the old lighthouse in1912.

In 1902, a rectory was begun and in 1904, foundations were laid for a new Saint Bernard convent. October 4, 1916 was the date of solemn consecration of Saint Bernard Church and its main altar by Most Reverend M. J. Gallagher, coadjutor Bishop of the Diocese of Grand Rapids.

The parish's beloved pastor, Monsignor Flannery, died January 4, 1921, at age 68 and was laid to rest in Alpena's Holy Cross Cemetery. He wished "to be buried among my people, those with whom I've spent my life — the best people on earth, barring none."

Following the passing of Monsignor Flannery, there were several priests who served at Saint Bernard and left the mark of their personality and faith with the people. Father Ignatius O'Brien, who served from 1961 to 1977, gained the reputation of being "on the cutting edge."

A new school was completed in 1963 and he himself worked on a team that built a new baptismal font in 1968. He sent youth to retreats in Saginaw, counseled Viet Nam conscientious objectors, housed homeless in the church basement, and encouraged charismatic responses among the faithful to cursillos and Life in the Spirit seminars.

Another pastor who had lasting impact was Father G. William Fischer who served from 1985 to 1991. Father Fischer's work in the church and community continue on in the spiritual richness of several small faith groups which he established and in "The Friendship Room," a soup kitchen at the parish center which serves meals five days a week to the needy of the community. Its pantry provides food bags for family needs. This project has expanded to include the whole community as volunteers and donors.

Father Joseph Graff, who took over in 1992, holding the dual role of Ecumenical officer for the diocese. He

works in the convening process with the Lutheran and Episcopal Churches and has been instrumental as Vicar in calling together the four Catholic parishes into a relationship of cooperation and unity. He was a driving force and catalyst in pulling area helping agencies together to begin "Call Us for Help," a triage agency of referral and appeal to assist those in emergency situations. In August, 1998, Father Graff moved to full-time pastor at Saint Anne, Alpena, and Father Patrick Bascio, C.S.Sp., was appointed pastor at Saint Barnard

Over the years Alpena changed from a lumbering town into a community with large factories and businesses. Saint Bernard has seen many changes also. We have had 19 pastors, 11 bishops and have been a part of four dioceses. We have decorated, redecorated, added to and torn down.

Good things have happened and mistakes were made but we have learned and grown from all of these experiences. Our forefathers left us many traditions; among them to pray, worship and praise God daily, to study and learn God's word, and to cherish our membership in the community of Alpena, the Catholic Church, and Saint Bernard Parish.

We can be certain that the future, also, will bring many changes. May our descendants still find value in the traditions that were passed on to us, and may Saint Bernard Church continue to play an intricate part in their lives and in the community of Alpena. ■

Saint Casimir, *Posen*

By Father Gerald F. Micketti

The Poles came to Presque Isle County to farm. They had heard about land available in the State of Michigan. Some of them lived in Detroit for a time; some came directly to Presque Isle County. The ports of entry were either Rogers City or Alpena. After arrival in Rogers City or Alpena, they most likely walked to the sites of their future farms in what became known as Posen.

The Poles were Catholic. They gloried in their faith. It wasn't long before they wanted a priest and the sacraments. In the early 1870s, after the immigrants arrived, the people would have their children baptized in Alpena. The first priest to visit the Posen area was Father Francis Xavier Szulak (pronounced Shulak), S.J. He was sent by Bishop Borgess of Detroit, and he came in 1874. He made only two visits in 1874. He celebrated the Mass in the home of Valentine Losinski during his first visit. On his second visit he said Mass in the home of Lawrence Kowalski. Father Szulak visited more often in the years 1876 and 1877.

Under the leadership of Father Szulak, a meeting of all the settlers was held and, after considerable debate, the present church site was agreed upon. The most important reason for this location was that it seemed the highest point in the township. Forty acres of land was donated by Frederick Denny Larke on January 15, 1874. Either the same year or 1875 a log church was built.

In the 1870s there were only two dioceses in Michigan — Detroit and Marquette. The Diocese of Grand Rapids was established in 1882. All of the lower peninsula of Michigan was in the Diocese of Detroit. Bishop Borgess of Detroit assigned Father Anthony Bogacki as the first pastor of the congregation in 1878. When the name for the parish was chosen is not known; the presumption, is that the Poles chose an honored Polish saint — Saint Casimir.

After his arrival, Father Bogacki built a log cabin for his residence and called it a "kitchen." This kitchen later was used for school purposes and still later for a residence of the sisters. Another pastor's residence was built in 1882, at a cost of $3,000; this residence was made of brick. The log church burned down January 28, 1883. A temporary frame building was constructed the same year.

Not in the least discouraged by the misfortune of 1883, the parishioners began to make preparations for a new brick church. When this building was completed is uncertain. Father Bogacki kept an account book of the finances during his years as pastor. The account seems to indicate that the brick veneer church was built in the early 1890s. Disaster struck this church. It burned to the ground on March 4, 1895. That same year a frame building was constructed which served the congregation until the present church building was constructed in 1971.

A school was never far from the thoughts of Father Bogacki. After his residence was built in 1882, the "kitchen" became a school. In his account book, Father Bogacki noted that a full-time lay teacher was employed and in September 1886, the school was opened. About 1890, the pastor put up, at his own expense, a frame school building. To this frame building a brick veneer structure was added in 1901. In 1895 the Felician Sisters came to Posen and took charge of the parish school. When they arrived, they lived in the log house — the first rectory.

In September 1896, Father Bogacki was transferred to Saint Stanislaus Parish, Bay City, and Father Joseph Lewandowski was in temporary charge of the parish until April of 1897, when Father Bogacki returned to Posen. Father Bogacki remained two days. From April 1897, to January 1, 1889, Saint Casimir had no pastor.

Father M. Matkowski was appointed pastor and served for one year. Father Joseph Lewandowski returned to the parish to serve the people of Posen for fifteen years. In 1901, during his regime, the brick veneer school building was constructed, adding seven classrooms to Father Bogacki's original school. Enrollment in the school increased. Boarding facilities were made available in 1904 because the priests and parents as well insisted on a Catholic education for their children. Most of the children lived on farms and were needed to work on the farms. Also, travel between the school and the farms was no short distance. Children ate meals, slept and shared chores during the week and spent only weekends at home. These arrangements continued also in the new school building until 1948 when buses provided transportation daily.

In January 1914, Father Lewandowski was transferred to Ludington. His successor was Father Chodkiewicz who came from Metz. He remained in Posen until May 1915. He was succeeded by Father Joseph Koss who served until 1933. A controversial and forceful pastor, Father Koss was responsible for the improvement and expansion of the parish and school. The problem was that not all agreed with his methods and philosophy of education. He planted the seeds of higher education that were reaped by the parish and his successor. During the tenure of Father Koss, the Felician Sisters relinquished the school and the Sisters of Mercy came to Posen to teach in the school. The curriculum was reorganized to suit the requirements of the day; new conveniences were installed in the parish buildings; the grounds were landscaped; a new convent was built; and cement sidewalks were built.

Under Father Koss, improvements were also made to the parish cemetery. The original location of the parish cemetery was one mile north of the present church property. According to Ann Mulka only two bodies were buried at the first cemetery site and that was with difficulty because the ground was too hard. The cemetery was relocated on the church property. Those two bodies were transferred to the present cemetery. When Father Koss left in 1931, there was $21,000 in the building fund.

The seeds planted by Father Koss were harvested by his successor, Father Kwasigroch, who came to Posen in 1931. Under this pastor the ninth grade was added to the school in 1932. The Posen Unit School Board leased two classrooms from Saint Casimir Parish and hired the nuns to teach the now expanded (the tenth grade was added in 1933) two years of high school. Students who wanted to continue in high school had to travel to Alpena to graduate.

Father Kwasigroch's stay was short; he left in 1935. His successor was Father Casimir Szyper. Under Father Szyper even more seeds of Father Koss's ideas were harvested. The high school expanded to four years and a new building in 1939. The first graduating class was June 9, 1941. *The Alpena News* carried a picture and news story about the first graduating class of Posen High School which was mistakenly captioned "Saint Casimir's High School." This incident caused some discord in the community or rather refueled the discord from the Father Koss era. This discord led to the formation of the Posen Consolidated School District #9 in 1955.

Father Szyper was a firm believer in the importance of religious education. He personally taught religion to children every day in the school. He visited the high school students before 9:00 a.m. and the elementary students at 11:00 a.m. Not only was a new school built while he was pastor, a new convent was also constructed. He was and is considered by the people who remember Father Szyper a scholar, teacher, builder and a saintly man of God.

In June of 1953, Father Stephen Kozak was installed as pastor succeeding Father Szyper. With Father Kozak, changes again became evident. The fifty-year-old school used as a high school was judged a safety hazard and the burden of financing both schools forced the parishioners to seek state aid for the high schools. In 1954 the last two nuns were released from teaching in the high school and the high school became a public school. The Posen Consolidated School District #9 was formed to build a new high school away from the church property. The old school building was demolished in 1957. Enrollment in the elementary grades continued to increase. A seventh grade was added and the acute shortage of sisters necessitated the hiring of three lay teachers.

The parish grounds received a new look in 1958. The men of the parish provided the labor for a spacious parking lot; cyclone fencing replaced the stone wall along Highway M-65; and a playground facility was added to the parish compound. A new rectory was built in 1960. Father Kozak continued making improvements in the parish cemetery.

Father Kozak was succeeded in January 1968, by a son of the parish, Father Clarence Smolinski, who had attended Posen High School in 1941-43. To him fell the task of building a new house of worship. The modern $450,000 church was constructed in 1971 with the first Mass celebrated at Christmas of that year. In tribute to the sincerity and hard work of Father Smolinski, the parishioners banded together to completely pay off the new church debt in two years.

Father Raymond Mulka followed Father Smolinski in 1980. Father Mulka was succeeded by Father Gerald Micketti in 1989. Father Stan Bereda, the present pastor, came to Posen in 1992. ■

Saint Catherine of Alexandria,

Ossineke (Nicholson Hill)

By Father Gerald F. Micketti

In Mikado, Black River, Harrisville and Oscoda, churches were established near large lumber operations. In these areas lumber barons often donated land for churches as well as financial support. They encouraged their employees to bring their families. The above mentioned churches were established before 1895.

After the large lumbering companies left, families purchased the cut over land. Former lumberjacks and loggers settled on farms with their families. Saint Catherine of Alexandria Parish at Ossineke was established in the midst of this farming territory after the turn of the century. Various small communities were represented in the congregation: South Ossineke, Spruce, Indian Reserve, Hubbard Lake Corners and Nicholson Hill.

In the decade prior to 1904, Father Godfrey Lenzen, formerly pastor of the Saint Joseph Parish at Klacking Creek, tended to the souls in the Nicholson Hill area. He lived in Alpena and traveled by horse and buggy as well as by bicycle over 15 rough miles. He offered Mass in the Tolson and the Saint Charles Schools. He had originally chosen a site for a church in Spruce. After consideration, the present site was chosen at the crest of Nicholson Hill. Five acres of land were donated by Lazaire Saint Charles. The hill received its name from one of the early lumbering companies in the area.

Father Joseph L. Poulin was given charge of the Nicholson Hill area as a mission of Saint Anne in Harrisville. The first church in the Nicholson Hill area was built in 1904. Thirty-eight families celebrated Mass on Christmas of the same year. The first child baptized in the church was Russell Louis LaLonde.

Father Louis Bouchard succeeded Father Poulin in 1905 as pastor of Saint Anne in Harrisville with Saint Catherine of Nicholson Hill as one of its missions. Father J. Arthur Houle followed Father Bouchard in 1913. After Father Houle died in 1919, Father Anthony Schumacher was the parish administrator for a very short time. While he was there, the rectory was built. Father Frederick W. Ryan came in 1919 and stayed until 1925. He was succeeded by Father Delehanty who stayed until 1934.

The first resident pastor of Saint Catherine Parish was installed in 1934. He was Father J.A. Moleski. He also took care of Saint Gabriel Church, the mission at Black River. Father Moleski was pastor for 18 months. Father Earl Denay followed him for one year. Father George Lavallee came in December of 1937 from Saint Mary of Manistee. He served longer than any other priest at Saint Catherine Parish.

He retired because of poor health in August 1953. Father Theodore LaMarre became the pastor and remained at Saint Catherine until October 1955. While he was pastor, the Saint Charles School was purchased and converted into a parish hall.

Father Robert Pelletier succeeded Father LaMarre. During the tenure of Father Pelletier a new church building was constructed. In the spring of 1956, architects were engaged and by fall of the year preliminary plans were approved. Final approval of the plans and authorization to submit the plans for bidding by the contractors was given in April of 1957. Bids for the new church were opened and accepted on May 21. The next day the ground was broken and construction began.

In December of 1957, bids were accepted for the purchase of the old church building. The last Mass in the old church was offered February 15, 1958. The old church was razed and the bell was placed in the new church. The new church was dedicated July 6, 1958, by Bishop Stephen S. Woznicki.

Father Julius Spleet, an Alpena native, was appointed pastor of Saint Catherine in June of 1967. He was installed as pastor by the dean of the Alpena Vicariate, Father Robert Pelletier. Father Spleet liked to work with the young people of the parish. Three years later Father Spleet was succeeded by Father Richard Seifferly. He carried on the youth activities started by Father Spleet. He also liked to hunt.

Father Seifferly served for five years. He was followed by Father Herman Kolenda, who served for two years when he transferred to Manistee. Father John Adomaitis followed Father Kolenda in 1977. Father John was born in Lithuania and immigrated to the United States in 1950. Due to poor health Father Adomaitis retired in 1988. He was succeeded by Father Gabriel Fox. Father Fox served until 1995 when Father Lawrence Kelleher became the pastor of Saint Catherine Parish. Father Kelleher brings a unique perspective into his pastorate. He was married for about 40 years. After his wife died, he decided God was calling him to be a priest. So he applied to Holy Apostles Seminary in Connecticut and was accepted. He was ordained for the Diocese of Gaylord in 1993. Now he is a father, grandfather and pastor. ■

Saint Clement, *Pellston*

By Father Gerald F. Micketti

Though we celebrated the dedication of the parish church of Saint Clement in 1985, the records of the parish began in 1901. Mass was celebrated in various homes prior to the construction of the church building. Before the present church was built, an attempt was made to build a church in Brutus. This came to an abrupt end when the walls collapsed in a wind storm.

Saint Clement Church.

On the 10th of February, 1908, four lots were donated by Colonel Bogardus of Pellston for church and school purposes. The deed was accepted by Bishop Henry J. Richter of Grand Rapids.

Work on the church commenced in May of the same year, after Bishop Richter and Cyprian Banscheid, O.F.M., Provincial, granted permission. Mr. N.J. Johnson was awarded the contract for the brick and George Lattimer was the carpenter. By the fall of the same year the church was under roof, but the work was discontinued for the winter due to lack of funds. Construction started again the following summer after receiving a gift of $250 from the Catholic Church Extension Society. Regular Sunday services started October 10, 1909. Twenty-four children and four converts, as well as a number of adults, attended the catechism instruction in the afternoon. The first three children baptized in the new church were Frederic, Mary and Margaret Slavin that same day.

The year 1910 saw more additions to and the dedication of the church. The belfry and steeple were completed by Charles Glenn and Joseph Zuber of Harbor Springs. New seats and the altar were installed. The church was wired for electricity and light fixtures installed through the kindness of Colonel Bogardus and the Pellston Electric Light and Power Company. The date of dedication was July 4, 1910. The church was blessed by Bishop Richter and named in honor of Saint Clement, Pope and martyr.

Saint Clements' Quonset Hut.

In the years following, the church building received more attention. The church also received much attention from its parish missions.

One way to raise funds for a parish is to have a Feather Party. In 1947, Saint Clement parish held a Feather Party. Fifteen live chickens were donated and then raffled off. The revenues were used to defray the cost of the sidewalk in front of the church.

How many churches have a Quonset hut? Father Cassian Nothbauer initiated efforts to secure a Quonset hut for the parish in 1950. The hut was used for catechism classes, dances, bingo, community services, the annual chicken dinner and other social events.

The church continues to be served by the O.F.M.'s in the person of Father Sylvester Micek. ■

Saint Dominic, *Metz*

By Father Gerald F. Micketti

The first residents of Metz and surrounding area arrived in 1873. Some of the first pioneers were John Nowicki, Andrew Burzych and Valentine Sytek followed by Frank Makowski and Nicholas Centala. Many of these first families were Catholic and would walk five to twelve mile to get to church at Posen.

Father Lenzen became interested in forming a parish at Metz in 1897. At that time Father Godfrey Lenzen from Alpena was doing mission work in the neighboring communities of Hillman, Indian Reserve, Posen, Rogers City and occasionally visiting Metz. He began to exchange letters with Mr. Watson Centala, who helped promote the idea in the Metz area, and with Bishop Henry J. Richter of Grand Rapids. At one point, there was a strong suggestion that the people of the Metz area attend Saint Casimir Church because the residents were of Polish descent and emigration. In 1898, the bishop granted permission to establish a parish at Metz.

December 8, 1898, Father Godfrey Lenzen offered his first Mass at the Nicholas Centala home. From that time on, the people had the opportunity to attend Mass from time to time. Donations were raised to erect a church building. The first church location was on land owned by Metz Township. The Township deeded over the land and a church was built in 1901. Bishop Richter wanted a church-school combination. The residents of Metz thought otherwise. A frame church was erected without a school. After a long wait the bishop accepted the property and blessed the church. Everyone turned

out for the occasion. The farm horses were groomed. A cavalcade was organized and this formidable array went to the station to welcome the bishop to Metz.

The story of the naming of the church at Metz may be apocryphal. There was some disagreement about what the name should be. Some people wanted to name the church after a particular saint; others wanted another name. As the story goes, Bishop Richter asked if anybody suggested the name "Dominic." No one had. The bishop said that will be its name — Saint Dominic.

In the same year of the church construction and dedication, Father Lenzen was transferred and Father Lewandowski of Saint Casimir administered Saint Dominic church until July 17. Then Bishop Richter sent Father Ladislaus Krakowski. He was followed in September by Father Stephen Banasiewicz who stayed until 1906. While he was pastor, a rectory was built behind the church. In June of 1906, Father Francis Kaczmarek was appointed the first pastor of Saint Dominic Church. He remained for two years; he also celebrated Mass in Rogers City during his stay in Metz.

The successor of Father Kaczmarek was Father Jan (John) Kaplanowski. While he was pastor, Metz was destroyed by a forest fire — the Metz fire of October 15, 1908. It was a tragic day! The fire started somewhere west of Metz and swept through part of Presque Isle County, cutting a path from around Millersburg to Lake Huron. The villages of Metz and South Rogers were destroyed. About 1,500 people were left homeless and 25 people were killed. Two of the worst incidents involved parish members: John Konieczny lost his wife and three children, and Saint Peter German Lutheran Church was destroyed. Through all of the fire and smoke, Saint Dominic Church and rectory were saved. After the fire, Pastor Thieme and Father Kaplanowski helped with the distribution of aid for those families left homeless and deprived by the fire.

In September 1909, Father Kaplanowski left and was replaced by Father Francis Piaskowski. While he was pastor, a two-classroom school was built and he was one of the teachers. Three years later, Father Chodkiewicz succeeded Father Piaskowski. Father Chodkiewicz was followed by Father Joseph Koss in 1914 and served for 18 months. His successor was Father James Czachorski. While he was pastor, he brought in three Sisters of Mercy to teach in the school. He was replaced in 1916 by Father Casimir T. Skowronski, who moved to Rogers City in 1919 to become the first pastor of Saint Ignatius Parish. Father Paul Felchnerowski followed Father Skowronski. He left in 1921 to be succeeded by Father Casimir Szyper.

Since its inception, Saint Dominic Parish had been used as a stepping stone for the young priests of the Diocese of Grand Rapids. It was in the year, 1925, that the parish came unto its own. Father Edward Szturmowski, Father Storm as he was addressed, led the congregation until 1939. He was an able speaker in English and Polish and was often asked by his friends to preach their services. Father Szturmowski was known for one thing; he loved to hear confessions. He would spend hours listening to confessions.

The year following Father Szturmowski's arrival, the rectory burned to the ground. At first he lived in the school; later he lived at the John Witulski home in Metz village. He endured many hardships, such as walking almost three miles to the church in all kinds of weather.

Father Szturmowski also began meeting with people for the purpose of moving the church to the village. The first site of Saint Dominic Church was on Centala Road, across from the Watson Centala farm, about three miles from the village. This was for him a great undertaking, since it was during the Great Depression and the farmers were getting so little for their produce. He was, however, a man of great determination.

Another struggle was with Bishop Pinten. After repeated trips to Grand Rapids, his patience and persistence were the winners. The pastor was given permission and the parish was urged to abandon the old site and build in the village.

Father Szturmowski kept a diary of the construction which began in earnest in March of 1930. The architect and contractor was Joseph Snow of Grand Rapids. The cost was about $18,000 and much of the work on the new rectory and new church was done by members of the parish and even by people who were not members of the parish. On September 7, Father Szturmowski moved into the new rectory. Work then began on the construction of Saint Dominic Church. On Thanksgiving Day of 1931 the new church was dedicated. The old church building was moved onto the premises and now serves as the parish hall. The old school building was also moved to the new church property and became a storage building. The school had been closed due to financial problems during the years of Father Paul Felchnerowski.

Father Szturmowski left in January of 1939; he was succeeded by Father Joseph Gorski. He made improvements on the grounds along with installing pews, pipe organ, stained glass windows, burning the mortgage. Father Gorski left in 1946. He was followed by Father Stanislaus Fron. With Father Fron, Saint Dominic Parish celebrated 50 years of worshiping as a community.

Father Fron was succeeded by Father Zygmunt Gaj in 1958; Father Bruno Kaczmarczyk in 1960; Father George Klimas in 1963; Father Lawrence Boks in 1970. Under Father Boks, the first parish council was formed and the old cemetery on Centala Road was spruced up.

In 1971, the Diocese of Gaylord was formed. Father James Brucksch succeeded Father Boks in 1973. The following year, Father Brucksch left and was replaced by Father Walter Derylo as the administrator while waiting his assignment to Samoa to do missionary work. After he left, Father Herman Kolenda became the pastor. He left the next year and Father Jan Baksik followed.

Father Baksik was ordained at Saint Ignatius Church. He was 66 at the time of his ordination, widowed and father of two grown children. He died in December of 1975. After his death, Father John Rushman, pastor of Saint Ignatius, Rogers City, became the temporary administrator of Saint Dominic. In 1976, Father Clarence Smolinski took over the administrative responsibilities of Saint Dominic from Father Rushman. He and his associate, Father Richard Sitar, took turns covering the Metz Parish. During this time, the church was completely remodeled for a cost of $140,000. The newly remodeled church was dedicated July 29, 1979, by Bishop Szoka.

When Father Smolinski was transferred in July of 1980, Father Martin Toolis came to Saint Dominic Church as the administrator. Father Raymond Mulka became the pastor of Saint Casimir Church, Posen. Father Mulka became the temporary administrator when Father Toolis left in 1981. Father Anthony Machcinski was assigned as administrator following Father Toolis. When Father Machcinski left in 1982, Father Mulka again assumed the role of administrator until his retirement in 1989. He was followed by Father Gerald Micketti who served until 1992. He was succeeded by Father Stanislaw Bereda, with Father Clarence Smolinski and Raymond Mulka helping at Saint Dominic on the weekends.

Bishop Robert Rose directed his staff to do extensive study on the role of the pastoral administrator whereby religious, lay persons or deacons, do the full administration of parishes and then priests are assigned to come in as sacramental ministers. Among those first appointments of pastoral administrators was Sister Anne Maslanka, S.S.J. T.O.S.F., who was the first pastoral administrator of Saint Dominic Parish. On September 3, 1993, Sister Rita Epple, R.S.M., became the second pastoral administrator and continues to serve in that capacity. ■

Saint Francis Solanus, *Bay Shore*
Saint Francis Xavier, *Petoskey*

From St. Francis Xavier Parish records

The first Catholic Church built in Petoskey was in 1848 or 1850 under the patronage of the famed Indian missionary, Saint Francis Solanus. Bishop Baraga, first bishop of Marquette, blessed the edifice and celebrated the liturgy in it. The church still stands on the shores of Little Traverse Bay, Lake Michigan. From its patron saint, it is obvious it was meant for the native Americans of this area. It served, however, also as a place of worship for the first non-Indian settlers. From it they received the light of faith. The church stands now as a monument to the intrepid faith of the first missionaries. The nostalgia of our past drifts over the land. It is a wholesome thought and a holy movement. Saint Francis Solanus, a parish church at Bay Shore, is served by Saint Francis Xavier, Petoskey. At the original Saint Francis Solanus Church, the priests of Petoskey celebrate Mass once a year on the feast of Saint Francis Solanus, July 14.

Saint Francis Xavier began its independent life three decades later. In 1877, ten Catholic families lived in Petoskey. The next year the number of families grew sufficiently large enough to warrant organizing a parish church apart from Saint Francis Solanus. In 1879, the Catholics of Petoskey translated their hopes into a visible reality. They established Saint Francis Xavier and built the first structure in 1879 under the supervision of Father Zorn of Harbor Springs. Father Zorn made it a practice to come to Petoskey once a month to serve the needs of the Catholics. Saint Francis Xavier was built on the corner of Howard and State Streets, the location of the present church. The lots were

purchased for $200. By 1881, the first church became inadequate and was replaced by a second church. The number of families had increased to an estimated 20 or 25. For an additional $100 another lot was purchased. As in the case of the first structure, so also in the second building, the parishioners provided both the material and the labor. Family names, still recognized today, appear on the work list of 1881. They are such names as John Wachtel, Casper Wegemer, Frank Wegemer, Adolph Fochtman, W.L. McManus, Aaron Kopp, Martin Feile, John Coveyou, Henry Fochtman, Gerhard Fochtman, Donatus Fettig, George Trautman, John Foerester, John Hofmann, F.X. Schultenhofer, Peter Meister and T.A. Bremmeyr. In that same year, 1881, Father Gustav Graf was appointed first pastor. Since the parish had no rectory, he lived with parishioners. The building of the rectory began in 1882. On July 25, 1886, Henry J. Richter, Bishop of Grand Rapids dedicated the church.

Laying of the cornerstone for present Church in Petoskey in 1903.

The early Catholics valued their faith and spared no cost or effort to have their children in a Catholic school. As early as 1883 Saint Francis Xavier opened a school with one classroom. It was situated in the rectory. The first teacher was Phillip Schmidt, who was assisted by Bessie Dunnigan. He continued in that capacity until 1890. In that year the Franciscan Sisters of Christian Charity from Manitowoc, Wisconsin, took over teaching in the school. Beginning with three sisters in a two-room classroom, the school grew to 16 classrooms in a grade school and a completely equipped high school. Over 300 Franciscan Sisters have taught at Saint Francis during their more than 100 years of service.

In the annals of the rectory there is a reference to a school being built in 1885. History is unclear in the matter. Seemingly, the parishioners built this first bona-fide school building facing Howard Street. In 1902 when it was moved into the present school yard, it faced Michigan Street. It was used until 1927, when it was replaced by the present grade school. It had nine classrooms. This is the older portion of the present building. A high school curriculum was added with the first class in 1941. The present new building was erected in 1954. An addition to the nine room grade school was built in 1963. Unfortunately, due to mounting costs, the high school closed its doors in 1971.

The year 1980, however, was a year when expansion again touched the community. Saint Francis Xavier had a kindergarten for the first time in its history. The school housed the Title I Programs, the Charlevoix-Emmet Intermediate School District classes and the Montessori School.

In conjunction with the coming of the Franciscan Sisters from Manitowoc, it is interesting to note that scarcity of sisters was not a new phenomenon. In 1889 the parish tried to obtain the services of the Notre Dame Sisters from Milwaukee. They considered the request impossible, not through lack of interest or dedication, but through their inability to free up any sisters. The Benedictine Sisters of Elk County, Pennsylvania, also found it impossible, not because of any reluctance on their part, but due to the resistance of their bishop. "This may be the holy will of God," they replied. "May it be done. Sometime, when our holy bishop goes on a trip to heaven, it may perhaps be possible for us to go to a mission outside of this area."

The Franciscan Sisters from Manitowoc have served well. Former students speak highly of the education they received at their feet. A few remember difficulties encountered and differences experienced. Teaching methods in an earlier day differed not only in Catholic schools under the sisters, but in all segments of education. Discipline in former days took a much harsher course than it does today. What has not changed is the lofty place of faith in the schools under Catholic auspices and in the presence of the Lord. In a Catholic school, that important presence can be explicitly articulated and encouraged. Saint Francis makes a difference. It is a faith-nourishing difference. It supports not only the child but the family as well, the parents, brothers and sisters.

The first pastor of Saint Francis Xavier was Father Gustav Graf in 1881. In 1884 the Franciscans of the Sacred Heart Province at Saint Louis, Missouri took charge of Saint Francis Xavier at the request of Bishop Richter of Grand Rapids. Petoskey was then in the Grand Rapids Diocese. Bishop Richter called upon the Franciscans to take over the Ottawa Indian missions in the northern lower peninsula including Harbor Springs and Petoskey. The pastor of Petoskey, however, lived in Harbor Springs and served Saint Francis Xavier as a mission. That arrangement continued until 1897 when Saint Francis Xavier was chosen as the Franciscan center. The Franciscans served missions henceforth out of Petoskey. This remains true today with stations at Bay Shore, Pellston and Cross Village, though the latter two are independent parishes.

In 1902, the parish of Saint Francis Xavier chose to build a new church to replace the second frame building on the corner of Howard and State Streets. Since the parish elected to build on the same spot, it moved both the church building and the priests' residence to Michigan Street. Two years later, in 1904, the convent and school were also moved to the back of the old church. The combined buildings were used as classrooms and a community hall until 1927. At that time all the buildings were torn down to make room for the new school. One of the classrooms in the old building held as many as 50 students.

As a note of historical significance it is revealing that the church of Saint Francis Xavier in 1902, when the new church was begun, counted only 200 families. They were an ambitious parish family. The farmers brought the building materials themselves. They were stone (hardheads) cut at home, timber, sand and gravel — all donated. Donated work included 504 days of labor, 451 days with teams, 87,000 feet of lumber, 112,000 feet of logs, 102 cords of stone, 1,000 loads of gravel, 2,000 loads of sand and all the posts for the scaffolding.

Quoting from the 1971 history of Saint Francis Xavier, Father Adolph Thillman, O.F.M., had the following to report: "In the excavation, dug by horse and scraped by the men of the parish, builders began laying the footings on April 6, 1903. Unlike the steel-reinforced solid concrete of today's technology, the footings of our church consist of large boulders placed in a trench with concrete poured around them. The stone basement walls measure about three feet thick. The dimensions of the church are: 160 feet in length, 60 feet wide and 84 feet through the transept. The cornerstone of the new Saint Francis Xavier Church was laid on May 21, 1903. In our friary the following was written: 'The 25th anniversary birthday of the village of Petoskey, typified in the Saint Francis cornerstone laying was a glorious remembrance for the future. From the first words of the Pontifical High Mass in the morning, May 21, Thursday to the closing remarks of the chairman of the evening, James Buckley, the celebration of the cornerstone laying for the new Saint Francis Church was an unqualified success. Joseph Richter, Bishop of Grand Rapids, celebrated the Pontifical Mass.' "

Included in the construction of the church is the present day friary attached to the church building. The Franciscan Friars paid for its erection at the cost of $16,728. The church was built for $45,389.56. Not all the work and construction was done, however, in 1904. Much of the interior was done in later years, most of it in the years between 1904 and 1908. In 1909, the main altar, side altars, the confessionals and the communion rail were installed. The bells came in 1915 as well as the pipe organ.

Besides the names of Franciscan Brother Adrian, the architect of the church and friary, Brother Sebastian, who did much of the wood selecting, Brother Christopher, who repaired the steeple, parishioners who played a prominent role in the construction and repairs of the buildings are: Charles Trautman; Mike Kopp; Henry Mania; Joe Hegener; Joe Paulus; Andrew, Eugene, Louis and Fred Hoffman; Henry Dombrowski; Gerry Grosskopf; and Mac McCarthy. This does not include the many other faithful parishioners from the Holy Name who spent many devoted hours on the maintenance of our buildings. They still do. The society presently conducts bingo for the support of the same projects.

Among the more recent and important improvements was the erection of the ramp on the south side of the church. It was constructed in 1976. Its users were most grateful for the convenience it afforded them. Entering the church had become so much easier. It was also a great asset for funerals and it obviated the need to struggle with the extended steps at the Howard Street entrance to the church. It is interesting to note that the ramp in 1976 cost as much to build as the entire church in 1903.

Complementing the ramp for usefulness was the most recent construction on the north side of the church: in 1980, the obsolete and dangerous north side stairway was replaced by a basement entrance into the church. The stairway was always icy in the winter and treacherous in every season. The parish felt good about the choice it made in improving the facility.

There were other happenings of note. On July 20, 1972, the Holy Name Society promoted the installation of electronic carillons in memory of E.A. Bremmeyr. The bells were the gift to the church on the part of Elizabeth Bremmeyr, the relatives and friends of the family.

Following the construction of the ramp, the trustees of that time, under the su-

pervision of the pastor, Father Robert Behnen, chose to continue the Ramp Fund under the new title of the Building Improvement Fund. It has served the parish extraordinarily well in the solicitation of donations and memorials for the support of further improvements of the buildings.

For years the Altar Society sponsored the annual August Dinner. It became a tradition at Saint Francis Xavier for the parishioners, summer residents, tourists and visitors. The financial gift the Society offers the church is an annual blessing.

Saint Francis Xavier in the course of her history experienced the thrust and the stress of many tongues. As letters in our files attest to in November of 1917, "another change was made in order to meet the just wishes of the Polish members of the congregation. Father Lullus Seeboth was transferred to Cleveland, Ohio, and Father Ladislaus Czech was assigned to the church to minister to the wants of the Polish members." The next year Virgil Walkowski, O.F.M., was "appointed to look after the spiritual needs of the Poles and Slovenians at Petoskey." The rhythm of the interest is still visible to those who study the patterns of the saints in the statues in the church. The variety of nationalities appear clearly in the variety of the patron saints.

An early elementary class with Sister Geraldine in 1901.

To enrich the life of the church we are blessed at Petoskey and at Saint Francis with the presence of the Sacramentine Sisters, a cloistered community of women dedicated to prayer and adoration of the Lord in the Eucharist. They came to Petoskey July 1, 1960. They are living sources in our midst in intercession and in grace. We are very fortunate to have them with us.

Fortunate is the parish which affords itself an accomplished organist. For 26 years Mr. August Huybrechts enhanced our liturgies with a special character. The church in her documents often tells us that good liturgies build up faith whereas poor liturgies destroy it. Saint Francis Xavier is blessed. Its choir under Mr. Huybrechts' leadership was known far beyond the limits of Petoskey.

On November 9, 1969, the Franciscan Sisters of Christian Charity of Manitowoc, Wisconsin, celebrated their centennial as a congregation of religious women in the church. They take the seraphic saint, Francis of Assisi, as their patron. In their work as teachers at Saint Francis Xavier since 1890 they have been the life blood of faith for the students and parents of Saint Francis. They have 90 years of devoted service in teaching at Saint Francis Grade and High School. The faith has flourished at Saint Francis because the sisters have been religious women witnessing to their own faith for others.

Saint Francis Xavier Cemetery began with a purchase of the oldest section of our cemetery from a Margaret Ani-waw-be, alias Margaret Nevbi, of Bear Creek Township for the sum of $240. It was deeded to Bishop Joseph Richter of Grand Rapids July 2, 1886. The present-day football field was purchased from Ralph Schluttenhofer, executor of the estate of Albert Schluttenhofer, deeded July 7, 1953, to Bishop Francis Haas of Grand Rapids. November 12, 1958, the church purchased the Kellogg Estate, the present day softball field. The cost was $5,450. Finally the property adjacent to the original cemetery and the complex known as the athletic field, comprising both ballfields, was purchased October 22, 1963, from Roselle Coveyou Sevener and deeded to Bishop Allen J. Babcock of Grand Rapids, courtesy of Jerry Lesher.

The Franciscans served the parishes of Saint Francis Xavier and Saint Francis Solanus since 1884 but, as of the summer of 1998, the order will no longer be able to assign priests for this ministry. This will be a significant change for these parishes and for the diocese, which will now assume full responsibility for staffing these churches. ■

Saint Gabriel, *Black River*

By Father Gerald F. Micketti

Black River started as a small fishing station at the mouth of the Black River. A man by the name of William Cullins and French-Canadian trappers came to the area from AuSable. William Cullins observed what he saw at the mouth of Black River and liked what he saw. That was in 1849. The Black River area also had stands of beautiful virgin white pine. That, too, was attractive. In the early 1870s Alger Smith and Company had moved in with its big operation of lumbering. The company owned 50,000 acres of pineland with an estimated stand of six hundred million board feet of pine. The river was dredged; a dock was built as was a sawmill and that which went with a sawmill. The company then proceeded to harvest pine timber spars and masts.

Black River as a community also grew and had everything a community in that day required or was felt necessary to have. It is believed that the population increased to about 2,000 families. Many of these families were French-Canadian and Catholic. It followed that they would want to build a church in their community. That became a reality in 1894.

Prior to 1894, Black River was visited by Father Cornelius J. Roche of AuSable in 1883. He came twice a year to minister to the needs of the Catholics. The following year, Father P. Charles Alphonse Winter increased the number of visits to every second month. He offered Mass in the three-room school house and would visit the men in the lumber camps. Two years later he offered Mass on every fifth Sunday when there was five in a month and occasionally first Mass on the second Sunday of the month.

In 1889 Father Frederick H. Ruessmann, who had just been appointed first pastor of Harrisville, attended to the needs of the Catholics at Black River about every fifth Monday. Father Ruessmann was noted for his beautiful singing voice and also his interest in teaching catechism. There were about 90 people who attended Mass in Black River in 1890.

Father James E. Mahar succeeded Father Ruessmann in 1892 and visited Black River every three months. Father Julien Doucet served the Catholics in Black River from 1893 to 1895. During his tenure, the present church building was constructed as well as the church in Mikado. Under the direction of Father Doucet, with volunteer help from the parishioners and a donation of land, all the lumber needed from Alger Smith and Company, and under the leadership of Mr. Cousineau, a sturdy frame building was erected. The building, seating 150, was built on cedar blocks at a cost of $1,375.80. Father Doucet was a small, French-speaking man and was admired by the people of Black River who could converse with him in their own language.

In 1895 Father Joseph L.Poulin was appointed the first resident pastor of Saint Anne in Harrisville along with the missions of Mikado, Black River, and Nicholson Hill. He carried on the work started by Father Doucet. He finished the church at Mikado and made preparations for the dedication of Saint Gabriel Church, Black River, which took place in November 1895. Father Poulin served the ten years at Harrisville. During those years he witnessed 36 marriages, buried 12, baptized adults and children. Long distances and bad roads still limited his service to every third and fifth Sundays of the month.

Father Poulin was succeeded by Father Louis Bouchard in 1905. He was from Muskegon and was ordained by Bishop Richter of Grand Rapids. He was very energetic and owned a 1911 Buick which helped him get around to visit parishioners. Father Bouchard served until 1913 when he was followed by Father J. Arthur Houle. He was a hard working priest who served until his death in 1919. After Father Houle's death, Father Frederick Ryan came to Harrisville as pastor. Under Father Ryan, the cedar block foundation of the church was replaced with a cement foundation. Father Ryan used a Dodge roadster for his pastoral work. He served until July 1924. His successor was Father Joseph Delehanty. Father Delehanty was appointed pastor of Saint Anne in Harrisville and served there until 1937. He covered the mission of Saint Gabriel until 1934 when Saint Catherine Parish received its first resident pastor and the care of Saint Gabriel Church, Black River was transferred to Saint Catherine of Nicholson Hill. Father Delehanty was remembered as a very good speaker; his sermons were remembered for their eloquence and subject matter. He, too, drove a car to and from Black River.

Father J.A. Moleski was the first resident pastor of Saint Catherine. He arrived from

Manistee and took charge November 1934 and left October 1936. He served the Catholics of Nicholson Hill, Black River and Lincoln. He was succeeded by Father Earl Denay for 18 months.

In 1937, Father George Lavallee followed Father Denay. He served for 16 years. He was a fatherly French priest who was held in high esteem by his parishioners. Under his leadership there was no excuse for missing religious education. He went from house to house picking up the children. There were as many as a dozen children in his big DeSoto at one time. During his tenure the church at Black River was remodeled and enlarged. A new altar was added, allowing more space for the sacristy and confessional. The church could now accommodate 200 people.

When Father Lavallee became so sick he could not serve as well as he would have liked, he resigned as pastor for health reasons and Father Theodore LaMarre was appointed the new pastor. One of his first tasks was to replace the old wood and coal furnace and build a permanent entrance to the church of Saint Gabriel.

Father Pelletier replaced Father LaMarre in 1955. He remained at Nicholson Hill and Black River for 12 years. He was very patient and understanding during the implementation of the decrees of the Second Vatican Council. When he left Nicholson Hill and Black River, Father Pelletier went to Saint Anne in Alpena. His successor at Saint Gabriel was Father Julius Spleet, an Alpena native. He served until 1970 when he was followed by Father Richard Seifferly. Father Herman Kolenda succeeded Father Seifferly in 1975 and served for two years. His successor was Father John Adomaitis. Father Adomaitis had been born in Lithuania and immigrated to the United States in 1950. He retired for health reasons in 1988 and was followed by Father Gabriel Fox. Under Father Fox, Saint Gabriel Parish celebrated its centennial and the church was thoroughly cleaned. Father Fox left Saint Gabriel in 1995 and was followed by Father Lawrence Kelleher who now serves as pastor of Saint Catherine, Ossineke, and Saint Gabriel, Black River. ■

Saint Ignatius, *Middle Village (Good Hart)*

By Kay Hughes

Driving along Shore Drive (M-119) between Harbor Springs and Cross Village, if one looks over the bluff at just the right time, one can see a pretty little church with a well-groomed graveyard down near the shore.

The first church here was built of birch bark by Father Baraga in 1833. The second church, built in 1861, was still standing when the Franciscans came in 1884. In 1889, a chimney fire destroyed it just before Mass was to start. Fortunately, no one was hurt. It was immediately rebuilt and still standing today. It was a mission station of Harbor Springs until 1928 when it became a mission station of Cross Village. It is open during the summer tourist season with one Mass a weekend.

Beside the pretty church is a graveyard filled with white crosses made from 2 x 4's. There's a story behind these crosses which have stood only a few years. Over the years, people have vandalized this little Indian cemetery until many of the graves were not marked. A decision was made to buy and paint 2 x 4's and see that each grave was identified. The gentleman who did this was Solomon Francis, who had been associated with the church since birth. His parents had been raised in the hewn log cabins next to the church. His mother played the organ, fed the priest when he came once a month, and his father warmed up the priest's quarters so it would be comfortable when he arrived. Solomon had the knowledge to rightly label the crosses. The late Solomon Francis was a veritable history book.

For years, the beach behind the church has been known as the best beach between Harbor Springs and Cross Village. Locals have grown to think of it as their own. In 1998, the Diocese of Gaylord sold the property to the two adjacent townships, who share the responsibility of maintaining it. Care was taken to hire experts to locate all the graves in this revered Indian cemetery, so that the beach property could be platted to avoid them. Sadly, though, vandals are already destroying Solomon's work. ■

Saint Ignatius, *Rogers City*

By Father Gerald F. Micketti

Father Francis X. Szulak (pronounced Shulak), was the first priest to regularly celebrate Mass in Rogers City, starting in 1874. Prior to his coming, a priest from Mackinac Island or other priests perhaps from Alpena, Bay City or Detroit came occasionally to Crawford's Quarry and Rogers City, which were about three miles apart on the Lake Huron shore. When the priest did come he would say the Mass in private homes. The first Mass to be offered in Crawford's Quarry was in the Dueltgen home. The first Mass offered in Rogers City was in the residence of Frederick Denny Larke, one of the founding fathers of Rogers City and a staunch Catholic. Subsequently, Mass was offered in the home of Frank Sommers at the corner of Third Street and Huron Avenue.

During his two years serving in Rogers City, Father Szulak brought together Catholics to form a parish. Albert Molitor and his wife donated three lots for a church site in 1872 on the corner of Second and Erie Streets. Three years later a frame structure was built and the congregation dedicated their church to Saint Ignatius, founder of the Society of Jesus, the Jesuits. Some complained that this church "was too far out of town" since, at that time, Huron Street was considered the "Main Street" and Erie Street, two blocks away, was considered a side street.

Although the congregation possessed a building, Saint Ignatius Church was considered a mission. In April of 1878, Father Bogacki was appointed the pastor of Saint Ignatius; however, he transferred to Saint Casimir Church in Posen because there were more Poles living in the Posen area. Father Bogacki cared for both communities until he left in 1898.

After Father Bogacki, Father Godfrey Lenzen assumed the pastoral care of all of the parishes and missions in Presque Isle County except Saint Casimir, Posen. For six years he visited Catholics in Rogers City, Metz, Ocqueoc, Millersburg, Hammond's Bay and Grace Harbor. Father Lenzen was from Saint Anne Church, Alpena. Once or twice he made his rounds with a bicycle just to show that it could be done if all other means of transportation failed.

Another priest from Alpena also served the congregation at Rogers City. Father Thomas W. Albin came to Rogers City during the years 1903-1906. Later Father Albin transferred to Onaway.

During the years 1906-1919, Saint Ignatius Parish was a mission to Saint Dominic Church in Metz. The first resident pastor of the Metz Parish was Father Francis Kaczmarek who served both Metz and Rogers City parishes for not quite two years. He was succeeded by Father Jan Kaplanowski. Between the years 1909 and 1916, the Metz and Rogers City parishes were served by Fathers Francis Piaskowski, Joseph Chodkiewicz, Joseph Koss. In April 1916, Father Casimir T. Skowronski arrived in Metz with the mission of Rogers City. On September 1, 1919, Father Skowronski, at the request of Bishop Kelly, transferred to Saint Ignatius Church to become the first resident pastor.

With the arrival of Father Skowronski, "C.T." as he was known to his intimates, Saint Ignatius took off. His transfer to Rogers City coincided with a period of growth in the community and in the parish. The catalyst for this growth came from the Michigan Limestone and Chemical Company, limestone quarry and related shipping operations.

In 1920, Mr. and Mrs. Paul H. Hoeft donated seven lots for a church-school building. Also a gift of $10,000 from the Michigan Limestone and Chemical Company and the generosity of numerous friends made possible the construction of a four-classroom school with a church auditorium upstairs as well as a rectory. There were also accommodations for the sisters teaching in the school. The school opened September 5, 1921, with 140 students taught by Sisters of Mercy who had moved from Saint Dominic Parish.

The joy and satisfaction of the church-school building for the parish was short-lived. On Sunday morning, January 6, 1924, both the church-school building and the rectory were destroyed by fire. Parishioners formed a bucket brigade in a futile attempt to stop

the fire. Just how the fire started is not certain; it was presumed that defective wiring was the cause. Gloom and sadness gripped the parish and the pastor.

Out of the ashes faith prevailed and help in many forms was forthcoming. The children resumed classes at the courthouse, the Maccabee Hall, the town hall and the Methodist church. The citizens of Rogers City took up a collection. Carl D. Bradley and John G. Munson of the Michigan Limestone and Chemical Company arranged for a substantial subsidy by their company. Father Koss at Posen collected $900; Father Gatzke of Saint Mary, Alpena collected $400; and Father Krakowski of Bay City collected $400. By August of the same year, the cornerstone for the new building was blessed and the building was completed by May of the next year.

The new Saint Ignatius Church and School was twice as large as the previous structure. There were eight classrooms and a school auditorium that was used as the church for worship. The total cost was $72,000. This structure is the present old portion of Saint Ignatius School.

Since the fire destroyed the rectory, Father Skowronski lived in a temporary rectory. In 1931, he felt inspired to issue a call from the pulpit for 25 friends who would volunteer to subscribe the full amount needed toward a new rectory. After making that announcement, Father Skowronski was filled with misgivings because the country was in the depths of the depression and many parishioners were surviving, sometimes just barely. Lo and behold, the following Thursday, one of the parishioners met him on the street and said, "Father, when are you coming to get your money? Clarence and I feel that we owe you $300." That did it. In a matter of ten days, 24 other families subscribed a sum of $9,000. That money plus another $3,500 obtained from the sale of the temporary rectory was enough to build a new rectory.

That left the sisters without a house. In 1939, a new convent was built by the parishioners at a cost of $21,000. The sisters had occupied two of the school classrooms. The school then expanded to include the ninth grade and kindergarten, both of which were discontinued when grade school enrollment increased.

Father Skowronski determined that the parish was in real need of a hall for purposes of gathering. In 1940, he looked at the vacant barn of the Bradley Farm, located within one block of the church. The barn was available and was accepted. The donors, however, attached so many stipulations to their gift that Bishop William Murphy of Saginaw was obliged to refuse the deed. Instead Bishop Murphy advised Father Skowronski to initiate plans for a new church. This was a blessing in disguise, although at the time it appeared as an insurmountable wall.

From 1940 to 1950, the parishioners prayed for and worked toward the goal of a new church. The parish prayed many novenas in honor of the Sacred Heart. Their reward? The beginning of the construction of a new church in 1950.

The new church was blessed on September 16, 1951, by Bishop Stephen Woznicki of Saginaw. The architect, Joseph Goddeyne of Bay City, had achieved a very imposing and unique edifice. The building resembles a Great Lakes ship. The tower resembles a lighthouse. Both resemblances reflect the maritime heritage of Rogers City — the Port of Calcite for limestone shipping and the three lighthouses in the county. The altar and communion rail are made of imported Italian marble and were consecrated on August 15, 1952.

After 33 years in Rogers City, Father Casimir T. Skowronski left Saint Ignatius at the end of 1952. He left his mark. Then assistant Kenneth Povish tells the story of C.T.'s ecumenism, Presque Isle style. Rogers City in the 1950s consisted basically of two congregations: Saint Ignatius with most of its membership south of Erie Street (the main east-west artery) and Saint John Lutheran Church with most of its membership living north of Erie Street. Father Skowronski's counterpart was Pastor Louis Linn. Both parishes had parochial schools. There was no communication of any kind between the pastors or churches. Pastor Linn was on the radio every Sunday morning and regularly-attacked Catholic teaching. Fathers C.T. and Povish took turns listening to him and replied in kind in their sermons. The Catholic radio program, "I Have A Question," was instituted on Sunday afternoons in part to counteract Pastor Linn's program. C.T. was born in Poland; Pastor Linn was born in Germany. That may explain their dislike for each other. In the halls of the hospital, they were barely civil to each other when their paths crossed.

One Thursday, C.T. invited Father Povish to go home to Alpena for the afternoon, to stay for supper there, and spend the evening, even stay overnight if he wished. This was awkward because his regular day off was Wednesday and he had just spent that day, ate supper and spent the last evening with his parents. So he bummed a meal in Rogers City, played cards with some friends and returned to the rectory about 11:00 p.m. The house was lit up, but all the window shades were drawn. A strange car was parked in front of the garage door behind the rectory.

Father Povish entered the back door and heard muffled voices coming from the pastor's study. He sneaked into the hall for a peek. There were C.T. and Pastor Linn poring over a chess board. C.T. later explained they were the only two people in town who knew how to play chess; and they had to play against each other. Twice a year they played chess, once at the rectory and once at the parsonage. Always the shades were drawn and the visitor's car was out of sight.

Father Adalbert Narloch succeeded Father Skowronski. During his tenure, he over-

saw the addition to the school, the landscaping of Mount Calvary Cemetery, and the acquisition of more land to enhance the property of the parish. The new school building opened with seven classrooms in September of 1961.

Father Narloch also was present to comfort the parishioners and the community during the loss of two Great Lakes vessels. The limestone carrier, *Carl D. Bradley*, sunk in Lake Michigan November 18, 1958. Thirty-three men lost their lives with that disaster. May 7, 1965, the steamer *Cedarville* collided with another vessel in the Straits of Mackinac and sank. Those losses hurt the parish and the community.

In 1970, after 17 years as pastor, Father Narloch retired at the age of 70. His successor, Father Zygmunt Gaj, took a long detour on his way to Rogers City. Born in Poland, Father Gaj spent five years in the concentration camps of Auschwitz and Dachau. In 1950 he arrived in Saginaw, eventually moving north to Rogers City.

Father Gaj stayed until 1974. He was succeeded by Father John Rushman, an assistant under Father Narloch from 1956 to 1959. He served the parish until his retirement in 1988. His successor was Father Arthur Mulka, a native son of the parish. He stayed for one year. He was followed by Father Richard Sitar who was pastor for three years. Father James Holtz came to Saint Ignatius to succeed Father Sitar. He served until 1996. He was followed by Father Thomas Dominiak, who served one year. The present pastor is Father Charles Donajkowski. ■

Saint John the Baptist, *Alpena*

Saint John the Baptist Parish was founded October 22, 1958, with one thought in mind — the need for a fourth parish and eventually a school in the city of Alpena. Because of the rapid increase in population in this part of the city and county, there was an urgency for the parish. When Father Edward Szturmowski arrived in Alpena, he was not only homeless, he was penniless. For lack of a building for Masses, Mass was offered at Ella White School only seven blocks from the property where the church building was to be erected. The first Mass was celebrated on November 10, 1957 with over 500 people in attendance.

Father "Storm" Szturmowski, with the aid of the church committee, purchased the property at the end of First Avenue bounded by Frederick, Franklin and North Streets. The winter of 1958 was utilized clearing the site for the church building. In March of 1958, the office buildings from the Abitibi site were moved to the parish grounds to be used as the pastor's residence as well as for meetings. A portion of the building was used as a chapel for daily Masses. Soon after acquiring the property, Father Storm organized a men's club to implement fund raising projects that would help the new parish realize their dream of their own "church."

Father Szturmowski was transferred in June 1960 and succeeded by Father John J, Kucinski. Under Father Kucinski more fund raising activities were encouraged and implemented. There were fish fries, dinners, bake sales, ponczki parties, rummage sales. What was also developing was a parish family. No longer was heard the familiar phrase "my former parish." New bonds were forming.

The present building was built as a school, which opened in 1964 with an enrollment of 84 students in grades 4 through 6. The school staff consisted of principal, Sister Danielita, with teachers Sisters Melitone and Redempta. Tragedy fell upon the community when two of the sisters were killed in an automobile accident in January 1965. The school carried on and in 1967, the first eighth grade class graduated from Saint John the Baptist School. There were 25 graduates. In 1971, the members of the school board petitioned Bishop Szoka to close the school because of declining enrollment and insufficient faculty. Bishop Szoka so ordered in August.

Father John Kucinski retired from active ministry in 1972 and he was succeeded by Father Ronald Gronowski. Other pastors who have served Saint John the Baptist include Fathers Terrence Raymond, Walter Derylo, Francis Partridge, and the present pastor Kenneth Stachnik. Saint John the Baptist Parish has grown over the years to over 800 families, many of whom are charter members of the parish. ■

Saint Joseph, *West Branch*

By Father Gerald Micketti

A view of Saint Joseph Church taken in the early 1900s.

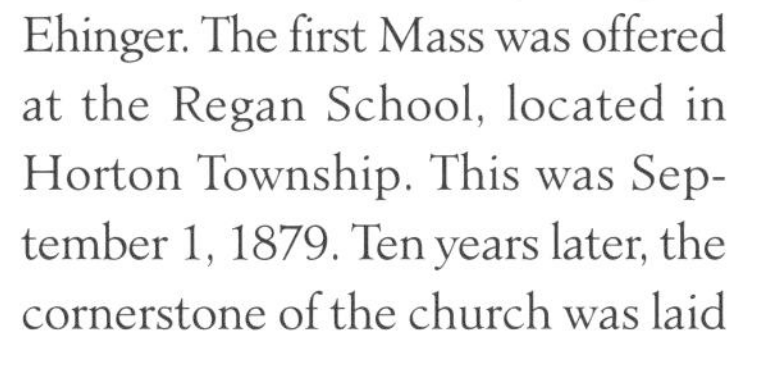

oly Family Parish was the neighbor of the West Branch parish. As indicated Father Francis X Szulak was the first missionary to the area. He came from Bay City and was invited to the area by August Ehinger. The first Mass was offered at the Regan School, located in Horton Township. This was September 1, 1879. Ten years later, the cornerstone of the church was laid and Saint Joseph Church became the house of worship for the parishioners in July of 1891. Lauretta Lehman recounts that many of the first parishioners were Lutheran by heritage who had migrated from Canada. When Father Szulak visited the area, he was instrumental in their joining the Catholic Church. Father Webeler followed Father Szulak and he was succeeded by Father Guthausen with Father Reiss as assistant.

In 1910, the construction of the school

Mass in the old church.

The women of the church pose at a 1950s parish function.

building was begun but it was not until the fall of 1917 that school was ready for occupancy. The first years saw 120 students and five Dominican sisters from Grand Rapids as the first teachers. The convent for the sisters was at the rear of the school building. By the school year of 1921-22, twelve grades were in session and the first class to graduate from the school totaled five in number. The graduation ceremony was held at the Opera House in West Branch.

This school eventually became overcrowded and the sisters' living quarters were needed for classrooms. A decision was made to purchase a dwelling across the street from the school for the sisters' living quarters. This decision was later questioned when several sisters were hit or nearly hit by motorists approaching the area over the hill from the west. It wasn't too many years later that the property for another convent was purchased from the Husted family. Father Aloysius O'Toole promoted the new school/church/convent and he was determined that there would be an Open House on Labor Day, even though there was no water or plumbing. Working until midnight the night before, Vic Niles installed the water and plumbing by a flashlight held by Marion Chadwick. The neighboring restaurant owner reported this to the State Highway Department in Alpena. The Highway Department would not allow them to erect a sign on the highway. Kent Chadwick, owner of a magazine/paper delivery service, brought his truck to the school and tacked a large sign that announced dinner and defied anyone to remove his vehicle. The Open House went on as planned. ■

Father Webeler

Saint Luke the Evangelist, *Bellaire*

By Father Gerald Micketti

Saint Luke the Evangelist Parish in its beginnings was associated with Saint Francis Xavier Parish in Petoskey. The Franciscan priests covered many small mission communities throughout northwestern Michigan. The first mention of the parish occurs around 1897. The priests from Petoskey made the trip to Bellaire via boat to Charlevoix and horse and buggy the remainder of the journey. Hence, Mass was not too frequent. Bishop Richter of Grand Rapids purchased seven lots in the village of Bellaire from Fletcher E. Turrell and Mary Turrell for the sum of $250. A small church was erected on this property. He remained interested in Bellaire because he came three years later to administer the sacrament of Confirmation. The Franciscan priests continued to serve the Bellaire mission, coming once a month to offer Mass, administer the sacraments and give instructions.

The first Saint Luke the Evangelist Church.

A severe blow fell upon the community in July 1921, when fire destroyed a major portion of the village of Bellaire. The church was also destroyed in that fire. The lots where the church stood were sold and two other lots were purchased still in the village. On this site, the Catholic church building which had formerly been used at Atwood, was dismantled, moved and reassembled. Since the Catholic families who had worshiped in the church were forced to seek employment elsewhere after the timber was gone, the priests from Petoskey discontinued their ministry in Bellaire.

When the Franciscan priests turned over the administration of many missions to the Grand Rapids Diocese, Saint Luke came under the ministry of Saint Joseph Church in East Jordan. This was in 1929. The pastor who arrived in East Jordan as pastor of Saint Joseph was Father Timothy Kroboth. He visited Saint Luke once a month. This arrangement continued until 1945 when Saint Luke became a mission of Saint Anthony Parish in Mancelona with Father Peter Jakubowski, pastor. Father Jakubowski offered Mass in Bellaire every other Sunday.

Father Walter Jude officiates at the groundbreaking for a new church in 1959.

First Communion in the new church.

With the increase in summer visitors and tourists in the area and growing pains becoming evident, efforts were made to raise money for an addition to the building. As the area continued to grow the need for a larger building was becoming apparent. Land was purchased at the north end of Bellaire and a new building was constructed. July 12, 1959, the cornerstone was blessed and laid with Msgr. Francis Kaminski, Dean of the Gaylord Deanery of the Diocese of Grand Rapids presiding. The pastor, Father Walter Jude, offered the first mass in the new church on Easter Sunday, April 17, 1960.

Sister Celine Goessl, SCSC, was appointed Pastoral Administrator at Saint Luke on August 19, 1991. Under her leadership, the parish built a rectory and is currently building a new parish hall. ■

History of the church in Alpena

Adapted from the Saint Mary Church of the Immaculate Conception Centennial Book

The history of the Catholic Church in northern Michigan goes back to April 13, 1861, the day after the Civil War began. On that day, the Most Reverend Frederick Baraga, Bishop of Sault Ste. Marie, paid $30 to James K. Lockwood for a lot on the north side of Chisholm Street, between Tenth and Eleventh Avenues. Mr. Lockwood made a gift of an adjoining lot.

Alpena, a lumbering settlement which had changed its name from Fremont only two years before, along with points on the north Huron Shore, lay in a kind of no-man's-land between the Dioceses of Sault Ste. Marie and Detroit. Bishop Baraga had clear jurisdiction over his former missions in the northwest lower peninsula. Cheboygan, one of five original counties in the north, had been assigned to Bishop Baraga in 1854, and Alpena at that time was a part of Cheboygan County. Alpena was separated in 1857 by an act of the Legislature. This uncertain status, at least about points south of Alpena, is indicated in a letter Bishop Baraga wrote to Father Patrick Murray of Beaver Island on November 20, 1867: "Visit the people along the shore as often as you can. I am sure that the Bishop of Detroit is unable to do anything for them."

Bishop Baraga felt the need for a Catholic church in Alpena. On Easter Monday, April 1, 1861, his diary relates that he left Sault Ste. Marie and started walking to Alpena. There, he intended to catch a fishing boat for Detroit and then go on to Cincinnati. The 64-year-old bishop, accompanied by a mail carrier, traveled the distance in nine days, arriving the evening of April 9, 1861. The following day, he held conversations with Mr. Lockwood and on April 13, he purchased a lot for a church. Bishop Baraga spent nine days waiting for a boat to Detroit in the house of a blacksmith named Samuel Ankers.

It was due to this visit of Bishop Baraga that the church got its start in Alpena. Father Patrick Murray came to Alpena at Bishop Baraga's direction on September 2, 1864, and remained until September 14. In that interval, he baptized seven children. Father Murray then returned to Beaver Island. There he received a letter from Bishop Baraga, dated November 27, 1864, saying: "I see by your letter that you remained only a short time in Alpena; much shorter than I intended you to stay." He wrote again on July 10, 1865: "I send you this letter from Samuel Ankers, by which you will see how necessary it is that somebody go to Alpena to raise up that church. I have nobody whom I can send but you. You have already worked there with good success; go again and do as much as you can." Father Murray complied, coming to Alpena on August 17, 1865, and remaining until September 22 of that year, recording five more baptisms. Bishop Baraga then asked Father Murray if he "would not like it better to be stationed at Alpena, than at Beaver Harbor." Finally, on February 15, 1866, Bishop Baraga wrote: "I received your letter of January 29th and am glad to see what a dutiful son you are. You are perfectly willing to go whither I shall send you. Make the necessary preparations at Beaver Harbor, and then leave for Alpena."

That was it. Father Patrick Murray came to Alpena to stay on May 11, 1866. He quickly decided that he wanted property closer to the village than that acquired by Bishop Baraga five years earlier. For $150, he bought from Gelos Potvin two lots on Chisholm Street between Fourth and Fifth Streets, almost directly opposite the present Saint Bernard Church. Father Murray moved swiftly on construction of a church and said Mass there for the first time on November 7, 1866.

The first Catholic church, named Saint Bernard, was a harbor of worship in this community for all nationalities: Irish, German, French, Swedes and Polish. The church directory listing in the *Alpena Weekly Argus*, indicates that two Masses were said on Sunday — one having a sermon in English and the other in French. Jurisdiction was exercised by Bishop Baraga, who had established his See at Sault Ste. Marie in November of 1853, but then moved it to Marquette in October of 1865. Upon his death on January 19, 1868, the northern part of the lower peninsula was transferred to the Detroit Diocese. Bishop Baraga never seemed to have conferred Confirmation at Alpena. On June 21, 1868, Bishop Paul LeFevre came from Detroit and confirmed 47 persons at Saint Bernard church ranging in age from 11 to 52 years old. His successor, Bishop Caspar H. Borgess, confirmed 44 persons on August 13, 1871. A letter from Bishop Borgess to Father Murray is a memento to that visit: "The generous surprise, which your congregation gave me, seems to oblige me to express to them my gratitude. It is the first token of filial affection with which I have been honored by the flock entrusted to my care since my unction. I beg to apprise you and your congregation that I shall offer my humble prayers to Almighty God for them, that He, in his infinite goodness, may bless them abundantly."

Father Murray then turned to the needs of the Catholic children of Alpena. On August 16, 1869, he purchased from D.D. Oliver, a lot 66 x 132 on the south side of Chisholm Street across from the church and rectory. Mr. Oliver donated $100 of the $300 purchase price toward the new school. A two-story frame building, 24 x 48 was erected. Even before opening Saint Bernard School in 1870, Father Murray worked at the instruction of parish youngsters, conducting a Sunday School from the start. He also ministered to the spiritual needs of Alpena's Catholic adults, who for the first time had a church and pastor.

Father Murray received an accolade for his achievements here in a letter from Bishop Baraga less than a year before the bishop's death, saying: "I received your excellent letter on the 24th of February, which gives me great consolation. I am surprised to see that you did so much about the building of your church in so short a time. You are useful wherever you move. I am very satisfied with the improvements which you are continually making, and I hereby give you a general approbation of any improvements you may wish to make for the future. You need not ask my permission."

Saint Mary Church of the Immaculate Conception.

Father Murray was succeeded by Father William Taaken on November 1, 1871. In turning the pastorate over to Father Taaken, together with the church, school, rectory and graveyard, Father Murray rendered an accounting that showed the parish debt totaled $820. Father Taaken's three-year tenure was highlighted by provision of a convent to house nuns who would teach in the school. On April 4, 1872, he acquired the lot on Chisholm Street just east of the school for this purpose. By the autumn of 1873, the small frame structure was complete, but no sisters were available. On May 17, 1872, Father Taaken also acquired the corner lot of Chisholm at Fifth, that is the site of the present Saint Bernard Church. It was purchased from Rod McKenzie for $800.

Beyond these facts, the record of his pastorate is slim, but his Hollander's stern and determined personality is indicated by the legend that comes down through the years. A certain parishioner had failed to pay his pew rent. After a due period of waiting, Father Taaken nailed a board across the entry to the pew. But the parishioner, a powerful man, ripped the board away and sat down. The following Sunday, the parishioner, finding that Father Taaken had caused the seat to be sawed out of the pew, went to a nearby hotel and brought back a chair, placed it in the pew and sat down, thereby winning that round.

On August 13, 1874, Father Taaken was succeeded as pastor by Father John VanGennip. The

school enrollment had grown from 100 students that first year in 1870, to 250 by 1875. Father Taaken, during his tenure, had prepared a convent for sisters to teach at Saint Bernard School, and had negotiated with the Sisters of Charity of Cincinnati for their coming in 1875. In the late summer of 1875, three Sisters of Charity came, which would launch 65 consecutive years of devoted service to Saint Bernard Parish.

Those first sisters were among the true pioneers of Alpena. They came carrying the torch of culture into the wilderness. They trudged through streets of sawdust on errands of mercy after school hours, drank water from a rough barrel hauled to their humble home on Chisholm Street, and melted snow to obtain wash water as the dread of winter gripped the primitive town. They put up with all the rough ways of the time, but brought to this environment an inspiration and promise of better things to come. After the first three came many others laboring in the same tradition of selfless service. Their influence upon the lives of thousands of people cannot be measured.

Father VanGennip, during his pastorate, did not add to parish land holdings nor erect any buildings, but concentrated rather on strengthening the spiritual life of his people. His efforts in this direction earned for him the nickname, "The Saint," as he was called by parishioners. Father VanGennip held night prayers in the church every evening of his pastorate, and continually exhorted his people to attend, an urging to which they gradually responded. Succeeding pastors ascribe, at least in part, the deep and abiding faith of the people of Saint Bernard to his ministry among them.

Father E.M. DeKiere was appointed to replace Father VanGennip on November 15, 1876, the first of two short periods in which he was pastor. His double tenure totals nearly two and a half years, but he was absent from the parish for months at a time due to ill health. There were now 300 families in the parish and 250 students in school.

When Father DeKiere left the parish for the first time in January of 1878, it was attended for about three months by Father Francis X. Shulak, a Jesuit priest from Chicago.

Father Shulak was well-known in the Alpena and Posen areas. Born on a small farm in Poland and receiving his education from his parents and the village priest, Father Shulak was ordained for the Society of Jesus in Krakow, Poland. In the year 1865, he was sent to the United States to further his English studies and to serve as a missionary to the Polish, Czechs and the non-Polish settlements in and around the area of Saint Louis, Missouri. After establishing a few libraries in Missouri, he was transferred to Chicago, Illinois, in 1869. In Illinois he immediately commenced traveling and sailing to establish posts on the Great Lakes. He traveled all areas of Lake Huron in northeastern Michigan holding Forty Hours Devotion, preaching at Missions, leading Novenas, and visiting lumber camps. In his travels to Indiana and Branch County, Michigan, he informed the Polish foresters and woodworkers that there was land in northeastern Michigan that could be homesteaded. The Poles took the advice of Father Shulak and purchased homesteads in Presque Isle and Alpena Counties.

Father Shulak could speak, read and write in English, Polish, Latin, German, Czech and French, so wherever he went, his missionary assignments were well received and appreciated. In this area, he attended particularly the people of the Polish settlement in Posen, a point confirmed by Baptism and other entries involving that community and signed by him in the Saint Bernard Parish Registry.

On June 15, 1874, Father Shulak purchased 40 acres of land adjacent to the present Saint Casimir Church in Posen, from the State of Michigan for $100. Under his direction, a log church was built in 1874-75. He continued to call at Posen until 1879, when Bishop C.H. Borgess of Detroit appointed Father Anthony Bogacki as first pastor.

Father Shulak is also given credit for establishing Saint Ignatius Parish in Rogers City, Michigan, naming the parish after his father. He gave many missions in Alpena, Bay City, Cheboygan, Saginaw, Port Huron and other posts, as he sailed the Great Lakes in the role as spiritual advisor.

By the year 1883, the city of Alpena had made much progress. Electric lights had been installed on Main Street; cedar blocks in the streets were a matter of pride; and a few brick buildings were beginning to compete with the prevailing frame structures. Some key industries had been established: Huron Portland Cement, a paper mill, and garment factory. With such a solid economic base, people were lured to Alpena, leading to the development of the town. The Polish people in Alpena, accustomed to hardship and struggle, contributed much to the growing community. One of their greatest contributions was to be Saint Mary Church, now located on Second Avenue, then known as Dock Street.

In May 1883, the Most Reverend Henry J. Richter was installed as bishop of the Grand Rapids Diocese. As one of his first pastoral assignments, Bishop Richter assigned Father Thomas D. Flannery to Saint Bernard parish. Father Flannery came to Saint Bernard on November 22, 1883. Father Flannery was joined at the original Saint Bernard Rectory on December 9, 1883, by Father P.C.A. Winter, who was to form a parish for the French-speaking families. They lived together there for a time, while a settlement was worked out. Under its terms, Father Winter's congregation kept the church and rectory, which stood at the east corner of Chisholm and Fifth, while Father

Flannery's congregation retained the parish name Saint Bernard and took the lands at the south corner of Chisholm and Fifth, on which stood the school, convent, and the beginnings of the new church.

At this same time, the large settlement of Poles in Alpena wanted to preserve their Polish heritage and grow spiritually with effective praise to God in their native tongue. They wanted a parish of their own. They were determined that the young generation be brought up in their own environment.

With the help of Father Francis Shulak and Father Joseph Kucinski, another Polish Jesuit from Chicago, a committee of 150 families worked to purchase an unused Methodist Church on what is now Second Avenue, the site of the present church. Negotiations were completed for the purchase of the building for the sum of $2,000, and title to the property, which was signed on July 2, 1883, and recorded July 3, 1883, was transferred from "Trustees of the Society of the First Methodist Episcopal Church of Alpena, Michigan to Trustees of the Society of the Polish Roman Catholic Church of Alpena, Michigan (to be organized)." The Polish people had much work to do on their new church before it could be used for services, since the Methodists had only sold them the building. The bell, pews and other furniture were removed for use in their own newly-constructed church on Chisholm Street. The Polish people worked strenuously gathering needed supplies and funds. Within six months, the needed renovations were completed.

The first Catholic church in Alpena.

The former Methodist Church was transformed into the Polish Catholic Church of the Immaculate Conception, in honor of Mary. On December 8, 1883, the first Holy Sacrifice of the Mass was offered in the renovated church. The first pastor was Father Candid Kozlowski. Since there was no formal rectory, the pastor had to "rough it" by living in a room adjoining the sacristy. Father Kozlowski did not "rough it" for long. Shortly, he left for a new pastorate in Lemont, Illinois. With his departure, he was succeeded by Father Matthew Grochowski but he, too, was quickly changed to Saint Joseph Church in Manistee. Even the third pastor, Father Kolasinski moved rapidly, staying only a few weeks. From January, 1885, to October, 1885, there was no priest at the parish. According to the records at Saint Bernard Church, most of the parishioners went there for services and the sacraments. Things seemed very unsettled indeed!

The period of vacancy ended when Father Augustine Sklorzyk, the fourth pastor, arrived in October of 1885. On February 21, 1886, Saint Mary Church was officially dedicated. It was customary in the Catholic Church not to dedicate any buildings until the debt was fully paid. The *Alpena Weekly Argus*, in its issue dated February 24, 1886, relates the following in regard to the dedication: "The Polish Church, on Dock Street, was dedicated the last Sunday. About nine o'clock in the morning, the men, belonging to the church, formed in line in front of the edifice; and then, headed by the Germania Band, marched up Dock and Second Streets to Chisholm Street, and then to the French Catholic Church. As it passed the *Argus* office, we counted the men in ranks and found there were 156 Polanders in the procession. They bore three banners...the first being the stars and stripes and the other two being Polish flags...red and white. The procession was under command of marshals mounted on horses. One of the marshals wore a white coat and a handsome sash. The men marched well and presented a good appearance. The weather was not very agreeable, and snow was falling."

"At Saint Anne Church, they were joined by 24 members of Saint Jean Baptiste Societe, and 18 Knights of Saint John, 16 of whom wore handsome uniforms. The procession, including the band, now numbered over 200 persons, marched back to the Polish church where the dedication services were held. The members of the French church were then escorted back to Saint Anne. During the march, the members of Saint John performed several marching maneuvers."

The new pastor showed a sense of development when in 1888 he purchased lots

9 and 10 in block 83 and built a two-room school on lot 10. This little school, the first Saint Mary Grade School, was staffed by himself and a lay teacher, Mr. Snick. This bright future was clouded by a terrible disaster that befell Alpena.

On July 11, 1888, a disastrous fire broke out on the north side of the Thunder Bay River,that destroyed Saint Mary Church and rectory, as well as 200 neighboring houses.

The *Alpena Weekly Argus* gave the following account of the fire: "Wednesday afternoon, July 11, 1888, will long be remembered by the citizens of Alpena. Then it was the 'fire fiend' swooped down on the north side, gathered a large portion of the residences in its fiery grasp, and in one short hour, had brought sorrow and destitution to from one thousand to fifteen hundred persons; had turned over two hundred families out of their comfortable homes, and left in its place, heaps of ashes, destitute families, and a hideous ruin.

"On the banks of the Mill Pond, about one mile and a half from the mouth of the river, on the north side, is a small ravine 10 feet deep. In this ravine, the edgings and other refuse from the lumber mill of H.R. Morse are burned. Last Wednesday, a gale of wind was blowing from the northwest, traveling at times at a velocity of 36 miles per hour. The wind traveled directly from the ravine, where the slabs were burning, towards the big sawdust heap, and then on to the residential area. Between the ravine and the sawdust pile, there is a road covered with sawdust, deposited by the mill carts. It seemed to observers, after the fire, that sparks from the burning slabs in the ravine must have set fire to the sawdust on the road, and then traveled to the sawdust heap.

"A large fire commenced. The fire department was sent, and in addition, the steam fire engines, as the fire was beyond reach of the water works. The round-house caught fire, then the Morse Boarding House, and from that point, the settled part of the city, on the north side, begins. The fire traveled from Fletcher Street to Walnut Street; then to Long Lake Avenue and on to Pine Street. Fire was now breaking out in various places, and although the fire boys and residents worked nobly to gain control of the flames, they were unable to be at all places at once. Residence after residence became wrapped in flames, and then the citizens were forced to behold a great conflagration, and see a large part of the city doomed to destruction; and that the fire's onward course could not be checked until the Bay was reached. The march of the fire to the Bay, after it got under full headway, took but a few minutes. Sparks and blazing shingles were carried, by the fierce gale, for blocks, and new fires would start up and then work backward and sideways.

An old classroom picture dated 1906.

"Desperate efforts were made to save at least part of household goods. In the center of the fire belt, houses were emptied of their goods, which were piled in the streets; but the fire came so quick, that the owners were forced to flee for their lives before they could remove their goods to a safe place. Very few of those, who lived along Miller and Lake Streets, saved anything except the clothes on their backs. Those persons who lived near the edge of the fire, on Oldfield and Clark, were more fortunate. As there was plenty of assistance, their household goods were removed to a place of safety. The scene along Oldfield Street was an excitable one. The street was dotted with tables, chairs, beds, organs, stoves, iron frames of sewing machines, and broken crockery ware. Women and children were running about, some crying, some half-crazed. Mothers had lost their children, husbands were separated from wives, and many more were tormented with fear that loved ones had perished in the flames.

"When the fire swept down to Dock Street, blazing brands set fire to the steeple of the Polish church, and soon that part of the structure was a mass of flames and presented a striking sight. The steeple was on fire before the main part of the church, and looked like a pillar of fire shining through the smoke-clouds.

"When darkness set in, the city on the north side of the river, from the dam to the river's mouth, was illuminated by the burning fires; reflection of the light extending hundreds of feet high, appearing like a long luminous cloud resting above the city. When the fire finally went out, everything consumable was destroyed, and what wood remained on the ground, would not make an ordinary dray load.

"In an hour, property to the amount of $300,000 had been destroyed, over one thousand rendered homeless, and hundreds left destitute; their only possessions were the clothes on their backs. The district burned was from 2 to 3 blocks wide, and 5 blocks long.

"Thursday afternoon, the ruined district was visited by thousands who wandered over the desolate area. It was a sad walk for those who had been expelled from their homes the preceding night. The work and toil of years lay before them, a Mass of ashes. The only death from the fire, was that of Mrs. Ann McLean, aged 57 years, who had come from Buffalo to visit relatives."

The tragic loss of their church and rectory did not deter the Polish congregation. Before the end of the year, they had built a new home for their pastor on lot 9. In March of 1889, Father Sklorzyk became ill, and due to a misunderstanding with the people, left the parish. He was replaced in October by a young energetic priest, Father Leopold Oprychalski, who imbued with zeal and concerned about the welfare of his parishioners, began planning the erection of a new church. Under his guidance, many fund-raising projects were successfully undertaken.

It was a time of growth and anticipation. Saint Mary Parish grew rapidly, with new families joining constantly, determined to preserve the Polish heritage. It was obvious that the increasing number of children meant new demands for a better school. Rich Polish customs and traditions were becoming strongly entrenched among the people. Their needs could be met only by organized schooling and a staff of dedicated teachers.

Father Oprychalski began a search for an order of religious sisters who would accept this responsibility to provide for the religious and educational welfare of the children and to preserve the Polish traditions and values of their parents. The pastor turned to the Felician Sisters of Detroit for help. Even though the school building continued to serve as a church, rectory, and school, the sisters were assured that proper accommodations would soon be provided. In 1889, three Felician sisters arrived by boat. What joy and royal welcome greeted the sisters! Even though their quarters were small and simple, the sisters made themselves comfortable and got ready for the opening of school.

Mr. Lad Filipiak, who attended the school from 1889-1892, recalls the first religious superior, Sister Mary Augustine. According to Mr. Filipiak, who was born in 1879, the school was on the first floor of the building, and the church and convent on the second. School records indicate that the first sisters lived in two rooms on the second floor of that original frame structure that was later remodeled as a convent and served as such until 1956.

Progress was being made not only educationally, but also religiously. On June 1, 1889, the first payment was made on the new church foundation, and the laying of the cornerstone took place on June 12, 1889. The *Alpena Weekly Argus* of June 12, 1889, reports the following: "The cornerstone of the new Polish Catholic Church, on Dock Street, was laid last Wednesday evening. There was an immense crowd present to witness the ceremonies. The stone bears the following inscription: 'Saint Mary Catholic Church, erected A.D. 1889." The church, which will be built of brick and stone, will be 106 feet and 2 inches in length, and the side walls will be 28 feet high. The width is 55 feet. From the foundation to the top of the spire will be 132 feet. The stone work is about completed."

During his vigorous pastorate, Father Oprychalski organized much in the parish: the Rosary Society in 1889 (still very active in the parish), a parish library with Polish literature imported from Poland and periodically enlarged. Much of the future success of Saint Mary depended not only upon a loving God but upon the gifts of this talented pastor.

Things were looking bright. On September 3, 1891, four sisters were assigned to the school: Sister M. Modesta, Principal, Sister M. Jutta, Sister Joanna Gorska, and Sister Valerie. The sisters were very excited and deeply impressed with the beauty and majesty of the entire area. Three sisters were to teach and one to do domestic work. ■

Saint Mary, *Burt Lake*

By Father Stanley Bur

The building of the first Saint Mary Church in 1909.

Saint Mary Church at Burt Lake is closely connected with early native American history. Saint Mary Church was and perhaps still is called the Indian Church. The present location of the church is connected with the dispossession of the native Americans from their reservation land on Indian Point. Indian Point is now called Colonial Point because of the Colonial Hotel on the land near Harbor Springs. In 1900, the Indians and their belongings were forcibly moved to the road and their houses set on fire. Twenty-five Indian families were left homeless. With no place to go, the Indians moved to "Indian Road." Today only a small burial ground remains where the Indian village once stood.

The present church building was constructed in the years 1909-10 and dedicated by Bishop Richter July 5, 1910. The present site is the second site of Saint Mary Church. There was a church opened two miles south. Since the Indians neglected to pay taxes, someone paid the back taxes and secured the title to the land where the church was located. The new owner had the Indians evicted. The native Americans lost their property, their homes and even their cemetery. After that, Mass was celebrated in private homes. Funds were slowly raised and land was donated for the church building. That was the church building dedicated July 5, 1910. Presently Saint Mary Church at Burt Lake is served by the pastor of Saint Clement Church, Pellston. ■

Saint Mary, *Charlevoix*

By David L. Knight

When the Most Reverend Henry Joseph Richter, Bishop of Grand Rapids, arrived for his first visit to Charlevoix on the morning of Monday, August 25,1890, he was welcomed by an enthusiastic delegation of Catholics eager to take their biggest step yet toward becoming a true parish family.

The occasion for Bishop Richter's trip north was the laying of the cornerstone for Saint Mary's Catholic Church. Though the Catholics of Charlevoix had been loosely organized for over two decades, they had yet to enjoy a permanent place of worship and a visible symbol of their faith.

Charlevoix had only been incorporated 11 years when Bishop Richter first visited but its location on the Pine River Channel linking Pine Lake to Lake Michigan had long made it a favored port for commercial and fishing vessels and a focal point for much regional commerce. Dominating the town's skyline at the time were steeples of its already established churches with the Congregational, Methodist and Baptist as the most prominent.

On the morning of the Saint Marys cornerstone laying, Bishop Richter arrived accompanied by Fathers Schmidt and Ignatius. The entourage must have arrived by horse-drawn coach as rail passenger service was not started in Charlevoix until two years later. The bishop was welcomed by Father Bruno Torka, O.F.M., who had recently been assigned as pastor of the Charlevoix parish by the Franciscan mission in Harbor Springs.

The Charles Zeitler family.

Mass was offered at 8:00 a.m. at Jefferies Hall downtown, one of the public venues used by the town's Catholic contingent for worship services before they had a church. Following Mass, the celebrants and congregation made their way up the South Hill to the church site. The cornerstone was laid in a solemn ceremony and Bishop Richter delivered a sermon exhorting parish members to persevere in their efforts to build a structure suitable for divine worship.

Some 23 years earlier, Father Philip Zorn had ridden into the Charlevoix area on the back of an Indian pony. His destination that day, March 10, 1867, was the homestead of William Graham in Marion Township where he celebrated the first recorded Catholic mass in the community.

Father Zorn gradually identified other Catholic families living in the vicinity and over the next 14 years he visited at set intervals to say mass in their homes and tend to their spiritual needs. When Father Gustav Graf assumed the duties of tending to Charlevoix Catholics in 1881, Father Zorn went on to other missionary pursuits and, by the time of his death in 1900, was one of Northern Michigan's most revered spiritual leaders.

In 1888, Father Norbert Wilhelm assumed

the pastorship and soon realized that his Charlevoix congregation was getting too large to be ministered to in homes and public meeting halls. He set about immediately to find a location for a church.

Father Wilhelm was succeeded the next year by Father Placidu Krekeler who continued the process of raising funds and securing a church site. Largely through the persistence of fund raising committee members M. Kehoe, William Woods and J. Woods, the financial resources were in place by 1889 to purchase one acre of land along the main thoroughfare of Charlevoix's south side.

The property purchased, efforts were now focused by Charlevoix area Catholics on the building of a church. By the time Father Bruno Torka arrived as pastor in 1890, enough contributions had been generated to start construction.

In the two years following the cornerstone laying, materials for the new church were gradually accumulated at the site as the Saint Mary parishioners continued to hold Mass at such places as Clark's meeting hall in Charlevoix and the Town Hall. By the summer of 1892, sufficient lumber was placed on the site to begin the project. The following winter and spring saw plasterers take up the job of interior finishing and within that period craftsman Jerome Heath completed a beautiful new altar.

The original Saint Mary Church on Bridge Street in Charlevoix.

In August, 1893, 26 years after Father Zorn had arrived on horseback, then-pastor Father Sabinus Mollitor deemed the church suitable enough for services and started holding monthly Mass there.

On May 31, 1894 Bishop Richter returned to Charlevoix to bless the new church. The event was reported as follows in the June 6, 1894 edition of the *Charlevoix Sentinel*.

"The new church edifice of the Catholic Society of Charlevoix was consecrated Thursday morning, May 31st, by Right Rev. H.J. Richter, Bishop of Grand Rapids, with the solemn and impressive ceremonial of the church. The Rt. Rev. Bishop was assisted by Rev. Fathers Sabinus Mollitor, Marion Glann and Bruno Torka, all of Harbor Springs. The attendance was large.

"At precisely ten o'clock, the Rt. Rev. Bishop, clothed in vestments with mitre and crosier, attended by the three priests, emerged from the church which had not yet been opened to the public. Followed by the waiting congregation, the Bishop and clergy passed around the edifice as the Bishop, from a silver chalice, sprinkled the walls of the church and the priests chanted the service of consecration.

"Again the prelate and fathers entered the sanctuary and with closed doors completed the holy service of consecration, after which the congregation was admitted and a solemn mass was celebrated with Father Mollitor as celebrant, assisted by His Grace the Bishop in cape and attending clergy.

"The music of the mass with Mr. Frank Coatta as organist and Mrs. M. Kehoe as leading soprano was credible. The beautiful Kyrie Eleison, Gloria, Credo, Respsonsoria, Sanctus and Benedictus were sung with an earnestness and skill surprising to one who is familiar with the difficult and dignified character of Catholic musical service.

"The Bishop occupied a throne on the gospel side of the altar in the purple vestments of his high office, rising from time to time as he participated in the mass. At the close of the mass, Bishop Richter preached a sermon on consecration and confirmed a class of 30 young people.

"During his discourse he complimented highly the zeal which characterized the labors of the Catholic people here in providing for themselves the neat and substantial house of worship in which they were gathered on this auspicious occasion.

"The Rt. Rev. Bishop was driven about town in the afternoon and before leaving expressed himself as delighted with Charlevoix and predicted for it a bright and prosperous future.

Final touches continued on Saint Mary Church over the next few years. In October, 1894, an important milestone was reached with the delivery of the church bell. Again, Father Mollitor presided over a solemn ceremony to dedicate this crowning part of the

church building. The bell weighed 521 pounds and was purchased mainly through a contribution from parishioner John Woods. Aside from the cornerstone, the bell is the only vestige of the original Saint Mary Church that was saved when the church was demolished in 1964. It was incorporated into the new church and is still used today.

In 1895, an addition to the church was built to serve as a vestry and temporary residence for the visiting priest.

On the night of August 29, 1896, the church which had been completed for barely two years, was almost lost. Following is the *Charlevoix Sentinel* account of the incident:

"Another severe electric storm occurred Saturday night last and for about two hours kept everybody in Charlevoix on the ragged edge of uncertainty. It was a veritable bombardment, so fierce and continuous were the flashes. At 11 o'clock, soon after a particularly startling flash and peal of heaven's artillery, the blood curdling shriek of the fire whistle was added to the turmoil.

"A gentleman who happened to be at his window opposite the Catholic Church saw a bolt of lightning strike the spire of that edifice and soon after saw flames issuing from it. He ran to the power house and gave the alarm. When the fire department reached the spot flames were pouring out of the front windows and on the interior of the belfry they were gaining rapid headway.

"The department was handicapped by a shortage of hose, the church being more than a block from the hydrant and the north side cart failing to arrive. But excellent work was done, the fire being practically confined to the front interior. At midnight the fire was under control and the church stands as evidence of the efficiency of the Charlevoix Fire Department. The damage will not exceed $600 which is fully covered by insurance.

After the fire, a top priority of the congregation was getting the church back in condition for Christmas services, which they did. Over the next few years, the additions and improvements continued. In 1897 Miss Mary O'Leary donated a new set of the ten Stations of the Cross.

In 1960 a campaign was started to build a new church. Louis S. Orlowski, a Detroit area architect who was also a Charlevoix native, an alumnus of Saint Mary Catholic School and a descendant of one of the parish's founding families, was selected to design the new church. Planned was a 500-capacity, 50 foot by 130 foot brick and stone building with a stylized roof featuring laminated wood arches. The site was right next to the old church in which services continued throughout construction. The total cost for the project eventually totaled $140,000.

Ground was broken for the new church September 4, 1963. Among those present was Mrs. Philip Lemieur who had been on hand 73 years before for the cornerstone laying of the first church.

On July 13,1964, Monsignor Francis Kaminski of Gaylord officiated over the dedication of the cornerstone. Deposited in the cornerstone were an historical outline of the parish, names of the pope, president and governor, names of all the priests who had served Saint Mary, a picture of the new church, a relic of Saint Martin DePorres, a coin depicting President John F. Kennedy, names of the architect and contractor and two copies of the *Charlevoix Courier*.

The following Sunday, Father Earl Denay held the first Mass in the new church. Some of its more distinctive features included an Italian marble altar and communion rail, hand-carved Stations of the Cross from Italy and a hand-carved Crucifix over the altar. Only a few days after the first mass at the new church, the old church was razed.

On Sunday, August 23, 1964, Bishop Allan J. Babcock, Bishop of Grand Rapids (the Gaylord Diocese was not established until 1971) presided over the dedication of the church. Assisting as deacon was Father Ulanowicz whose dream of a new church for Saint Mary was finally realized.

The church, Saint Mary School, rectory and convent were revitalized in a major capital improvement program undertaken by Father James Gardiner in 1990-94 and stands today as a strong symbol of the enduring Catholic faith in Charlevoix. ■

Saint Mary of the Woods, *Kalkaska*
Saint Aloysius, *Fife Lake, Mission of Saint Mary of the Woods*
Saint Mary, *Lake Leelanau*

By Father Joseph Wiekierak

A little Saint Mary wood frame church, with its little cemetery occupied about a quarter of an acre on a hillside in Barker Creek, was a mission located about ten miles northeast of Traverse City.

Father Peter Jakubowski, Pastor of Saint Anthony Church in Mancelona, moved the church six miles east to the village of Kalkaska, and set it upon two lots alongside U.S. 131. It became his mission church.

While Father Joseph Wiekierak was Administrator of Saint Rita, Maple City and of Saint Joseph Bohemian Settlement, he was appointed Administrator of Saint Mary in Kalkaska and Saint Aloysius in Fife Lake on June 24, 1955, by Bishop Allen Babcock, who left it to his discretion to decide where to establish his residence. Both were mission churches, and had forty and thirty-five families, respectively. Since the Village of Kalkaska was ideally situated for growth and development, it was selected as the parish with Saint Aloysius as the mission. Truly, by divine providence a field stone house directly across the highway from the church was available and became the rectory.

The little church at Barker Creek.

Saint Mary Church seated about sixty persons. With two Masses on Sunday, it was adequate for the local Catholics. However, because the abundance of lakes and forests in the area made it a tourist attraction, the need for larger seating capacity was quickly apparent.

In 1956, Carlton Miller (Marie) a parishioner and vice-president of the Wayne Wire Industrial plant obtained twenty acres in a wooded area about a quarter of mile east of U.S. 131 on County Road 612. With a loan of $80,000 at three percent from the Diocese of Grand Rapids, the 40 families courageously ventured upon their building project. Medals of the Blessed Virgin Mary were buried in the four corners of the construction at the ground breaking ceremony and Saint Mary — now of the "Woods" — was erected.

Simultaneously, a rectory was also built. The total cost of the project was about $115,000. It was the generosity of the summer and winter visitors and a $5,000 grant from the Catholic Extension Society that greatly aided the small congregation to reach its goal — the "burning of the mortgage celebration." After several years the church basement was developed into sound proof Confraternity of Christian Doctrine (C.C.D.) classrooms for the combined students of Saint Mary and Saint Aloysius. The folding door construction made it possible to open up the area for parish social and fund raising events.

Saint Aloysius Church in Fife Lake was larger in size and in seating capacity than Saint Mary of the Woods in Kalkaska. It had been served over the years from Saint Mary of Hannah and by priests residing at the Convent of Holy Angels in Traverse City.

The cemetery alongside the church was a special blessing. Each year the parishioners — even non-Catholic relatives — would gather for a "clean up" project. It was a bonding experience as they united in work and then shared an enjoyable potluck luncheon.

As a mission church it was its lot for a time to have Sunday Mass only once a month. However, the people, being a faith-filled congregation, would gather on Sunday to pray the rosary.

While a new church was built in Kalkaska, the church in Fife Lake was renovated. The walls were paneled, a new rug covered the sanctuary and a new free standing altar with a hanging crucifix were installed. Then due to an increase of tourists an addition was attached to the Gospel side of the sanctuary. It was closed off during the winter months.

Saint Mary School 1930 graduating class.

Inside Saint Mary Parish.

Kalkaska and Fife Lake bid farewell to Father Wiekierak on July 8, 1969. He left to become pastor of Saint Mary Parish in Lake Leelanau.

At the time of his new appointment Father Joseph Podhajski contacted him since Bishop Allen Babcock was seriously ill, to inform him that the grammar-high school would remain open for the approaching school year, thereafter, it would be discontinued.

During that first year, the parishioners were distressed over the scheduled closure. They were reluctant to abandon their school, which was so much an integral part of their parish lives. Hence, a delegation met with Monsignor Herman Zerfas, the Superintendent of Schools in Grand Rapids, and was able to convince him to permit Saint Mary to continue its Catholic education ministry. Permission was granted with the proviso that the school maintain financial viability.

Immediately, a fund drive was started, and in three weeks $45,000 was raised. The school's debt was paid off and the financial situation improved.

Today, a quarter of a century later, Saint Mary School in Lake Leelanau is still passing on the Catholic faith through education. ■

Saint Mary – Our Lady of Mount Carmel, *Gaylord*

A history excerpted and written from "Sown On Good Ground" by Sister Alice O'Rourke, O.P.

Migrants and immigrants who moved their hopes northward during Michigan's lumbering era became the foundation for the Catholic Church which emerged in Otsego County, Saint Mary-Our Lady of Mount Carmel, a church which nearly 100 years later would become a cathedral, the cornerstone for a new diocese.

Father Francis Xavier Szulak, S.J., worked among Polish settlers in the northern counties of lower Michigan from 1876 to 1887. Among those were the settlers of Otsego County. He began visiting growing Otsego County around 1878, when Gaylord's population boasted several tradesmen, retailers and a few professionals. "As lumbering operations moved northward...the diversity of occupations probably helped Gaylord prosper while other towns almost disappeared."

Szulak soon purchased three lots, for a total of $31, that would eventually become the site of Our Lady of Mount Carmel, a house of prayer for the 28 Catholic families reportedly living in the Gaylord area in 1878.

The old Saint Mary Cathedral.

In 1882, about a year after Bishop Caspar Borgess assigned jurisdiction for Gaylord to Father J.H. Schutjes, pastor of West Bay City, Rome established the Diocese of Grand Rapids, which was to include Otsego County.

On his first visit to Gaylord on July 24, 1883, Bishop Henry J. Richter, first bishop of the Diocese of Grand Rapids, dedicated Gaylord's first Catholic church, built a year or two earlier under Father Szulak's guidance. He also confirmed 50 people that day.

While the church's value was listed at $1,450 for insurance purposes, its value was much greater to the more than 100 families it would serve.

In 1888, 150 families joined in an effort to build a rectory for their newly-assigned, full-time pastor, Father Leopold Oprychalski. They generously helped to buy candlesticks, an organ, cassocks for altar boys and vestments for their new pastor.

He served sixteen months before his transfer to Alpena. It was not until 1891, after several priests served the parish temporarily, that Father Alexander Lipinski was assigned as pastor. In 1892, 40 mothers in a heartfelt letter to the bishop begged Lipinski be allowed to remain in Gaylord.

"We will do anything to keep Father Lipinski. We beg of you, your Lordship, please let Father Lipinski stay in Gaylord."

But in 1892, Father Lipinski was transferred to Saginaw.

His successor, Father Casimir Skory, however, served the parish a dozen years. During Father Skory's tenure, Otsego County and Gaylord grew and so, too, did Saint Mary Parish. "Between 1892 and 1899, the number of families increased from 140 to 201, all but 34 of whom were Polish..."

Under Father Skory's pastorate, several parish societies and mutual aid groups were

established. It was under his leadership that Saint Mary School was built, at a cost of $1,875, and opened in 1894 with 50 pupils.

Additionally, Father Skory led the parish in building its second church. He asked each family to pledge $40 over three years, and on September 15, 1901, Bishop Richter dedicated the new red-brick and stained-glass-windowed church with a bell tower from which rang the bell of the first Saint Mary.

Three years later, the bell tolled the end of Father Skory's service in Gaylord, and he was assigned to Grand Rapids.

Father Simon Ponganis arrived for a brief pastorate from 1904 to 1907. At the time, 700 of Saint Mary's 1,050 parishioners did not understand English, therefore, church services were almost exclusively in Polish. Many parishioners of other descent, however, felt neglected and appealed to the bishop to intervene.

Ponganis returned to Saginaw in 1907 and Father Francis Kaczmarek was named his temporary replacement. In 1908, he moved into a newly-constructed rectory. The old rectory became a convent for the Grand Rapids Dominican Sisters, who began staffing the school, now boasting more than 100 students.

In 1913, Father Ponganis returned to Gaylord where he would serve until 1935. His parish was growing in numbers and in faith.

From among the roughly 220 families at Saint Mary came the first ordination from within the parish. Ladislaus Czapran, son of Mr. and Mrs. Francis Czapran of Gaylord, was ordained February 11, 1923, and celebrated his first Mass at Saint Mary on February 13, 1923.

Bishop Szoka and Msgr. Kaminski at the groundbreaking for the new cathedral in 1975.

It was Ponganis who guided his flock through sometimes turbulent years. During World War I, the "Polish people of Gaylord joined their counterparts elsewhere in collecting funds for relief of those in their homeland."

And, as if to slap prejudice in the face as the Ku Klux Klan called for an amendment requiring all children attend public school, Ponganis pushed to remodel and add onto his parish's school. In 1929, Saint Mary graduated its first high school class.

Among the graduates was Regina (Gruszczynski) Latuszek. "We started out early in the morning at 8:00 a.m. Mass at church and sang in the choir..." recalled Latuszek on the occasion of the school's centennial. "Then we all marched to the school. At lunch if we stayed, as a rule we were assigned chores to do," which did not please Latuszek, who often found herself mopping floors or cleaning blackboards.

The Great Depression three years later took its toll on everyone, including Ponganis. During a brief leave of absence, Father Francis Kaminski was assigned assistant to Ponganis. The young priest left but returned in 1936, when Ponganis relinquished his pastoral duties to Kaminski.

As the parish grew, so did the need for a parish hall. It wasn't until 1946, after World War II, the men of the parish dug a full basement under the church, providing space for such a hall. And, with the prosperity that flourished after the war, Gaylord and Otsego County also thrived. Saint Mary had served 250 families in 1945; in 1950 it served 430. The growth demanded an assistant pastor.

A $300,000 addition to the high school addressed the needs of the growing school in 1954. On November 30, 1960, a fire destroyed the elementary school, though staff and students escaped without injury. Everyone, including six-year-old Ann Huff who gave Monsignor Kaminski her 26 cents, helped rebuild the school, which reopened in September of 1962.

Within a matter of a few years, planning was under way for a new diocese, and on June 15, 1971, the Diocese of Gaylord was established. Saint Mary Parish, which had begun as a tiny church for immigrants and lumbermen, was to become the smallest See City in the United States. Edmund C. Szoka was installed as bishop.

And with the creation of a new diocese and a growing population came a new cathedral for the parishioners of Saint Mary. The contemporary $1.6 million cathedral, including a rectory and parish hall, was dedicated July 25, 1976, with much ritual and fanfare.

As rector of the cathedral parish, the jovial, white-haired Kaminski stayed busy and several priests served as his assistants. The Monsignor, with the parishioners and the com-

munity who loved him, celebrated his 50th jubilee as a priest in 1978.

When Kaminski's health began to deteriorate, he and the bishop decided he should retire in 1980, though he remained in residence at Saint Mary.

Upon Kaminski's retirement came the assignment of Father James Suchocki, Father Jim as he would be known to his parishioners, as rector.

Father Jim and his parishioners witnessed many milestones: elevation of Szoka to archbishop; installation of Robert Rose as bishop; the death of Monsignor Kaminski; the school's designation as a National Exemplary School, and together they marked the centennial celebration of Saint Mary Cathedral Parish on January 1, 1984.

First Mass in Saint Mary's Cathedral.

In 1992, Father Francis Murphy became rector of the parish. During his tenure, the community marked the centennial of the school, which brought with it the distinction of being named honored industry during the community's annual Alpenfest. Under his guidance, the parish undertook a $600,000 addition to the school in 1996.

Murphy was reassigned in 1997, with Father John McCracken named his successor.

"Saint Mary Cathedral parishioners...are reaping the harvest of seeds sown in generations past. As they move into a new century, they are aware of the heritage of faith they have received and are conscious of their responsibility for maintaining that heritage and bequeathing it to future generations." ■

Saint Matthew, *Boyne City*
Saint Augustine, *Boyne Falls*

By Father Gerald F. Micketti

The Catholic Church did not officially come to Boyne City and Boyne Falls until rather late in local history. In 1887, there was certainly a Catholic presence in the Emmet and Charlevoix Counties. There were, for instance, parishes on Beaver Island and at, Cross Village, Harbor Springs and Petoskey. There were also churches at East Jordan and Gaylord. There were also stations at the time where Mass was offered occasionally, such as the Boynes, Advance, Charlevoix, Elmira, Mount Bliss (Praga), Bay Shore and South Arm. These stations were served by the Franciscan priests out of Harbor Springs and later Petoskey. Both parishes in the Boynes owe their establishment to Father Bruno Torka, O.F.M.

Boyne Falls is the older of the two parishes, tracing its origins to 1900 when the construction of a church began. This church was blessed in 1901 by Bishop Richter. The organization of the parish in Boyne City started in 1904 and the original church on Grant Street was built in 1907.

Saint Matthew had outgrown the Grant Street building. In 1962, the present church building was built. Also in the same decade, Saint Augustine was enlarged by widening the main structure. The pastor of both parishes at that time was Father Jerome Szydlowski. He was pastor from 1956 until his death in 1977. Father Dennis Stilwell succeeded Father Szydlowski, staying in the area until 1985 when he was transferred to Immaculate Conception Church in Traverse City. While he was pastor, Saint Augustine Church was completely remodeled in 1982. Father John O. Ladd succeeded Father Stilwell and served for four years. Father Thomas Neis followed Father Ladd and served until 1993, when he was transferred to Saint Mary in Charlevoix. Father Francis Partridge is the present pastor. ■

Saint Michael the Archangel, *Suttons Bay*

Father Ignatius Mrak celebrated the first Mass in the area called Suttons Bay in 1845 when he established his Indian mission at Peshawbestown, about three miles north of Suttons Bay. Like many other places and communities without a Catholic church building, the first Masses were offered in the homes of the settlers. The first settlers were mostly of German descent with a few Irish families mixed in. Agriculture and lumbering drew the men and later families to the area. Some of the early families included were Steimels, Walters, Beuerle, Fehrenbach, Herman and Kuemin.

Father Andrew Herbstret followed Father Mrak in 1870. The first church building in Suttons Bay was a small frame structure possibly built through the efforts of Father Mrak. The present parish of Saint Michael the Archangel was established by Father Herbstret and another frame building erected in 1873 on the site of the present church. Father Herbstret was responsible for some of the immigration to the area when he launched a real estate boom and brought families from Ohio, where he served as a member of the Congregation of the Precious Blood. He also had dreams of establishing a Catholic "National University" on the bay.

Students at the Omena School in 1920.

Father Philip S. Zorn succeeded Father Herbstret during the years 1875 through 1879. He visited the community from Harbor Springs. After Father Zorn, Father George Zeigler, who was assigned to Saint Francis Church in Traverse City, served the Catholic families at Suttons Bay. After the Diocese of Grand Rapids was established, Saint Michael Parish was placed in the care of Saint Mary of Lake Leelanau, at that time called Provemont. This relationship continued for 20 years with Masses offered on the second, fourth and fifth Sundays of each month. The priests that cared for the two parishes in the following years included Fathers Charles J. Votypka, Frederick H. Ruessmann, Alexander F. Zugelder.

Father Ruessmann served twice at Saint Michael. His second term started in August of 1899 and the community experienced growth and disaster. While he was the pastor, the parish could began building a combination schools and convent. Sisters of Saint Dominic of Grand Rapids were the first teachers in the school. The disaster was the destruction of the church by fire Sunday, October 30, 1904. The church was rebuilt in 1905. That same year, Saint Michael the Archangel Parish received its own resident pastor, Father John D. Engemann. From that point Saint Michael grew and prospered. ■

Saint Patrick, *Traverse City*

By Father Gerald F. Micketti

It was a warm beautiful afternoon in August of 1984. Don Miles and his family were living at Long Lake south of Traverse City. His eleven-year-old son, called out, "Hey, Dad, some guy on a motorcycle is coming up the drive!"

Wondering who it might be, Don got up, opened the door and met a man standing there. He put out his hand, smiled and said, "Hi! I'm Father Frank Murphy."

After entering the house, Father Murphy explained that Bishop Rose had authorized the creation of a new parish in the southeast corner of Grand Traverse County. This meant taking portions of Immaculate Conception, Saint Francis and Saint Mary of Hannah parishes to form a new parish. The more Father Murphy talked the more excited Don became about being a part of the new parish.

Thus began the process to establish a new Catholic parish, Saint Patrick Church. The church's first location was the Blair Township Hall and the parish grew with each weekend Mass. Members had to set up and take down after all the Masses. Don was one of the first lectors and it always seemed to him that he was standing in the middle of the congregation when he was proclaiming the reading.

The congregation soon outgrew the township hall and moved to the Interlochen grade school in the village of Interlochen. Mass was also celebrated on Saturday nights at Dendrinos Chapel of the Interlochen Center for the Arts. Participating in the Masses was like gathering with the extended family. People arrived at the chapel, set up and prepared the altar, decided who was going to be the lector, eucharistic ministers, ushers and what hymns to sing.

Father Frank Murphy breaks ground for Saint Patrick Church in 1986.

Each week chores were divided among various families including the Hammers, Molers and Wambolds. Everyone was eager to participate. Interlochen students joined the congregation on Saturdays, sometimes providing the music. Alice Hammer and Stephany Moler undertook the ministry of passing out bulletins every weekend. One Saturday a "professional usher" helped with the collection at Dendrinos Chapel. After the Mass he stood at the back of the chapel and passed out bulletins. Stephany was very upset. She came to her mother and said, "Mom, he's doing our job!"

During the second summer a student came to play the organ for the Mass. When he came on stage, he never looked at the congregation; he immediately sat at the organ and began to play the music for the first hymn. After the Mass he wanted to run off the stage but people kept getting in his way because they wanted to tell him what a great job he did. By the end of the summer he had changed completely. When Father Murphy announced the last weekend of the summer was the final appearance for the young man, he strode on the stage, waved to congregation, seated himself and played the music for the hymns chosen. The final piece of music was a trumpet recessional. At the end of the piece he stood up, turned to the congregation and bowed to a standing ovation.

There were about 120 families who initially registered as parishioners in 1984. As the number of members increased, the idea of a building to call home became important. In the summer of 1986, the ground was broken to begin construction of Saint Patrick Catholic Church building.

Parishioners were promised that the first Mass in the new church would be Christmas Eve, 1986. Week by week it looked as if they were going to meet the deadline. Then, a snag! Two days before Christmas Eve, it was discovered the parish had no occupancy permit. Phone calls were made. The permit was issued on the spot by the inspector who had arrived like the police were chasing him. Christmas Eve, 1986 witnessed the first Mass celebrated in the new building. The church was dedicated March 17, 1987.

During construction of the new parish facilities, Father Murphy was constantly on the scene checking progress. He wore one particular flannel shirt that had seen its better days, probably several years ago. That shirt became his trademark. It was decided that at least a part of that shirt had to be in the cornerstone. His sister had other thoughts. The weekend of the dedication Father Murphy's sister went through his closets and destroyed the old flannel shirt. She said that every time she visited with Frank she would go through his clothing and get rid of his rags.

The church construction.

Growth continued through the years for Saint Patrick Church. By the spring of 1997 the parish had a thousand registered families. A conference room was added to the rectory. The store room and the kitchen of the social hall were expanded and two restrooms added to the social hall.

In September, 1992, Father Murphy moved to the Cathedral in Gaylord and Father Gerald Micketti became the pastor at Saint Patrick. ■

Saint Philip Neri, *Empire*

By Father Gerald F. Micketti

He traveled from Peshawbestown to attend to the spiritual needs of the settlers. His name was Father Ignatius Mrak. He had come from Austria and arrived in the United States in 1845. He offered his services as a priest to the Bishop of Detroit. He was sent to succeed Father Frederick Baraga at L'Arbre Croche, probably near present day Cross Village. He served the Native Americans there as well as the settlers in the surrounding counties. One of the those communities was Empire. So begins the history of Saint Philip Neri Parish in Empire.

Empire was first settled in the mid-1850s by John LaRue. The village is believed to have been named for the schooner, *Empire*, which went aground near the present site of Empire in 1865 and served as the village school that winter. In December of 1887, the T. Wilce Company formed the Empire Lumber Company to provide hardwood for their flooring company in Chicago. About 1890 the lumber company expanded into one of the largest hardwood mills in the state, converting Empire into a booming lumber town with a population reaching up to one thousand around 1900. The last mill burned in 1917 and ended the boom of Empire.

Some of the settlers of Empire and the area were Catholics. They had spiritual needs that required the attention of a priest. Father Mrak offered Mass in the year 1855 in the home of Richard Tobin, located just south of the Glen Lake narrows. The Tobin land became the gathering place of the settlers in the area who were Catholic. A

small church built of logs was constructed on the southeast corner of the cemetery in 1867 on the Benzonia Trail, now county road 677. The early Catholic settlers were buried at this location, too; the first grave was that of Richard Tobin himself. Father Mrak continued to meet the spiritual needs of the settlers until 1869 when he was appointed the second bishop of the Diocese of Sault Ste Marie and Marquette, succeeding Frederick Baraga.

During this time the area was becoming more populated. Frank Payment sailed the Great Lakes and landed at Glen Haven. Impressed with the area, he encouraged several people from his hometown of Ogdensburg, New York, to emigrate to what became East Empire, five miles east of the present day Empire. This was in 1867. Soon Mass was offered in the homes of Pat Karns and Tom Deering in East Empire.

When Father Mrak left for Sault Ste. Marie, he was followed by Father A. Herbstret. Father Herbstret lived in Suttons Bay and visited all the missions in his territory. In the fall of 1870, Father Philip Zorn succeeded Father Herbstret who was transferred to Big Rapids. When Father Zorn visited the Empire area, he offered Mass at the Dunn farm. He also baptized Pat Gordon, Frank Daly, Joseph Verno and John Deering at the Dunn farm.

For about eight months Father Schacken came from Traverse City to serve in Empire. Then for about three months Father Zassa came to the area also from Traverse City. Then the responsibility fell to Father Zorn. He remained until 1877, living at Suttons Bay.

Father Ziegler followed Father Zorn in 1877. Father Ziegler was the first resident pastor of Saint Francis Church in Traverse City. He also came to Empire to offer the Mass. In 1885 Father Nyssen, who followed Father Ziegler in Traverse City, served the Catholics of Empire.

During this time the only road of any sort was the Benzonia Trail. Families traveled during the day to the sites of the homes where Mass was offered and then returned the next day. Sometimes they blazed new trails through the forest to get to the Mass.

Another homesteader in the area was Philip J. Sullivan. He arrived in Glen Haven by boat, came to Empire and homesteaded the land that became the site of the first Saint Philip Neri Church. He donated the land where the old church stood. The location of that building is immediately behind the present rectory. The foundation or part of the foundation is visible. The building was about 20' x 40'. He also donated the land for the adjoining cemetery. The church was named Saint Philip in honor of Mr. Sullivan.

The first Saint Philip church building was begun in June of 1894 by Burr Getman. It was partially completed when strong winds leveled it to the ground. It was soon reconstructed. Benches served as the first pews and the communion rail was made of 2 x 4's. Mass was offered by Father Joseph Bauer coming from Saint Francis Church in Traverse City. One woman remembers that it was a real treat to dress up on Sunday mornings and drive the horses seven miles to Mass, which was always at 10:30 a.m. People going to Holy Communion would have a big treat of doing numerous farm chores and fasting from midnight before having breakfast.

In 1906 a horse barn was built on the northeast corner of the property to keep the horses dry and warm. The barn could accommodate about 20 teams. The barn was a necessity because the number of confessions before Mass delayed the start of Mass, sometimes for two hours. During this time a priest came from "the Polish settlement," about 15 miles further north. "The Polish settlement" was Isadore, Holy Rosary Parish.

One of the priests was Father Stephen Nowakowski. He usually traveled on a fat little pony which he let saunter along. The next priest to come from Isadore was Father Bieniaowski. He drove the horses like mad and the ponies, skinny and tired, would be puffing when they reached Saint Philip Neri Church on summer mornings. Father Bieniawski came on Saturday afternoons in the winter. There was also a Father Niadowski who also visited from Isadore. Fathers Downs and Golden followed the priests from Isadore; both priests came from the Nessen City area. When Saint Philip church became a mission of Saint Ann of Frankfort, Father Flajole was the visiting priest. He was followed by Father Bauman. Another visiting priest was Father Kosnik. During his time of visitation, Popa Builders of Cedar built the altar sanctuary and sacristies for the old church in 1921.

Father Joseph Bocek became the first resident pastor in 1940 and served Saint Philip church until his death in September 9, 1954. He was a frequent dinner guest of his parishioners.

The present rectory was built in 1956 under the direction of Father Leo Zielinski. A local builder and parishioner, Harold Schaub, built the rectory. Father David Drinan followed Father Zielinski and Father Francis Hackett followed Father Drinan.

Father Joseph Battersby succeeded Father Hackett. At this time Saint Philip parish was feeling the growing pains of summer visitors and their attendance at Mass. The Mass schedule increased to five Masses for the summer. Eventually sliding glass doors were added to the south wall of the old church and the pews were rearranged at the beginning of each summer to accommodate people inside and out. This growth and accommodation were happening while Father Battersby was the pastor. He also started the planning for a new church. He was not to build the new church. Father Edward Roczen, his successor, was to see the new building constructed.

In January 1969, parishioners met with Father Roczen and Edward Gutierrez, architect from Muskegon and contractor, Bud Johnson, of Suttons Bay. They decided to build the new church on property donated by Mark and Warren Deering. The building would seat 331 in the nave and over 200 in the overflow. In February, the Building and Finance Committee launched a fund drive. Less than four months later, ground was broken and construction began. The cost was $185,000.

Father Roczen left Saint Philip Neri Church in 1980. He was succeeded by Father Joseph Wiekierak. During his tenure, the parish hall was enlarged. Later on the hall was enlarged again, with a new wing added for eight classrooms, an office for the director of religious education, and a chapel for use in the winter months.

Father Wiekierak left in 1988 and was followed Father Charles Goentges. He was succeeded by Father Jerome Tuller, O.F.M., Cap, in 1990. Because of ill health he left in 1994. Interim pastor was Father Larry Kelleher until Father John Tupper, the present pastor, arrived. ■

Saint Raphael, *Mikado*

By Father Gerald F. Micketti

Daniel Bruce was the community pioneer in the village of Mikado. He actually founded the community by talking with the railroad and convincing them to build tracks from Tawas to Mikado and north. A train stop was established and the Bruces built a large hotel. This railroad passed through a farming area where many people lived who later became the parishioners of the Catholic Church in Mikado. The business in the village catered to the farming community. Much later, residents found employment in Oscoda and at Wurtsmith Air Force Base.

The first priest to celebrate Mass in Mikado was Father P.C. Winter, pastor of Sacred Heart Church, AuSable. He took care of the Catholic residents of the Mikado area during the years 1884-1892. He would say the Mass monthly about 1888-1889, when Father Ruessmann became his assistant. The Mass at that time was said in the northeast corner room of the residence of "Red-Dan" McDonald. This home is one-half mile east and one-half mile south of the present town of Mikado; in those days this home was at the west end of the logging area and the end of the road. Mrs. Albert Broadwood was baptized in this residence in 1889 and Gertrude McGillis, daughter of Mr. and Mrs. William McGillis, was baptized in the same residence in 1892.

Father J.E. Mahar succeeded Father Winter in February 1892, as pastor of Sacred Heart Church, AuSable. He had Fathers E. Langlois and Edward LeFevre as assistants. Mass continued to be celebrated monthly in Mikado.

From the year 1893, through 1895, Father Mahar continued on in AuSable but as pastor of the English-speaking parishioners. Father J.A. Doucet was appointed pastor of the French-speaking parishioners also in AuSable. The two pastors of Sacred Heart Church shared the same rectory and used the same church, alternating for early and late Masses on succeeding Sundays.

During the year 1893, Father Doucet became interested in Mikado. Since the parish in AuSable had dwindled from 900 families in Father Winter's time to 175 families in the early 1890s and since many of the sawmills went out of business, Father Doucet closed the school in AuSable, sold the school building and sisters' house, then tore down the short-lived school-church building in Oscoda. From some of the material of the church-school building a church was built in Mikado. Two brothers, Dan and John Cameron, together with Gillis McDonald and his brother, James, dug the holes for the large cedar blocks and put them in to hold the three-wall cedar timbers as the foundation of the Mikado

church. This activity was in the spring of 1893.

Two years later Father Mahar was transferred and Father Doucet became the only pastor of Sacred Heart Parish. The Harrisville parish was transferred from Alpena and made a mission to AuSable along with Mikado. Father Poulin was sent as an assistant to Father Doucet, and he immediately took charge of the task of completing the church in Mikado. Bishop Richter of Grand Rapids dedicated the church to Saint Raphael Sunday, August 13, 1895.

In 1901, Father Doucet was sent to Standish and Father L.A. Montagne who had been an assistant to Father LeFevre in Pinconning, became the new pastor of Sacred Heart, AuSable and the missions of Harrisville and Mikado. Father Montagne stayed until the terrible AuSable-Oscoda fire of July 11, 1911, when everything in the parish and town burned to the ground.

In 1905, however, Father Poulin was appointed pastor of Saint Anne church in Harrisville with the mission at Mikado. Saint Raphael Parish would remain a mission attached to Saint Anne Parish, Harrisville until 1950, when Father Lawrence Greiner was made the pastor of Sacred Heart Parish in Oscoda and Mikado was attached to Oscoda. During the tenure of Father Greiner a new foundation was built for the church building. In the fall of 1951 Edward Loyer and his son-in-law, Stanley Waszkiewicz, Amil Dumont, Ernest Michaud, William Stewart and Roy Lindzy together with other parishioners raised the church building and built a cement foundation and block wall for a permanent foundation. All but a few of the old cedar blocks had rotted away and the church was beginning to tilt and slip eastward. A good strong wind would have blown the church over. During this same time period, in the early 1950s, a new entrance was built and Mr. and Mrs. Edward Greenwood donated a Reed organ for the church.

When Father Raymond Mulka became pastor of Saint Anne Parish, Harrisville, Saint Raphael Church was attached to Saint Anne Parish and remained attached to Saint Anne Parish. As the pastors changed at Harrisville so did the pastors at Saint Raphael. During the following years, additions and renovations were made to the church.

Another addition to the Mikado community came through the parish. The Saint Raphael Vincent de Paul Society came into existence in June of 1987. Based in the church, it started out with just a few members who felt a need to help the people in the area. With Nancy Schisler as the president, members of the parish decided to have a clothes closet and food pantry. But, as donations of clothes came in, the society outgrew the church. A thrift store was opened and the surplus spilled over in the church's basement. Through grants, Sunday collection and donations, they were able to help people not only with food and clothing but rent, utilities, heat and medical aid.

A group of parishioners in Harrisville concentrated mainly on visiting the sick and elderly. They saw a need for services and with the help of many, in the fall of 1991, with the backing of Saint Raphael and Saint Anne Parishes, construction of a new building was started. This building is located in Mikado and has helped numerous people in the Mikado area. ■

Saint Rita, *Maple City*

Many interesting events make up the history of the lovely Saint Rita Church high on a hill overlooking the village of Maple City.

In the year 1873, Catholics of this small community were served by Reverend Zorn and later by the Reverend Mrak, who in time was elevated to bishop.

Sometime before 1884, a group of Bohemian Catholics had come to Cleveland Township and settled in what is now called "the Bohemian Settlement," where in 1884 they built a church and Father Mrak became pastor.

Father Bieniawski of Isadore, at present in charge of the church in Mackinaw City, was then appointed to take over the Bohemian Settlement and Empire churches as his missions, and he said Mass once a month in each of these churches.

In 1901 David A. Clavette and Charles Bloom of Ludington moved their families to Maple City where they had purchased the Stanley and Young General Store. The Clavette family were Catholics and became interested in bringing Holy Mass directly to their little community. In 1914, Matthew Sullivan, son of the pioneer settler, and Dave Clavette went to Grand Rapids where they beseeched Bishop Gallagher to allow them the privilege of having Mass at least once a month in their village. The Clavette family were then proprietors of the Hotel DeClavette and arrangements were completed whereby a small altar was to be erected in the hotel for Mass to be celebrated once a month by Father Flajole, pastor of Saint Ann Church in Frankfort. He also acquired the Bohemian Church as one of his missions.

It soon became apparent that a larger place was needed to accommodate the many Catholics attending the monthly services. The group rented a large room in the Bellinger building across the street from the hotel. Once again Matthew Sullivan, Dave Clavette, and another enthusiast, Stanley Peplinski, journeyed to Grand Rapids to request permission of Bishop Gallagher to allow them to purchase the property. The Bishop assured them he would "look into the matter."

Upon their return to Maple City a Novena was made to Saint Rita asking her to assist them in their prayers asking God for this great favor. Before the close of the Novena, Father Flajole received word to proceed with the purchase and to make necessary alterations.

It was at one of their frequent planning meetings that Mrs. Clavette suggested that their church be called Saint Rita in thanksgiving for the many favors they had received through her intercession. There was justifiable pride by all when Mass was offered for the first time at Saint Rita in 1914.

Saint Rita's history would not be complete without the story of the religious education of the children of the community. Classes were held three times a week, and on September 8, 1918, the momentous day arrived when 24 children received their First Holy Communion.

This was just the beginning of the religious education of the children. In 1920, Father Albert Bauman requested permission to have the Sisters of Mercy send four nuns for the duration of six or eight weeks during the summer vacation to teach catechism to another First Communion class; and to confer the Sacrament of Confirmation, another first for the parish. His request was granted and two nuns were sent to teach in Maple City, and two in Empire.

Saint Rita was served as a mission church from Frankfort by Father Flajole from 1914 to 1919; Father Albert Bauman from 1919 to 1924; Father Roman Kosnik from 1924 until it was made a mission of Empire with Father Bocek on August 1, 1951. He was authorized to build a rectory next to the church in Maple City. He resided in Cedar until the parish house was ready for occupancy in January 1952. Father Sniegowski was

pastor until April 6, 1953, when Father Joseph Wiekierak was placed in charge. On July 1, 1955, another change was made when Father Wiekierak was transferred to Kalkaska and was succeeded again by Father Sniegowski, who had been pastor of White Cloud.

In the fall of 1958 Father John Najdowski became the pastor, and remained at Saint Rita/Saint Joseph until Father Stanislaus Bur came in the summer of 1960. A parish hall was constructed during Father Bur's pastorate; and Saint Rita and Saint Joseph parishes merged. Former pastor of Saint Jean Baptiste Parish, Muskegon, Monsignor William Frazier, arrived in the summer of 1970 to become pastor of Saint Rita/Saint Joseph Parish. During this time, these parishes became a part of the new Diocese of Gaylord.

Father G. Wm. Fischer served from 1974-76, followed by Father Martin J. Toolis from 1976-78. Father Toolis directed the renovation of Saint Ritas Church. Father Arthur Mulka served temporarily from October 1976 to February 1977 with Father Ron Gronowski, while they were pastors of Holy Rosary church at Cedar. Father David A. Romzek served from 1978-82 and Father Casimir J. Zawacki from 1982 to August 1984. During his stay, an addition to the parish hall was realized.

Father James A. Holtz was assigned to Holy Rosary Church in Cedar in August 1984 as well as the co-parish of Saint Rita/Saint Joseph. Since the merger of the three parishes, the community has grown under the spiritual guidance of Father Albin J. Gietzen who arrived in August 1985, followed by Father Charles Zeeb in August 1993; Father Martin Schaub from August 1995-October 1996; and Father Edward Boucher from November 1996 until the present.

Monsignor Bonaface Winowiecki served as substitute priest over the years. Retired Father Walter Anthony has also served as substitute priest for many years. ■

Saint Rose of Lima, *Herron*

By Father Gerald F. Micketti

Saint Rose of Lima Parish is situated about halfway in Alpena County on highway M-32. The parish was served by a priest who lived at Saint Anne Church in Alpena. In 1886 Bishop Richter assigned Father Joseph Thadee Hudon, the newly arrived pastor of Saint Anne, to establish preaching stations in the King Settlement, Presque Isle and Ossineke areas. The King Settlement Mission was the beginning of the church which later became known as Saint Rose of Lima Parish in Herron.

Father Hudon was young, only 28. That was fortunate because it took a vigorous man to make the difficult treks to the outlying missions of King Settlement, Presque Isle and Ossineke. The few existing wagon roads were often impossible and a great deal of traveling was confined to tote roads. "Tote roads" were trails branching off in many directions over high ground in the wilderness.

Father Hudon served the 41 families (12 English, 26 French and three German) in King Settlement for one-and-one-half years, saying Mass twice a year, before he was succeeded by Father Theodule Blais. Father Blais was installed as the pastor of Saint Anne Parish in Alpena. He unfortunately, found himself in trouble with Bishop Richter and was removed in January of 1893. Father Napoleon Nazaire Poulin was sent to Alpena for three months as administrator until Father Charles H. DeQuoy became the pastor.

Regardless of that situation, Father Blais is credited with securing the initial parcel of land now owned by Saint Rose of Lima Parish. On June 20, 1890, Samuel Clearwood deeded a small corner portion of his farm for the mission. For the next four years, whenever weather permitted and the country roads were fit for travel, Father DeQuoy trudged out to minister to the families in the Herron area. That changed when Bishop Richter assigned Father Godfrey Lenzen as pastor of the newly named Saint Rose of Lima Parish. ■

Saint Stephen, *Lake City*

By Willard M.J. Baird

The Catholic Church in Lake City is dedicated to Saint Stephen, the first martyr, as recorded in the Acts of Apostles. The first church building bearing his name was built in 1896. The Catholic presence in Missaukee County goes back further, probably ten years prior to the building the church. Newspaper reports indicate that "Catholic Services" were offered in 1887. County Records show that in 1885 Bishop Henry Richter acquired two adjoining residential lots in Lake City, one block north of the present United Methodist Church. The land was not utilized by the Diocese of Grand Rapids.

The first Catholic families in Lake City assembled periodically for Mass in a private home, the county courthouse, or the Grand Central Hotel. The priest would come either from Reed City or Cadillac at irregular intervals. Father Baroux visited Lake City in the late 1880s to offer Mass. A fire in Lake City, July 4, 1888, nearly destroyed the entire city, including the Grand Central Hotel. After the fire the hotel was rebuilt and Mass was offered in the new hotel building. Father Baroux was succeeded as pastor of Saint Ann in Cadillac by Father Louis M. Prud'homme; it was from Cadillac that Father Baroux served the Catholic families in Lake City. Not only was Father Prud'homme serving as pastor of Saint Ann, he was also ministering to the needs of several missions which included Lake City, Marion and Frankfort. In 1897 Father Godfried Guthausen arrived at Cadillac to assist Father Prud'homme. The assistant served eight missions in six counties, one of which was Saint Stephen. It was during the pastorate of Father Prud'homme that the first Catholic church was built in Lake City and Saint Stephen Parish was organized. Property was purchased, construction started and completed in one year — 1896. Until 1950, Saint Stephen was a mission but that year it became a parish. The first resident pastor was Father Edmund J. Farrell. ■

The original Saint Stephen church.

An interior view.

Saint Thomas Aquinas, *Elmira*

Hotel man William S. Hartwell became the first postmaster, on September 3, 1877, with the office named Elmira, after its township. The village of Elmira was originally platted and recorded as Windsor, on September 4, 1880. The Grand Rapids & Indiana Railroad came through in 1887 and established a station here, called Eaton.

In the late 1800s, logging companies moved into this area to harvest the virgin timber. Many young Polish men and their families migrated into the area to harvest the virgin timber and find a better life for their families. These Polish families were devoted Catholics and sensed the need of a church for their families to grow spiritually. The parish began with a nucleus of six families. Mass was celebrated in different homes by the Franciscans from Petoskey or Harbor Springs until the first church was built in 1895. It was a small frame structure at the south end of the village with a seating capacity of 100. Bishop Henry J. Richter, of the Grand Rapids Diocese, blessed this building on October 11, 1895, naming the Mission in honor of Saint Thomas Aquinas. At the same time, he confirmed a class of 20. On November 15, 1898, under the direction of Father Bruno Torka, O.F.M., a three-acre parcel of land was purchased for a cemetery by the Grand Rapids Diocese for $30 from William & Celia Wood. Bishop Richter visited again on October 14, 1899, confirming another class of 20. On June 29, 1905, the bishop blessed the church bell and confirmed 32 people.

For some years in the early part of the 20th century, the number of households fluctuated between 25 and 40, nearly all Polish speaking. Mass was celebrated the first Sunday of each month, then the third Sunday and any fifth Sunday. Beginning in October 1922, with the congregation having grown to 64 families, Mass was celebrated at Elmira every Sunday and Holy Day. Attendance at the weekend catechism classes grew from an average of 30 in 1915 to an average of 75 by 1922. With the appointment of Father Ceslaus Lipinski as the first resident pastor of Mancelona in July 1929, the many years of service at Elmira by the Franciscans from Petoskey and Harbor Springs came to an end.

Father Jerome A. Szydlowski, was appointed first resident pastor in 1946 and lived for seven years in a single room attached to the church. He increased the building fund from $900 to $22,000 during his six-year tenure. Non-Catholics joined Catholics in making the construction of a new church possible. The land, ten acres, was donated by Mr. Darius Buell, a non-Catholic, who also did the excavating free of charge and later donated the majestic blue spruce which surround the church.

Construction of the new church and rectory was started on May 4, 1953, and was completed a year later. Members of the parish contributed one day's work every two weeks. Farmers gave an acre or more of potatoes which were sold and the proceeds turned over to the church fund. Two parishioners, Casimir Skowronski and Joseph Kucharek, each contributed more than 1,000 hours of work on the church. With this cooperation and donated labor, the estimated cost of $80,000 was cut in half.

The first Mass in the new church was celebrated on Saturday, May 8, 1954. The Mass was preceded by a procession which was led by Father (Chester) Ceslaus Klimowicz who hand-carried the Blessed Sacrament to the new church. The procession was viewed by many non-Catholic neighbors and friends as it made its way to the new church. The procession included: Otsego County Sheriff Ralph Holewinski and 250 to 300 parishioners and friends. This was a joyful, heartrending and exciting day but also a sad day for some of the older members of the parish whose spiritual lives were centered around the old church. Father Klimowicz moved into the new rectory at about the same time.

On Sunday, August 15, 1954, Bishop Allen J. Babcock laid the cornerstone and dedicated the church and rectory at a 4:00 p.m. ceremony. The ceremony was a community event, attended by 30 priests and 350 parishioners and guests.

Prior to the ceremonies inside the church, Bishop Babcock officiated at the laying of the cornerstone. Sealed within the stone was a copper carton containing official documents including the history of the parish, current issues of the *Western Michigan Catholic*, the *Otsego County Herald Times* and coins of various denominations.

In a brief address to the parishioners before the closing benediction, Bishop Babcock praised the leadership of Father Klimowicz in inspiring the parish to undertake and complete the construction of the beautiful church and an appropriate rectory. He said that such praise was due because willingness to give not only money but also time and energy indicated true faith. He declared that the pounding of every nail and the carrying of every board by a parishioner was in fact a prayer and an act of faith. He remarked that such spirit to give time and labor toward churches and schools unfortunately is lacking in many urban areas. He reminded the congregation that by providing a beautiful church for worship, they will inspire children toward greater prayer and reverence, and perhaps will lead some of the youngsters to the priesthood or sisterhood.

Deacon at the benediction was Father Methodius Dobrzelewski, O.F.M., a native son of the parish stationed in Lake Geneva, Wisconsin. Subdeacon was Father Jerome A. Szydlowski, the first resident pastor. Also present were: Brother Religious Dobrzelewski, O.F.M., of Pulaski, Wisconsin, a brother of Father Methodius and a seminarian, Casimir Kucharek, studying in Edmonton, Alberta, for the Ukrainian Diocese in Saskatchewan. In September 1968, Reverend Lionginas (Father Leo) Dieninis was appointed pastor.

In 1979, under the leadership of Father David Gemuend, a major remodeling project took place. The pews were removed and Mass was celebrated in the basement until the completion of this project which included: A new oak altar, pulpit, tabernacle base and oak trim throughout the church (by Mr. Guy Baker, a parishioner); new needlepoint "Stations of the Cross" were completed by several ladies of the parish.

Raising the steeple.

Twelve new stained-glass windows were created and installed by Tom Woodruff, owner of Suttons Bay Stain Glass Company. The most sensational piece is a five-feet-by-five-feet window. This panel is a symbolic approach toward the Holy Spirit in full descent in the form of a white dove. In the background is a tunnel representing the passage between life and death, a tunnel whose surface is composed of a mosaic of human faces. The borders feature images of the heart of Christ, consumed by Pentecostal fires. A series of eight windows depict the biblical creation and there are three floral panels which decorate the choir loft. Mr. Woodruff also carved the nine-foot wooden risen Christ; a "triptych (three panel) oil painting of the holy family was commissioned to a lady artist in New Jersey; a new insulated ceiling was installed. The icon of "Our Lady of Czestochowa," at the entrance of the church, was donated by Mr. and Mrs. Ted Makarewicz. There were also many smaller projects which were completed by many members of the parish.

On August 12, 1979, the parish church at Elmira was solemnly rededicated according to the rites of the Holy Roman Catholic Church. The Most Reverend Edmund Casimir Szoka, D.D., J.C.L., First Bishop of Gaylord, officiated.

The altar of sacrifice was anointed with holy chrism and dedicated for worship by the Most Reverend Bishop. In the crypt of this altar were sealed relics of the holy apostles Peter and Paul and a relic from the bones of the holy patron of this edifice, Saint Thomas Aquinas, Doctor of the Church and Confessor of the Faith. To fulfill the liturgical requirements for dedication of an altar, a relic from the bones of the bishop and martyr, Saint Stanislaus of Crakow, was buried here in peace. Included in addition, were the bones of the sainted Prince of Poland, Saint Casimir and the relics of an unknown martyr which had been removed from the former altar stone of this church and placed now in this crypt.

Reverend Martin Toolis, Reverend Robert Nalley, Deacons Jeff Cannon and Andrew LePain have served the parish and currently Reverend Richard Hannon serves as pastor. ■

Saint Wenceslaus, *Gills Pier*

By Helen Korson

Over 100 years ago the Bohemian Community of Saint Wenceslaus, Gills Pier, became a parish in the beautiful farming area of Leelanau County overlooking Lake Michigan and only a short distance from Lake Leelanau (formerly Carp Lake). All of the families who formed this group were of the Catholic faith and hard working farmers. Most of these were young married couples, friends or related in some form, arriving with a small child or two. The next generation married; this neighbor's young son courted his neighbor's daughter, later marrying his sweetheart and so it went. After two generations, this group could no longer continue to marry their neighbors. They traveled to neighboring parishes, finding life long partners among the French, German, Polish and Swede communities. Even though this has taken place, the parish Saint Wenceslaus has remained predominantly of Bohemian heritage, being entrepreneurs, self-supporting and giving. The names of the original families one can very much find on the parish roster. Such names as Kalchik, Korson, Kolarik, Kovarik, Houdek, Sedlacek, Jelinek, Reicha, Kiessel and Roubal. An annual dinner in the summer and a fall festival have always been great fund raisers for the parish necessities and upkeep of its church and buildings.

Sixteen years ago another fund raiser was begun. Father James McLaughlin was the pastor; something had to be done to revitalize this parish of committed, dedicated people during the cold winter months. A special Mass and dinner was held for all former retired senior members living away from the community and also members of the parish. The hall was filled with guests, happy to be present, remembering days of old, and getting reacquainted with people they had not seen in years.

Father McLaughlin had another idea. The men of the parish were asked to make and serve a soup supper. So in Lent one year, Julius Kolarik, Jr., living west of the church, dressed out a steer. All of the bones (with meat on, of course) were brought to the church kitchen and cooked. Groups of men workers were assigned to remove the meat from the bones when the bones was cool. Vegetables were donated, cleaned, scrubbed and chopped for the soup. The men made two kinds of soup — cream of potato and vegetable beef. Both were delicious when served with homemade bread. For a treat each guest was served a choice of cake or brownies.

There was fun in the midst of the work. While the bones were cooking and the vegetables were made ready, there was plenty of camaraderie amongst the men. Some of the cherry farmers made cherry wine. A jug or two helped the men prepare and cook the soup. The card games became livelier, laughter was more prevalent and the soup simmered on. What better way to make soup, have fun and raise a little money, too.

God bless you, Father McLaughlin, for this great idea of yours. ■

Historical Glimpses

By Father Gerald F. Micketti

Diocesan historian and pastor Father Gerald Micketti compiled the following sketches of some of the historically significant parishes in the Gaylord Diocese.

Saint Joseph, Onekama

Before Saint Joseph Catholic Church of Onekama was established as a parish, Catholics of the area gathered for Mass, first, at a farm on Kerry Road and, later, at a log cabin home on the corner of roads 598 and US-31. They were considered to be a mission of Saint Mary Church of Manistee and were served by the priests from that parish.

In 1887, permission to establish a parish in Onekama was granted by Bishop Henry Joseph Richter of the Diocese of Grand Rapids and the church cornerstone was laid soon after that. When the church, an outhouse and a barn were finished, Saint Joseph became a mission of Holy Family Church of Nessen City. And in 1916, James Kenny became the first parishioner to be ordained as a priest.

In 1938, Saint Joseph became a parish with a resident priest and with a mission: Saint Raphael of Copemish. In 1967, the present Saint Joseph was built and, in 1971, it became a part of the Diocese of Gaylord.

The bell and stained glass windows from the old church are now a part of the present Saint Joseph and they stand as a fitting memorial to the spirit and faith of those who started the parish and to those who have sustained it.

Saint Paul, Onaway.

Saint Paul, Onaway

On the western end of Presque Isle County is the city of Onaway. The first recorded Mass in Onaway was said at the home of James Burbey in 1898. Saint Paul Parish was established in 1900. The first resident pastor of Saint Paul Parish was Father Thomas Albin. The first church building burned in November of 1925. Two years later Saint Paul School, which was dedicated in September 1911, was closed for lack of funds.

The present church structure is built on land purchased in 1944. Construction began in June of 1950 and the first Mass was said in Sunday, April 29, 1951.

Saint Monica, Afton

Also established in 1900 was Saint Monica Parish in Afton west of Onaway in Cheboygan County. The church building is a wooded structure constructed around 1900. The church met the needs of the French and Irish immigrants who came to Michigan through Canada to cut trees and clear the land. There has been no resident pastor. The priests who came to offer Mass at Saint Monica came from Saint Mary Church, Cheboy-

gan, Saint Anthony Church, Mackinaw City, Saint Paul, Onaway, Saint Francis, Alverno, the Catholic Shrine, Indian River, and presently, Saint Paul, Onaway.

Saint Pius X, Hale

Saint Pius X parish started as a mission from the mother parish of Saint James parish located in Whittemore. The status of parish was bestowed in February of 1995. It was in the 1930s that a small number of Catholic families in the Hale area would make their trip to a Catholic church either in Whittemore or Turner. The first Mass said in the Hale area was May 30, 1954 in the Plainfield Township Hall in Hale. The next year ground was broken for a church building. In May of 1956, the cornerstone of the church was laid and the membership of the church continued to grow. In 1967 a hall and kitchen were added to the church building. Today Saint Pius X Parish is a blend of members from some of the earliest families, resorters who now call Hale home and members of the former parish of Saint Francis in Glennie.

Our Lady of the Lake, Prudenville/Houghton Lake

Houghton Lake, Michigan's largest inland body of water, had become a "summer mecca" for tourists from the booming auto cities of Flint, Detroit, Lansing and Pontiac. Former logging roads that became state and federal highways and a dependable rail system made Houghton Lake a natural gathering spot to get away from the hustle and bustle of city life. The population of Houghton Lake was growing during the 1930s. Some of that growing population were members of Catholic churches. They now worshiped in Houghton Lake. The priest, Father Al Bauman, who cared for the small number of Catholics in Houghton Lake came from the parish at Gladwin. He obtained permission to use the Roscommon Township Hall for Masses during the summer.

When the Diocese of Saginaw was established in 1938, the parish at Gladwin was separated from Houghton Lake, because Houghton Lake in a different county remained a part of the Diocese of Grand Rapids. Bishop Joseph Pinten of Grand Rapids designated Houghton Lake as a mission of the Cathedral of Saint Andrew. That meant a round trip of nearly 300 miles. The rector of the cathedral, Msgr. D.E. Malone appointed Father Daniel Izzo, an assistant pastor as administrator of the mission parish of Our Lady of the Lake.

Father Izzo now said Mass in the Denton Township Hall and in the Houghton Lake School auditorium each Sunday. He expanded the Mass schedule from "summers only" to include twice monthly visits through fall, winter and spring seasons as well. "Fog, icy roads, snow and sleet storms were big enough obstacles to prevent Masses from being offered at the lake on the first and third Sundays of every month," reported an article in the local paper.

Saint Francis of Assisi, Lewiston

Another parish that was founded after the Diocese of Saginaw was established was Saint Francis of Assisi. Prior to the year 1946, priests from Saginaw and Mio came to the Lewiston area to celebrate Mass in private homes. Bishop William Murphy directed that a parish be started to meet the needs of the Catholic families in the area. Father Pancratius of the Franciscan order in Saginaw was assigned the task of building a community and a church for the eight Catholic families and the summer visitors. Father Pan, as he was known, arrived in Lewiston carrying a battered suitcase. He sought temporary shelter for himself with the Catholic families and began to say the Mass in the their homes and in a quonset hut until a church building could be built.

Saint Mary, Grayling

The formative years of Saint Mary Parish in Grayling were influenced by three priests — Fathers Szulak, Webeler and Reiss. The first was Francis Xavier Szulak, S.J., a missionary out of Saint Mary Parish in Bay City. He visited the isolated communities in various counties and the lumbering camps caring for the sacramental and spiritual needs of Catholics. In 1885, under his direction, Saint Mary Church was erected. Mr. Joseph Charron purchased and donated to the parish four lots where the parish buildings now stand. He was also active in the construction of the original church.

After the establishment of the Diocese of Grand Rapids, Saint Mary Parish was attached as a mission to Saint Mary Parish in Cheboygan. From September of 1887 to February of 1888, Father Aloysius Webeler, pastor of Saint Mary Parish in Cheboygan, ministered to the needs of the Catholics in Crawford County. During this time the church construction was completed. In 1888, Father Webeler was transferred to Saint Joseph Church in West Branch. He continued to visit the Grayling parish from West Branch until October 1900. In 1891, the church at Grayling was dedicated and Bishop Richter administered the sacrament of Confirmation. When Father Godfrey Guthausen succeeded Father Webeler at Saint Joseph in 1900, Saint Mary in Grayling remained with Saint Joseph. In July of 1903, Father John J. Reiss was appointed assistant to Father Guthausen. Father Reiss took care of Saint Mary church in Grayling. Five years later Father Reiss became the first permanent pastor of the Grayling parish. Now Saint Mary Parish found herself the hub of missionary activity. Attached to the parish as missions were Roscommon, Lewiston, Frederic, Deward and Lovells. Under Father Reiss' ministerial care, the parish grew both physically and spiritually. While he was the pastor he was instrumental in the beginning of Grayling Mercy Hospital in 1910. He labored in Grayling for 15 years and was remembered as the beloved pastor long after he Grayling.

Saint Nicholas, Larks Lake

The first settlers in the area called Larks Lake were Baltser and Catherine Lark. They had a business in Center Township of Emmet County. Round Lake was renamed Larks Lake after this family. There were several stores located at one time or another in or near the village. Catholicism was the faith of many of the early German and Polish families who settled in the area. Cross Village was the nearest Catholic Church. Travel in those days could be slow. Winter travel was even slower if at all possible.

Nicholas Dusseldorf set aside five acres of his land to be used as the future site of a Catholic Church and cemetery. A wood structure was erected about one half mile west of the village of Larks Lake. This church was dedicated on September 18, 1905 and was named Saint Nicholas, after the man who donated the land. Bishop Richter at the time of the dedication also confirmed 27 person. Father Bruno Torka, O.F.M. was the first pastor.

By 1945, the building was becoming run down and inadequate. Lumber had been bought and stored. The old church was dismantled and a new one was erected about two miles to the northwest on land donated by Frank Skiba. Some of the furniture and some of the religious fixtures donated by the early settlers were moved to the new building and Mass was offered in the new Saint Nicholas Church in 1946.

Saint Joseph, Mapleton

Mapleton is located on the Old Mission Peninsula of Grand Traverse County. The peninsula is a narrow strip of land jutting out from what is now Traverse City. The early pioneer life the Grand Traverse area commenced in Old Mission. Up to 1853, Old Mission was the only trading post and center of human habitation in the area. It was first settled 12 years earlier and consisted of a few Indian wigwams and four log dwelling houses.

Father Ignatius Mrak was the first Catholic priest to visit Old Mission in the early 1850s. He said Masses in the homes of the settlers and in the wigwams two or three times a year. When he retired in 1891, Father Zorn continued the mission activity and said Mass at the residence of George Lardie in Old Mission and in the houses of Oliver Lardie and Richard Johnson of Mapleton.

In 1880, the Catholics living on the peninsula decided to build a chapel and selected Mapleton as the location. Oliver Lardie generously donated the land for the site of the church. The chapel, 24 by 30 feet, was erected and blessed by Father George Ziegler the following year. After the church was built Father Ziegler came from Traverse City and began to celebrate the Mass in Mapleton every alternate month. Since that time priests from Saint Francis Church in Traverse City regularly came to Saint Joseph Church to say the Mass. Eventually Saint Joseph Parish became a parish with its own pastor.

Saint Mary, Hannah

People started to move into the area now called Hannah in 1862. That was the year George and Julia Nickerson, along with their two sons, started to homestead 160 acres. Several years later more families moved into the area. This led to the creation of Mayfield Township of what is now Grand Traverse County. Eventually some Catholic families also came to the area to stake out a claim in Mayfield Township. Among the first Catholic families were Klinkner, Stienebach, Schmuckal, Younglas, Krueger, Hendges, Cavitch and some of the Weber families. Many of the settlers came from North Dorr, an area east of Holland, Michigan and also from the Byron Center area. After the railroad was completed, settlers came in greater numbers. Word finally reached Father Ignatius Mrak, a circuit riding priest, later Bishop of Marquette, then circuit riding bishop out of Peshawbestown. His territory covered seven counties traveling any way he could to meet the needs of the Catholic families. After Bishop Mrak, Fathers Zorn, Zeigler and Nyssen continued to minister to the Catholics in the area working out of Suttons Bay and then out of Saint Francis Church in Traverse City.

Saint Theresa, Manton

Until 1973, the Catholic families in and around Manton worshiped at surrounding churches, such as Cadillac, Harrietta, Fife Lake and Lake City. On Sunday afternoon, March 11, 1973, Father Edwin Thome, pastor of Saint Ann Church, Cadillac, offered the first Mass for the Catholic families in the Manton area at the V.F.W. Hall in Manton. With the approval of Bishop Edmund Szoka, the congregation was given permission to exist as a canonical station as long as priests from Cadillac were available to serve the sacramental and spiritual needs of the community. The community moved from the V.F.W. Hall to the First Christian Church on a rental basis in March of 1973.

A community needs a place to call home. Manton was no different. Land was

purchased and ground was broken for a church building June 18, 1978. The new building is indeed new. After much homework, the building committee decided to use the Geodesic Dome design. This new structure is the home for Saint Theresa Parish in Manton.

Saint Edward, Harrietta

In 1912, Catholic families of the area of Harrietta were celebrating Mass at the home of Constable Phil Tobin, first at his farm house, later at his Harrietta home. Thus a congregation was forming. Preparation for a church building began with Father Edward Lefevre. The Saint Ambrose Church building in Jennings was no longer needed so the building was purchased by the Catholics of Harrietta. With Cadillac Saint Ann Parish pastor Father Frederick J. Williams approval, the building was dissembled and moved by rail from Jennings to Harrietta where the foundation was laid and the structure rebuilt by the parishioners. In 1922, the finished church was blessed by Bishop Edward D. Kelly.

Until the 1970s Saint Edward parish continued to serve the Catholic residents and visitors to the area as a mission of Saint Ann in Cadillac. One Mass on Sunday was celebrated at the church. When the status of mission churches was discontinued, Saint Edward became a parish church without a resident priest. Until 1985 the Sunday Mass schedule was continued with the help of Father Edwin Thome of Saint Ann and Father Clarence Smolinski of Saint Joseph Parish, Manistee. After Father Thome's transfer to Acme to start a new parish, Father Bissot combined the two parishes into Saint Ann/Saint Edward for administrative purposes and Sunday Mass was discontinued except for the summer months when Father John Tamulis came from his retirement home on Pleasant Lake to celebrate the Mass. Father Bissot retained the bimonthly Thursday Mass schedule for Saint Edward.

Saint Gertrude, Northport

In 1901, the present property for Saint Gertrude Church was procured. The community was ministered by Father Bruno Torka, O.F.M., from Petoskey. In May, Father Torka called a meeting of the parishioners. A decision was made to build a church. In the autumn of the following year the construction began.

Prior to this building, Mass was offered in the loghouse home of Charles Verreau probably by Father Mrak in 1865. Mass continued to be said in the Verreau home until 1882, when Bishop Mrak began to offer Mass at the home of Sam Gagnon. After Bishop Mrak, Northport was ministered to by Father Torka from Petoskey.

The first Mass in the new church was offered in 1903. Two years later Saint Gertrude was attached to Saint Michael the Archangel Parish in Suttons Bay. Sunday Mass was discontinued around that time. In the 1930s Sunday Mass was restored to Saint Gertrude during the summer season. In 1946 Bishop Babcock of Grand Rapids granted permission for Sunday Masses every week. Again the parish was served by the priests from Petoskey. In 1948 Saint Gertrude was attached to Saint Wenceslaus of Gill's Pier. In 1972, with Father James Gardiner as pastor, Saint Gertrude entered a new phase of life. At a church meeting in the fall of 1973, the community decided to build a new building. The new church was dedicated by Bishop Szoka August 15, 1976. ■

Past and present parishes in the Diocese of Gaylord

Alphabetical by city (county) with the date of establishment

ACME *(Grand Traverse)* — Christ the King, 1984

ADVANCE *(Charlevoix)* — 1884-1889

AFTON *(Cheboygan)* — St. Monica, 1903

AGAMING *(Emmet)* — 1857-1860

AGANING *(Leelanau)* — 1892-1893

ALABASTER *(Iosco)* — St. Mary Star of the Sea, 1877-1931

ALCONA *(Alcona)* — 1884-1890

ALPENA *(Alpena)* — St. Anne, 1885
— St. Bernard, 1866
— St. John the Baptist, 1958
— St. Mary, 1885

ALVERNO *(Cheboygan)* — St. Francis, 1880-1990

ARCADIA *(Manistee)* — St. Susanna, 1912-1951

ATLANTA *(Montmorency)* — Jesus the Good Shepherd, 1979

ATWOOD *(Antrim)* — St. Louis, 1881-1924

AU SABLE *(Iosco)* — 1892-1894 — Sacred Heart, 1869-1929

BARTON CITY/MUD LAKE *(Alcona)* — 1891-1908

BAY SHORE *(Emmet)* — St. Francis Solanus, 1896

BEAR LAKE *(Manistee)* — 1885-1888

BEAVER ISLAND *(St. James) (Charlevoix)* — Holy Cross, 1861
— Indian missions, 1886-1893
— St. Ignatius, 1832-1899

BELLAIRE *(Antrim)* — St. Luke, 1888

BLACK RIVER *(Alcona)* — St. Gabriel, 1885

BLISS *(Emmet)* — St. Patrick, 1900-1924

BOWERS HARBOR *(Grand Traverse)* — 1880-1882

BOYNE CITY *(Charlevoix)* — St. Mark, 1906-1917
— name changed to St. Matthew, 1917

BOYNE FALLS *(Charlevoix)* — St. Augustine, 1886

BRUTUS *(Emmet)* — 1896-1904

BURT LAKE *(Cheboygan)* — Assumption of Our Lady (St. Mary) , 1829

CADILLAC *(Wexford)* — St. Ann, 1882

CARP LAKE *(Emmet)* — 1900-1914

CEDAR *(Leelanau)* — Holy Rosary, 1876

CHARLEVOIX *(Charlevoix)*
— Assumption of the Blessed Virgin Mary (St. Mary), 1877

CHEBOYGAN *(Cheboygan)*
— St. Charles, 1896-1989
— St. Lawrence, 1896-1966
— St. Mary, 1855-1989
— St. Mary-St. Charles, 1989

CLARION *(Charlevoix)* — 1891-1894

CLEON *(Manistee)* — 1884-1893

COLFAX *(Wexford)* — 1877-1889

CONWAY *(Emmett)* — Sacramentine Monastery; Augustine Center, 1951

COPEMISH *(Manistee)* — St. Raphael, 1934

CROSS VILLAGE *(Emmet)* — Holy Cross, 1827

EAST BAY (*Grand Traverse)* — 1877-1873

EAST JORDAN *(Charlevoix)* — St. Joseph, 1877

EAST TAWAS *(Iosco)* — St. Joseph, 1869-1997

ECHO *(Antrim)* — 1888-1889

ELK RAPIDS *(Antrim)* — Blessed Sacrament (Indian mission), 1897-1920
— Sacred Heart, 1877

ELLSWORTH *(Antrim)* — 1895-1901

ELMIRA *(Otsego)* — St. Thomas Aquinas, 1887

EMPIRE *(Leelanau)* — St. Philip Neri, 1872

FIFE LAKE *(Grand Traverse)* — St. Aloysius, 1884

FIVE MILE CREEK *(Emmet)* — St. Joseph, 1900-1931

FRANKFORT *(Benzie)* — St. Ann, 1864

FREDERIC *(Crawford)* — St. Leo, 19090-1942

FURNACE *(Antrim)* — 1884-1888

GARDEN ISLAND *(Charlevoix)* — Sacred Heart, 1861-1938

GAYLORD *(Otsego)* — St Mary Our Lady of Mount Carmel, 1884

GILLS PIER *(Leelanau)* — St. Wenceslaus, 1891

GLEN HARBOR *(Leelanau)* — 1864-1888

GLENNIE *(Alcona)* — St. Francis of Assisi, 1972-1991

GOOD HARBOR *(Leelanau)* — St. John Nepomucene, 1877-1889

GOOD HART/MIDDLE VILLAGE *(Emmet)* — St. Ignatius, 1833

GRAYLING *(Crawford)* — St. Mary, 1884

GREENBUSH *(Alcona)* — 1877-1890

HALE *(Iosco)* — St. Pius X, 1912

HARBOR SPRINGS *(Emmet)* — St. Peter, 1829-1851
— Holy Childhood of Jesus, 1851

HARRIETTA *(Wexford)* — St. Edward, 1922

HARRISVILLE *(Alcona)* — St. Anne, 1869

HERRON *(Dafoe) (Alpena)* — St. Rose of Lima, 1897

HIGGINS LAKE *(Roscommon)* — St. Hubert, 1947

HIGH ISLAND *(Charlevoix)* — St. Joseph, 1884-1939

HILLMAN *(Montmorency)* — St. Augustine, 1897

HOG ISLAND *(Charlevoix)* — 1884-1887

HORTON'S BAY *(Charlevoix)* — 1892-1901

HOUGHTON LAKE *(Roscommon)* — St. James, 1940

INDIAN RESERVE *(Hubbard Lake) (Alpena)* — St. Mary, 1901-1930's

INDIAN RIVER *(Cheboygan)* — Catholic Shrine, 1946

IRONTON *(Charlevoix)* — 1884-1894

JENNINGS *(Missaukee)* — St. Ambrose, 1905-1920

KALKASKA *(Barker Creek) (Kalkaska)* — St. Mary of the Woods, 1884

KARLIN *(Grand Traverse)* — St. Joseph, 1912-1981

KASSON *(Leelanau)* — 1877-1889

KINGSLEY *(Hannah) (Grand Traverse)* — St. Mary, 1877

KLACKING CREEK *(Ogemaw)* — Holy Family, 1892

LAKE CITY *(Missaukee)* — St. Stephen, 1884

LAKE LEELANAU *(Provemont) (Leelanau)* — St. Mary of the Assumption, 1864

LARKS LAKE *(or Centre Township) (Emmet)* — St. Nicholas, 1895

LELAND *(Leelanau)* — Holy Trinity, 1864-1886

LEWISTON *(Montmorency)* — St. Francis of Assisi, 1897

LINCOLN *(Alcona)* — 1935-1938

LOGAN TOWNSHIP *(Ogemaw)* — 1913-1914

MACKINAW CITY *(Emmet)* — St. Anthony of Padua, 1884

MANCELONA *(Mancelona)* — St. Anthony of Padua, 1882

MANISTEE *(Manistee)* — Guardian Angels, 1889
— St. Joseph, 1885
— St. Mary of Mount Carmel Shrine, 1844

MANITOU ISLANDS *(Leelanau)* — 1864-1868

MANTON *(Wexford)* — St. Theresa, 1973

MAPLE CITY *(Leelanau)* — St. Joseph, 1886-1970
— St. Rita, 1917-1970
— St. Rita-St. Joseph, 1970

MAPLETON *(Grand Traverse)* — St. Joseph, 1864

MAYFIELD *(Grand Traverse)* — 1884-1894

METZ *(Presque Isle)* — St. Dominic, 1900

MIKADO *(Alcona)* — St. Raphael, 1889

MILLERSBURG *(Presque Isle)* — St. Stephen, 1901-1947

MIO *(Oscoda)* — St. Mary, 1914

NESSEN CITY *(Benzie)(Oscoda)* — Holy Family, 1892-1933

NORTHPORT *(Leelanau)(Oscoda)* — St. Gertrude, 1865

NORTHPORT POINT *(Leelanau)(Oscoda)* — 1922-1928

NORTH UNITY *(Leelanau)* — 1864-1871

NORWOOD *(Charlevoix)* — 1877-1889

OCQUEOC *(Presque Isle)* — St. Elizabeth, 1901-1938

OGEMAW *(Ogemaw)* — 1884-1889

OLD MISSION *(Grand Traverse)* — 1864-1871

OMENA *(Leelanau)* — 1886-1888

ONAWAY *(Presque Isle)* — St. Paul, 1901

ONEKAMA *(Manistee)* — St. Joseph, 1891

OSCODA *(Iosco)* — Sacred Heart, 1915
— Wurtsmith AF Base

OSSINEKE *(Alpena)* — St. Catherine of Alexandria, 1901

PELLSTON *(Emmet)* — St. Clement, 1900

PESHAWBESTOWN *(Leelanau)* — Immaculate Conception, 1846-1991
— name changed to Blessed Kateri Tekakwitha 1991

PETOSKEY *(Emmet)* — St. Francis Solanus, 1859
— St. Francis Xavier, 1879

PORCUPINE RIDGE *(Charlevoix)* — 1884-1888

PORTAGE *(Manistee)* — 1888-1889

POSEN *(Presque Isle)* — St. Casimir, 1879

PRAGA *(or Mount Bliss) (Antrim)* — St. John Nepomucene, 1882

PRESCOTT *(Ogemaw)* — St. Alban, 1912-1913

PRESQUE ISLE *(Presque Isle)* — 1877-1878

PRUDENVILLE *(Roscommon)* — Our Lady of the Lake, 1941

RIGGSVILLE *(Cheboygan)* — Sacred Heart, 1884

ROGERS CITY *(Presque Isle)* — St. Ignatius, 1877

ROSCOMMON *(Roscommon)* — St. Michael, 1880

ROSE CITY *(Ogemaw)* — 1910-1911

ROUND LAKE *(Missaukee)* — 1900-14

ST. HELEN *(Roscommon)* — St. Helen, 1884

SHERMAN *(Wexford)* — 1897-1914

SKIDWAY LAKE *(Prescott) (Ogemaw)* — St. Stephen, 1961

SOUTH ARM *(Charlevoix)* — 1877-1888

SOUTH BOARDMAN *(Kalkaska)* — 1897-1914

SPENCER CREEK *(Antrim)* — 1877-1889

SUMMIT CITY *(Grand Traverse)* — 1892-1894

SUTTONS BAY *(Leelanau)* — St. Michael the Archangel, 1874

TAWAS CITY *(Iosco)* — Immaculate Heart of Mary, 1953-1997
— Holy Family, 1997

TORCH LAKE *(Antrim)* — 1887-1889

TRAVERSE CITY *(Grand Traverse)* — Immaculate Conception, 1902
— St. Francis of Assisi, 1864
— St. Patrick, 1984

UNDINE *(Charlevoix)* — 1887-1891

VANDERBILT *(Otsego)* — Holt Redeemer, 1968

WATERS *(Otsego)* — 1913-1914

WEST BRANCH *(Ogemaw)* — St. Joseph, 1880

WHITTEMORE *(Iosco)* — St. James, 1886

WILLIAMSBURG *(Grand Traverse)* — 1877-1883

WOLVERINE *(Cheboygan)* — St. Aloysius, 1891-1951

YUBA *(Grand Traverse)* — 1914-1915

Vicariate Map

The 11,171 square miles of the Diocese includes the 21 most northern counties of Michigan's Lower Peninsula:

Alcona
Alpena
Antrim
Benzie
Charlevoix
Cheboygan
Crawford
Emmet
Grand Traverse
Iosco
Kalkaska
Leelanau
Manistee
Missaukee
Montmorency
Ogemaw
Oscoda
Otsego
Presque Isle
Roscommon
Wexford

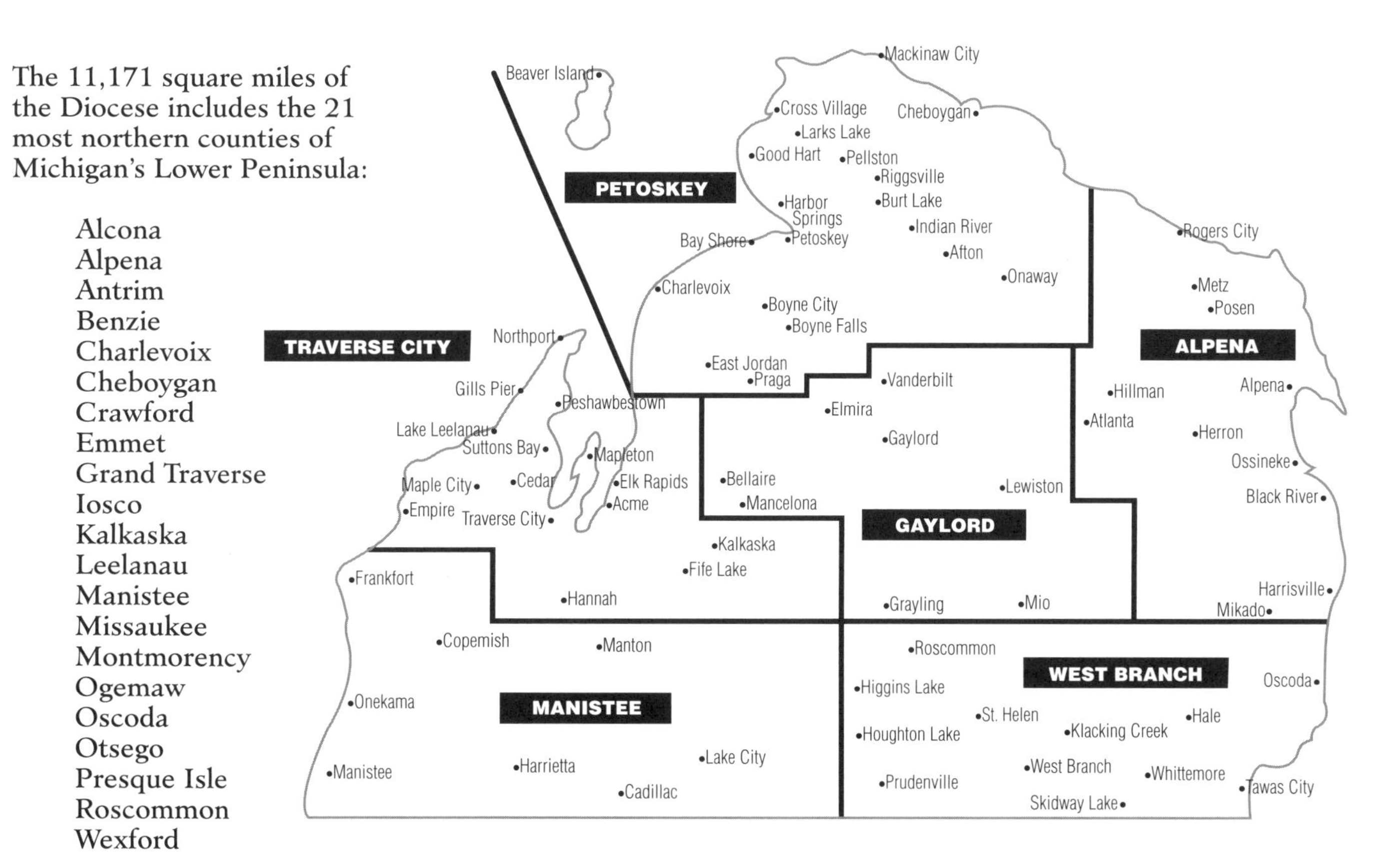

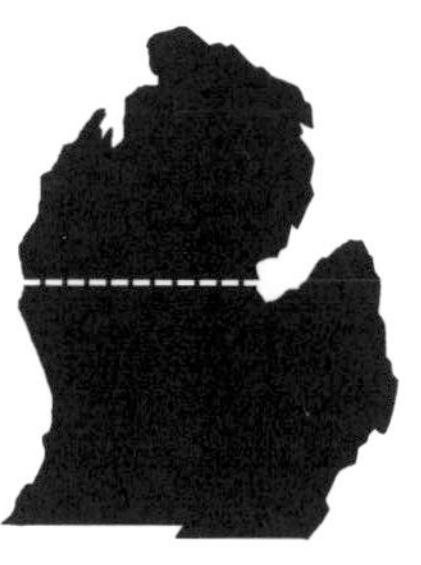

FACTS OF INTEREST

The Diocese of Gaylord was established on July 20, 1971, by His Holiness, Paul VI. The territory had originally been part of the Dioceses of Saginaw and Grand Rapids.

Total population of the 21-county area is 421,449 of which more than 82,000 are Catholics.

A very special word of gratitude *to the authors of the various stories on the history of the Diocese of Gaylord. They have given us a flavor and experience we will cherish for a long time. They have helped us link up with the incredible stories of faith from long ago and give us courage to go forth into the next millennium. They have made the stones cry out.*

A message from Bishop Patrick R. Cooney

I thank you for taking the necessary time and effort to travel the long path that is the church history of the people—laity, religious and clergy—who have lived and worked within these 21 counties that form the Diocese of Gaylord.

The wonderful work of God is aptly described on each page. It was He who inspired all of these, our forbearers in the faith, to take all the risks so that vibrant parishes might exist throughout the area that now makes up this diocese. We give Him thanks and praise for all the wonderful blessings He has given to us throughout this history.

At the same time, I hope you have been amazed at all the heroic acts that were done by these people—men and women. Without their efforts we would not exist as a church today. To them we are grateful and from them we have taken a lesson. That lesson is, simply, that the building of the church has always required great effort. Therefore, each one of us is challenged to do for those who will follow us what has been done for us.

It has often been quoted that the person who does not know history is doomed to repeat all of its mistakes. I hope that the reading of this history might contribute to our knowledge and that we will be able to avoid at least some of the mistakes as we walk into the future.

God bless each of you.

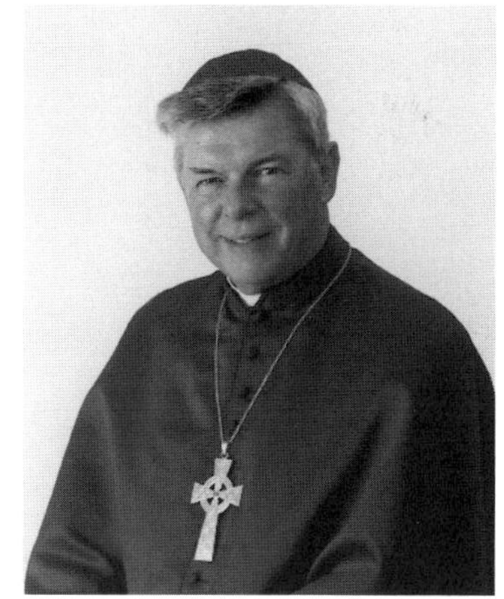